Targeting Maths

AUSTRALIAN CURRICULUM EDITION

3

Garda Turner

PASCAL PRESS

Contents

Term 1

Numbers to 1000	2
Addition	6
Subtraction	10
Length	15
Fractions	18
Investigation 1	22
Measure with People Measures	
Revision	24
Number Facts	26
Patterns	28
Time	32
3D Space	35
Data and Chance	39
Term 1 Revision	44

Term 2

NAPLAN* practice	46
Numbers over 1000	54
Tables	58
Subtraction	60
Subtraction strategies	64
Fractions	68
Investigation 2	72
Cakes and Biscuits	
Revision	74
Money	76
Patterns	80
2D Space	84
Capacity	88
Time facts	92
Presenting data	94
Term 2 Revision	96

Term 3

Addition	98
Multiplication	102
Sharing	108
Fractions	112
Investigation 3	116
Holidays	
Revision	118
Patterns and Multiples	120
Position	124
Mass	128
Symmetry	132
Time	134
Data	136
Term 3 Revision	140

Term 4

Four digit numbers	142
Multiplication	146
Division	152
Fractions	156
Length and Area	160
Investigation 4	164
Farmer Zoop's Farm	
Revision	166
Number Patterns	168
Angles	171
Timetable	174
Position	175
Chance	179
Term 4 Revision	182

New Edition

Targeting Maths Australia's Favourite Maths Program

NEW — **Australian Curriculum alignment**

Complete coverage of the Australian Curriculum with content descriptions appearing on each page.

The proficiency strands coverage is shown by these 4 icons:

Understanding   Fluency   Problem solving   Reasoning

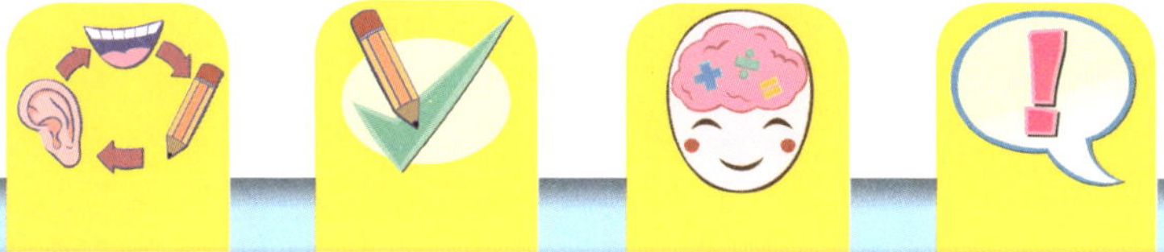

NEW  — **iPad Apps**

With an app for each Year level Kinder/Prep – 6, the Targeting Maths Apps include all the essential maths content that children need to know in an amazing NEW app that makes learning maths fun, motivating and full of rewards. Look for it in the App store today! Made especially for the iPad and aligned to each student page.

NEW — **Integrated Problem-solving Program**

Includes an integrated problem-solving program that actively builds students' problem solving capabilities.

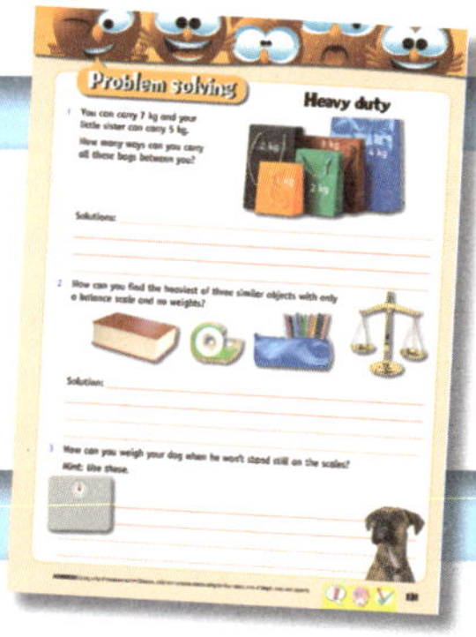

NEW — **Term Investigations**

Each term includes an investigation that will get students planning and working through an extended problem.

NEW — **In-stage topic alignment for composite classes**

Great for composite classes too, the contents of each book in one stage, eg Year 1 and Year 2, match topic by topic.

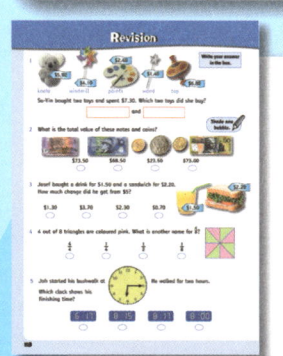

NEW — **Regular revision and NAPLAN* practice**

Mid-term revisions are in the form of a multiple choice NAPLAN*–style practice test for Years 2 – 6.

* These are not officially endorsed publications of the NAPLAN program and are produced by Pascal Press independently of Australian Governments.

Australian Curriculum Alignment

Year 3 Content Descriptions	Targeting Maths 3 Student Pages
Number and place value	
ACMNA051 Investigate the conditions required for a number to be odd and even and identify odd and even numbers.	27
ACMNA052 Recognise, model, represent and order numbers to at least 10 000.	2, 3, 4, 5, 54, 56, 142, 144, 145
ACMNA053 Apply place value to partition, rearrange and regroup numbers to at least 10 000 to assist calculations and solve problems.	2, 4, 6, 7, 8, 9, 10, 11, 13, 14, 54, 55, 56, 57, 60, 62, 63, 64, 65, 67, 101, 102, 103, 143, 144
ACMNA054 Recognise and explain the connection between addition and subtraction.	3, 12, 55, 57, 61, 66
ACMNA055 Recall addition facts for single-digit numbers and related subtraction facts to develop increasingly efficient mental strategies for computation.	6, 7, 8, 9, 11, 12, 13, 14, 60, 62, 63, 64, 65, 66, 67, 79, 101, 102, 103, 169
ACMNA056 Recall multiplication facts of two, three, five and ten and related division facts.	26, 58, 59, 98, 99, 104, 105, 106, 108, 109, 110, 169
ACMNA057 Represent and solve problems involving multiplication using efficient mental and written strategies and appropriate digital technologies.	58, 59, 72, 73, 83, 98, 99, 104, 105, 106, 107, 111, 146, 147, 148, 149, 150, 151, 152, 153, 154, 155
Fractions and decimals	
ACMNA058 Model and represent unit fractions including $\frac{1}{2}$, $\frac{1}{4}$, $\frac{1}{3}$, $\frac{1}{5}$ and their multiples to a complete whole.	18, 19, 20, 21, 68, 69, 70, 71, 112, 113, 114, 115, 156, 157, 158, 159
Money and financial mathematics	
ACMNA059 Represent money values in multiple ways and count the change required for simple transactions to the nearest five cents.	10, 61, 76, 77, 78, 79, 100
Patterns and algebra	
ACMNA060 Describe, continue, and create number patterns resulting from performing addition or subtraction.	5, 27, 28, 29, 30, 31, 80, 81, 82, 120, 121, 122, 123, 168, 169, 170
Using units of measurement	
ACMMG061 Measure, order and compare objects using familiar metric units of length, mass and capacity.	15, 16, 17, 22, 23, 72, 73, 88, 89, 90, 91, 128, 129, 130, 131, 160, 161, 162, 163, 164, 165
ACMMG062 Tell time to the minute and investigate the relationship between units of time.	32, 33, 34, 92, 93, 134, 135, 174
Shape	
ACMMG063 Make models of three-dimensional objects and describe key features.	35, 36, 37, 38
Location and transformation	
ACMMG065 Create and interpret simple grid maps to show position and pathways.	124, 125, 126, 127, 175, 176, 177, 178
ACMMG066 Identify symmetry in the environment.	132, 133
Geometric reasoning	
ACMMG064 Identify angles as measures of turn and compare angle sizes in everyday situations.	171, 172, 173
Chance	
ACMSP067 Conduct chance experiments, identify and describe possible outcomes and recognise variation in results.	42, 43, 116, 117, 139, 179, 180, 181
Data representation and interpretation	
ACMSP068 Identify questions or issues for categorical variables. Identify data sources and plan methods of data collection and recording.	41, 116
ACMSP069 Collect data, organise into categories and create displays using lists, tables, picture graphs and simple column graphs, with and without the use of digital technologies.	39, 41, 116, 117, 138
ACMSP070 Interpret and compare data displays.	39, 40, 41, 94, 95, 136, 137

How to Solve a Problem

Read • Plan • Work • Check

Read the problem carefully. Read it again. Underline important words.
Plan what you are going to do — add, subtract, multiply or divide.
Work Write the steps you take to work out the answer. Write your answer in full.
Check your answer! Make sure that your answer makes sense and that you answered the question.

Draw a diagram

Draw a simple picture.
Use symbols if you can.

12 − 5 = 7

3 × 4 = 12

Trial and Error

Make a guess and write it down. Check if it is right. If not, work out if your guess should be higher or lower. Make another guess and write it down. Check if it's right. Keep going until you have the correct answer.

Look for patterns

Study the numbers in the problem. Write them down in a list.
Can you see a pattern?
What comes next in the pattern.
Write it as your answer.

Bundy runs 2 km, then 4 km, then 6 km on 3 days. How far should he run on the 4th day to keep to his pattern?

2, 4, 6, ?   2, 4, 6, 8
Bundy should run 8 km.

Use a table

Put the information from the problem in columns. Can you see the pattern? The information is clearer in a table.
Use this to work out the answer.

Jerry	5 mins	10 cakes	2 in 1 min.
Cam	4 mins	8 cakes	2 in 1 min.
Tilly	3 mins	9 cakes	3 in 1 min.

Who eats the fastest?
Answer: Tilly eats fastest.

Work backwards

Read the problem all the way through. Find one piece of information. Write it down. Find another piece of information that relates and put them together. Write it down. Keep working backwards until you solve all the pieces of the problem.

Kell has $2 more than Greg, who has $3 less than Dee. Dee has $5. How much do they each have?

Dee = $5
Greg = $5 − $3 = $2
Kell = $2 + $2 = $4

v

Dictionary

am (ante meridiem)
The time from midnight to midday

angle
The amount of turning between two lines that meet at a point

angle   right angle

area
The size of the surface. It is measured in square units.
cm² = square centimetre
m² = square metre

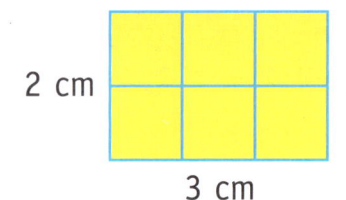

2 cm   Area = 6 cm²
3 cm

ascending order
In order from smallest to largest
1, 7, 11, 19, 32

capacity
The amount a container can hold 
The capacity of this bottle is 1 litre.

centimetre (cm)
A unit of length
10 mm = 1 cm
100 cm = 1 m

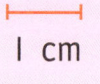

1 cm

certain
Something that is definite. It will happen.

compass points
Marks on a map that show direction.

North
West East
South

cone
A solid shape that tapers to a point and has a circular base

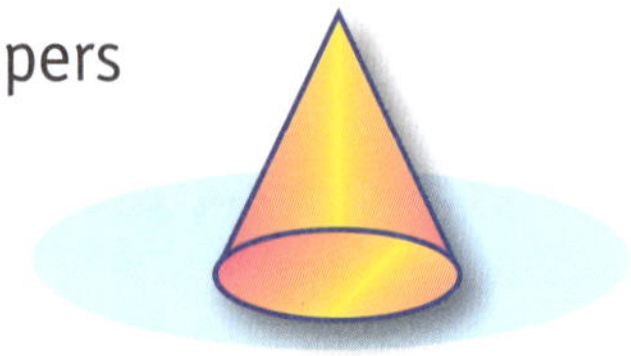

cube
A solid shape which has six square faces

cylinder
A solid shape which has two circular ends and a curved surface

decimal number
A number that has a decimal point
eg 0·3, 75·16

descending order
In order from largest to smallest
96, 84, 61, 37, 11

diagonal
A line that joins two corners in a polygon but does not make a side

diagonal   diagonal

Dictionary

division (÷)
Sharing into equal groups

4 groups of 2
8 ÷ 2 = 4

edge
Where two surfaces meet

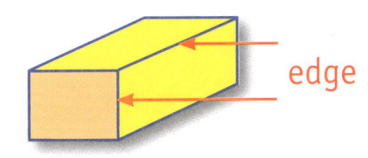

even number
When you multiply a whole number by 2 you get an even number.

eg 14 (7 × 2)   20 (10 × 2)

Even numbers end in 0, 2, 4, 6, 8.

face
A flat surface of a solid shape

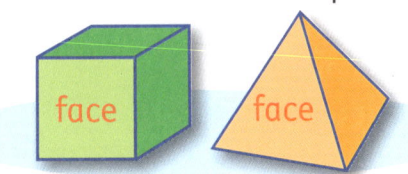

fraction
A part of a whole or a group

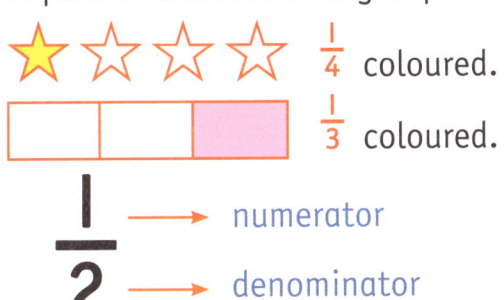

$\frac{1}{4}$ coloured.

$\frac{1}{3}$ coloured.

$\frac{1}{2}$ → numerator
    → denominator

graph
A diagram that shows a collection of data

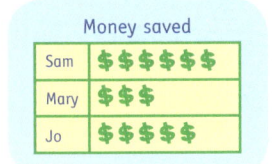

column graph   picture graph

hexagon
A 2D shape with 6 straight sides

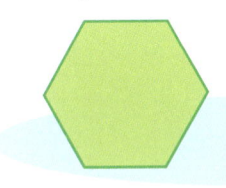

regular hexagon   irregular hexagon

kilogram (kg)
A unit of mass for weighing things

line
straight line

parallel lines

curved line

litre (L)
A unit of capacity

1 L = 1000 millilitres (mL)

metre (m)
A unit of length

1 m = 100 cm
1000 m = 1 km

millimetre (mm)
A unit of length

10 mm = 1 cm

Dictionary

multiplication (×)
Find the total of a number of equal groups or equal rows

5 × 4 = 20

4 × 6 = 24

octagon
A 2D shape with 8 straight sides

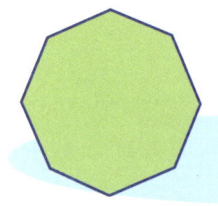

regular octagon   irregular octagon

parallelogram
A quadrilateral with opposite sides parallel

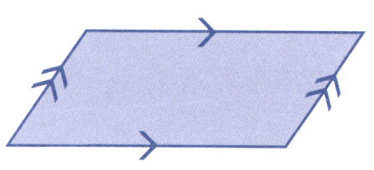

pentagon
A 2D shape with 5 straight sides

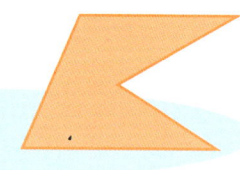

regular pentagon   irregular pentagon

place value
The value of a numeral depending on its position in a number

396 = 300 + 90 + 6
754 = 7 hundreds + 5 tens + 4 ones

pm (post meridiem)
The time from midday to midnight

polygon
A shape with 3 or more straight sides
eg

prism
A 3D shape with identical ends. All other faces are rectangles. The ends give a prism its name.

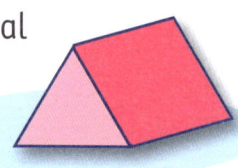

triangular prism

product
When numbers are multiplied, the answer is called the product.

pyramid
A 3D object with one flat base. All other faces are triangles coming to a point. The base shape gives a pyramid its name.

square pyramid

quadrilateral
A 2D shape with 4 straight sides

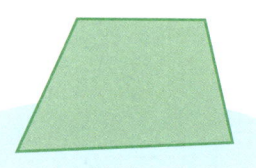

rhombus
A quadrilateral with all sides equal and opposite sides parallel. It is a special parallelogram.

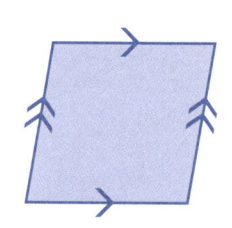

Dictionary

rounding (to nearest 10)

0 Round down → ← Round up 0
1 2 3 4   5 6 7 8 9

eg 675 → 700
(rounded to the nearest 100)

4492 → 4000
(rounded to the nearest 1000)

symmetry

A shape has symmetry if both halves match exactly when it is folded on the line of symmetry

line of symmetry

three-dimensional objects (3D)

Solid shapes that have length, width and height

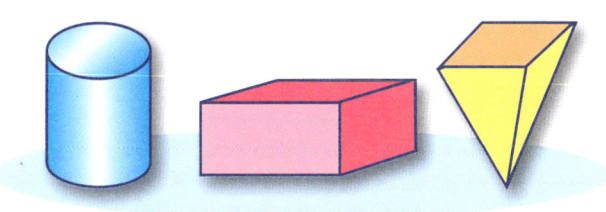

time

analogue

digital

trapezium

A quadrilateral that has one pair of parallel sides

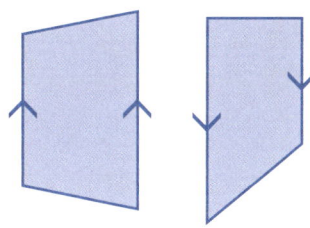

triangle

A 2D shape with 3 straight sides

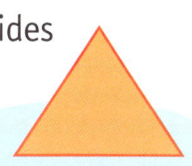

two-dimensional shapes (2D)

Shapes that only have length and width

vertex

The point where the arms of an angle meet

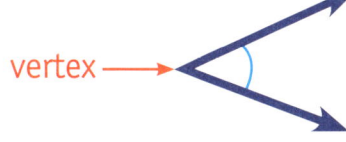

vertex →

volume

The amount of space a solid object takes up

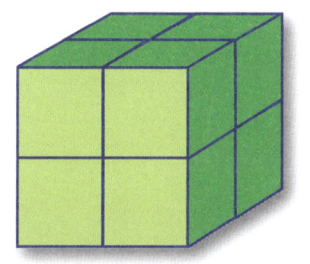

ix

Lab 3 — ordering numbers

Numbers to 1000

Numbers to 1000

10	20	30	40	50	60	70	80	90	100
110	120	130	140	150	160	170	180	190	200
210	220	230	240	250	260	270	280	290	300
310	320	330	340	350	360	370	380	390	400
410	420	430	440	450	460	470	480	490	500
510	520	530	540	550	560	570	580	590	600
610	620	630		650	660	670	680	690	700
710	720			760	770	780	790	800
810	820	830		850	860	870	880	890	900
910	920	930	940	950	960	970	980	990	1000

1 Write:
  a the 5 missing numbers.
  b the numbers between 360 and 370. _361, 362_ _____

  c 10 more than 160. _____   d 10 less than 700. _____

  e 100 more than 180. _____   f 100 less than 910. _____

2 Count in 10s from 740 to 800. _____

3 Count in 100s from 440 to 840. _____

4 a Circle the numbers 10 more than 600, 770, 510, 850.

  b Are the numbers odd or even? _____

2 ACMNA052 & ACMNA053 Number and place value • Recognise, model represent and order numbers to at least 10 000. • Apply place value to partition, rearrange and regroup numbers to at least 10 000 to assist calculations and solve problems.

Counting in tens and hundreds

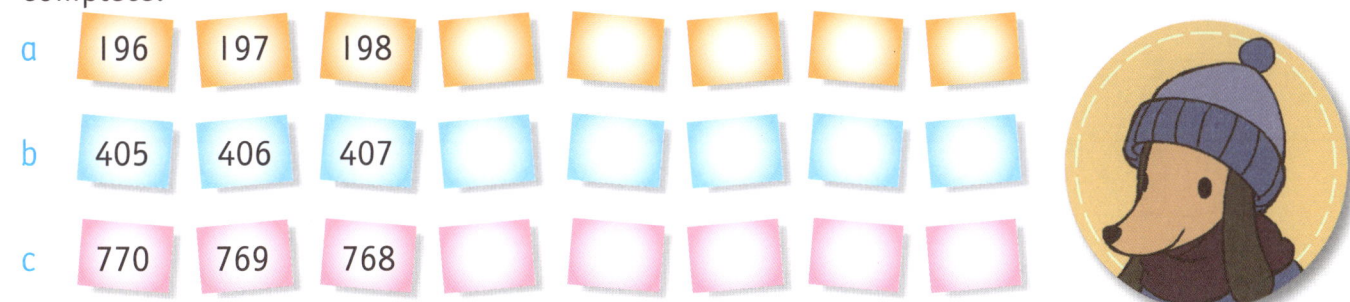

1 Complete.

a 196 197 198 ☐ ☐ ☐ ☐ ☐

b 405 406 407 ☐ ☐ ☐ ☐ ☐

c 770 769 768 ☐ ☐ ☐ ☐ ☐

2 Complete the table.

Number	1 more	10 more	100 more
a 57			
b 300			
c 690			
d 799			
e 205			

3 Write the number 10 less than:

a 70 _____   b 330 _____   c 500 _____   d 405 _____

4
a 340 +10→ ☐ +10→ ☐ +10→ ☐

b 572 +10→ ☐ +10→ ☐ +10→ ☐

c 870 −10→ ☐ −10→ ☐ −10→ ☐

d 600 −10→ ☐ −10→ ☐ −10→ ☐

Challenge! Who will land on 850? _____
Flea jumps in tens, Grasshopper jumps in 20s, Frog jumps in 50s.

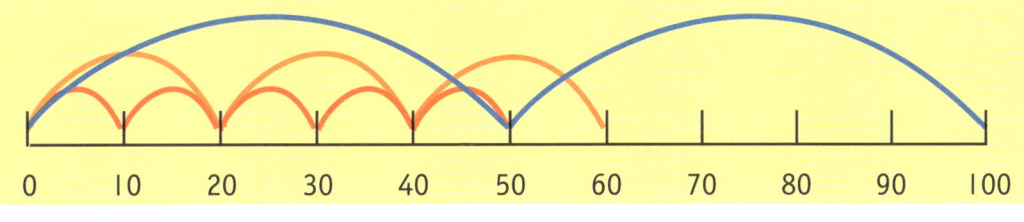

Place value

1 How many?

a
Hundreds	Tens	Ones
100 100 100 100 100	10 10 10 10 10 10	1 1 1

_____

b
Hundreds	Tens	Ones
100 100 100 100 100 100		1 1 1 1 1 1 1

_____

2 Complete: eg 549 = five hundreds, four tens and nine ones

a 362 = _____

b 791 = _____

c _____ = six hundreds, 3 tens and 7 ones

d _____ = eight hundreds and 4 tens

3 Beware! These are not in place value order. Write the number:

a _____ = two hundreds, four ones and three tens

b _____ = eight ones, six tens and four hundreds

c _____ = 9 ones and seven hundreds

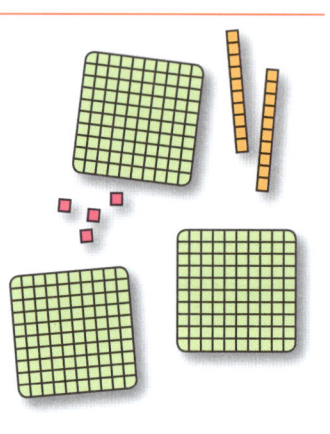

4 How much altogether?

a $100, $10, $100, $10, $10 _____

b $100, $100, $1, $100, $100, $1, $10, $10 _____

c $100, $100, $10, $1, $100, $100, $10, $1, $1, $10, $10, $1, $1 _____

5 Complete.

a 264 = 200 + 60 + ☐

b 670 = ☐ + 70 + 0

c 712 = ☐ + 10 + ☐

d 354 = ☐ + ☐ + ☐

e 617 = 600 + ☐ + ☐

f 409 = ☐ + ☐ + 9

g 555 = ☐ + ☐ + ☐

h 830 = ☐ + ☐ + ☐

Challenge! About how many marbles would fill the tray? ☐

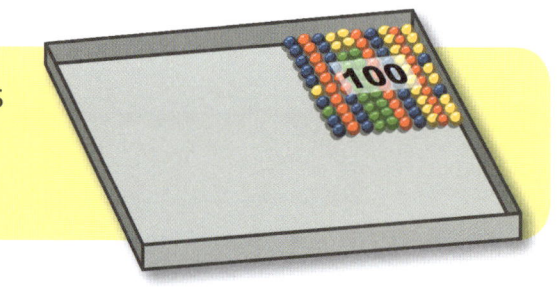

Write and order 3-digit numbers

1 Complete each counting pattern.

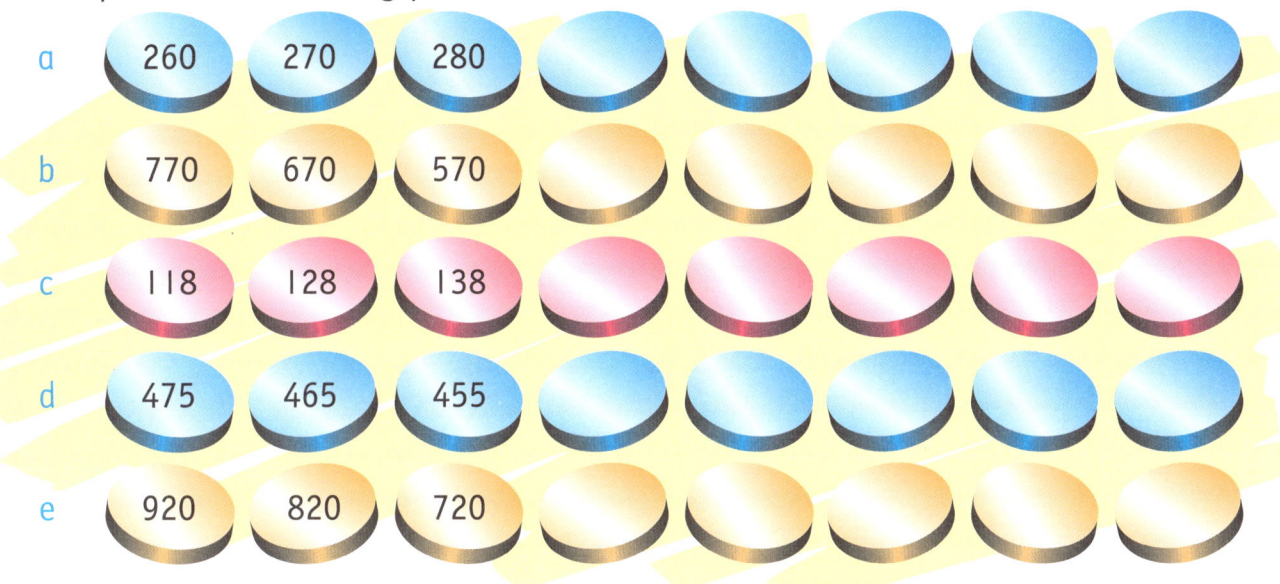

a 260 270 280 ___ ___ ___ ___ ___

b 770 670 570 ___ ___ ___ ___ ___

c 118 128 138 ___ ___ ___ ___ ___

d 475 465 455 ___ ___ ___ ___ ___

e 920 820 720 ___ ___ ___ ___ ___

2 Write each number.

   a three hundred and forty-two _____   b seven hundred and sixty-five _____

   c nine hundred and one _____   d four hundred and fourteen _____

3 Write in words.

   a 509 _____

   b 213 _____

4 Underline the larger number. Use **less than <** or **greater than >** to compare the two numbers.

   a 269 ___ 312   b 786 ___ 867   c 499 ___ 501   d 301 ___ 199

   e 614 ___ 641   f 221 ___ 212   g 550 ___ 505   h 888 ___ 900

5 Write in order. Start with the smallest number.

   a 673 212 754 704   ___ ___ ___ ___

   b 655 529 601 599   ___ ___ ___ ___

Looking for Patterns

Make different 3-digit numbers with these numbers. How many numbers can you make? How many are odd? How many are even? Repeat with 3 different numbers. Can you see a pattern?

2 4 5

Addition

Lab 3 patterns 1

Jump

1 Fill in the boxes.

2 Start at:

   a 46 and go forward 8. ____   b 46 and go back 15. ____   c 46 and go forward 23. ____

3 Start at:

   a 57 and go back 6. ____   b 57 and go forward 15. ____   c 57 and go forward 29. ____

4 Start at:

   a 28 and go forward 2. ____   b 28 and go back 18. ____   c 28 and go forward 26. ____

5 This time keep hopping. Start at 81 and

   a go back 5, ____   b now go forward 1, ____   c now go forward 9. ____

6 Start at 6 and

   a go forward 14, ____   b now go back 6, ____   c now go forward 20. ____

ACMNA053 & ACMNA055 Number and place value • Apply place value to partition, rearrange and regroup numbers to at least 10 000 to assist calculations and solve problems.
• Recall addition facts for single-digit numbers and related subtraction facts to develop increasingly efficient mental strategies for computation.

Counting in 5s and 10s

1 Five more than:

a 20 _____   b 40 _____   c 75 _____   d 25 _____   e 10 _____
f 15 _____   g 35 _____   h 50 _____   i 11 _____   j 79 _____
k 17 _____   l 93 _____   m 44 _____   n 58 _____   o 86 _____

2 Ten less than:

a 60 _____   b 85 _____   c 30 _____   d 45 _____   e 95 _____
f 39 _____   g 91 _____   h 63 _____   i 13 _____   j 27 _____

3 Fill in the blanks and write a number sentence.

eg I start at 37, go __forward__ __30__ and stop at 67. | 37 | + | 30 | = 67

a I start at 48, go _____ _____ and stop at 88. | | | | = 88

b I start at 64, go _____ _____ and stop at 94. | | | | = 94

c I start at 22, go _____ _____ and stop at 72. | | | | = 72

4 Fill in the missing numbers.

Rule

a 14, __, 24, 29, __, 39, 44, __   Rule: + 5

b 68, __, 88, __, __, 118, __, __

c 65, __, 55, 50, __, __, 35, __

d 32, 37, __, 47, __, 57, __, __

e 129, __, __, 114, __, __, 99, __

Challenge! A springbok can leap 5 m. If it travels 50 m, how many leaps does it make? ☐

A cougar can jump 10 m. If it jumps 7 times, how far does it travel? ☐

Doubles and near doubles

1.
   a double 2   ☐ + ☐ = ☐
   b double 8   ☐ + ☐ = ☐
   c double 5   ☐ + ☐ = ☐
   d double 10 ☐ + ☐ = ☐
   e double 9   ☐ + ☐ = ☐
   f double 16 ☐ + ☐ = ☐

2.
   a 4 + 4
   b 7 + 7
   c 11 + 11
   d 13 + 13
   e 0 + 0
   f 9 + 9

Sometimes numbers are near doubles!

8 + 7
↓
8 + 8 − 1

8 + 7
↓
7 + 7 + 1

3. Show the near double you used.
   a 4 + 5 = _4 + 4 + 1_ = ___
   b 10 + 9 = ___ = ___
   c 3 + 2 = ___ = ___
   d 8 + 9 = ___ = ___
   e 7 + 6 = ___ = ___
   f 6 + 5 = ___ = ___
   g 12 + 13 = ___ = ___
   h 17 + 16 = ___ = ___
   i 15 + 14 = ___ = ___
   j 19 + 18 = ___ = ___

4.
   a A cake costs $9. How much for 2 cakes? ___
   b One puppy weighs 5 kg. What is the mass of two puppies? ___
   c One bottle of cordial makes 18 drinks. How many drinks will two bottles make? ___
   d I bought two books. One book cost $14 and the other cost $13. How much did I spend? ___

5. Keep doubling.
   a 2   _4_   _8_   ___ ___ ___ ___
   b 3   ___ ___ ___ ___ ___ ___
   c 5   ___ ___ ___ ___ ___ ___

Challenge! If one box holds 6 watermelons, how many watermelons will 8 boxes hold? ☐

Addition facts to 10 and 20

1 Look for the ten then find the total.

a. [7][5][3] = 15 (with 10 bracket over 7 and 3)

b. [5][5][1] = ___

c. [9][6][4] = ___

d. [6][8][2] = ___

e. [1][3][9] = ___

f. [9][1][7] = ___

g. [4][6][2] = ___

h. [2][4][8] = ___

i. [3][8][7] = ___

2 Addition table (empty grid to fill in)

3

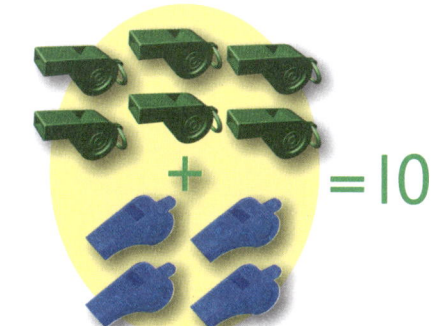

a. 6 + 7 = ___
   16 + 7 = ___
   26 + 7 = ___

b. 5 + 8 = ___
   15 + 8 = ___
   25 + 8 = ___

c. 9 + 4 = ___
   9 + 14 = ___
   9 + 24 = ___

d. 5 + 6 = ___
   25 + 6 = ___
   65 + 6 = ___

e. 8 + 7 = ___
   8 + 37 = ___
   8 + 57 = ___

f. 3 + 8 = ___
   43 + 8 = ___
   83 + 8 = ___

4 Look for tens.

a. 6 + 3 + 7 + 4 = ___

b. 8 + 5 + 2 + 5 = ___

c. 9 + 7 + 1 + 5 = ___

d. 4 + 9 + 6 + 9 = ___

e. 3 + 8 + 7 + 6 = ___

f. 2 + 9 + 7 + 8 = ___

ACMNA053 & ACMNA055 Number and place value • Apply place value to partition, rearrange and regroup numbers to at least 10 000 to assist calculations and solve problems. • Recall addition facts for single-digit numbers and related subtraction facts to develop increasingly efficient mental strategies for computation.

Lab 3 — Subtraction

TEN BIN ten bins

Change

Prices:
- Top: 50c
- Fake nose/glasses: 75c
- Teddy bear: 65c
- Star cookie: 45c
- Doll: 90c
- Duck: 25c
- Windmill: 15c
- Wand: 80c
- Goggle eyes: 35c

John has $1 to spend at the fair.

1 How much change will he get if he buys:

   a the teddy bear? _____   b the goggle eyes? _____
   c the duck? _____   d the star cookie? _____
   e the wand? _____   f the doll? _____
   g the fake nose and the toy windmill? _____
   h the top and the duck? _____

2 a Choose three items you would buy.
      _____

   b How much change would you get from $2?
      _____

ACMNA059 Money and financial mathematics • Represent money values in multiple ways and count the change required for simple transactions to the nearest five cents.
ACMNA053 Number and place value • Apply place value to partition, rearrange and regroup numbers to at least 10 000 to assist calculations and solve problems.

Subtraction on a number line

— is the take away sign. It means take away, subtract, difference between, minus or less.

0 — 10 — 20 — 30

1 Use the number line to find the difference.

a 17 − 9 = ___   b 12 − 4 = ___   c 10 − 3 = ___   d 16 − 7 = ___

e 15 − 8 = ___   f 26 − 9 = ___   g 18 − 12 = ___   h 23 − 5 = ___

i 19 − 7 = ___   j 29 − 17 = ___   k 15 − 9 = ___   l 21 − 7 = ___

2
a 15 pencils, 3 broke. How many not broken? ☐ − ☐ = ☐

b 29 jellybeans, 8 eaten. How many left? ☐ − ☐ = ☐

c 36 books, 5 torn. How many not torn? ☐ − ☐ = ☐

d 22 keys, 0 lost. How many keys? ☐ − ☐ = ☐

e 17 cakes, all eaten. How many left? ☐ − ☐ = ☐

f $48, $12 spent. How much left? ☐ − ☐ = ☐

3 Write a story for each. Then write a number sentence.

a ☐ − ☐ = ☐

b ☐ − ☐ = ☐

Challenge! You have 36 lollies.
If you eat 3 every afternoon, how many days will they last? ☐
What if you ate 4 each night? ☐   Or 6 each night? ☐

Subtraction patterns

1

a 9 – 4 = 5
   90 – 40 = 50
   900 – 400 = 500

b 7 – 3 = ___
   70 – 30 = ___
   700 – 300 = ___

c 5 – 2 = ___
   ___ – ___ = ___
   ___ – ___ = ___

d 8 – 6 = ___
   ___ – ___ = ___
   ___ – ___ = ___

e 9 – 8 = ___
   ___ – ___ = ___
   ___ – ___ = ___

f 6 – 1 = ___
   ___ – ___ = ___
   ___ – ___ = ___

Can you see the pattern?

2 One addition fact tells us 4 things.

eg 5 + 3 = 8   3 + 5 = 8   8 – 5 = 3   8 – 3 = 5

a 7 + 2 = ___ , ___ + ___ = ___ , ___ – ___ = ___ , ___ – ___ = ___
b 5 + 6 = ___ , ___ + ___ = ___ , ___ – ___ = ___ , ___ – ___ = ___
c 8 + 5 = ___ , ___ + ___ = ___ , ___ – ___ = ___ , ___ – ___ = ___
d 9 + 7 = ___ , ___ + ___ = ___ , ___ – ___ = ___ , ___ – ___ = ___
e 6 + 7 = ___ , ___ + ___ = ___ , ___ – ___ = ___ , ___ – ___ = ___
f 4 + 9 = ___ , ___ + ___ = ___ , ___ – ___ = ___ , ___ – ___ = ___

3 a Cross out some dolls. Write a number story and a number sentence.

___ – ___ = ___

b Write the 3 other number facts.

Challenge! Zac had 14 marbles. He gave 2 away and had 16 left.

What is wrong with Zac's story? ___

How many did Zac give away if he had 2 left? ___

Two-digit subtraction

Subtract to 100

1 Use a number line.

eg 56 − 24 = 32

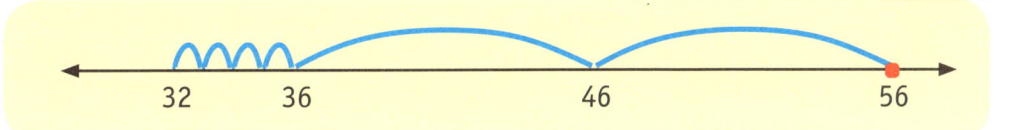

32   36   46   56

a 75 − 31 = _____

b 89 − 47 = _____

c 38 − 23 = _____

d 64 − 42 = _____

e 98 − 65 = _____

f 46 − 15 = _____

g 57 − 23 = _____

h 79 − 34 = _____

2 a 48 − 21 = _____
```
  4 8
− 2 1
```

b 66 − 36 = _____
```
  6 6
− 3 6
```

c 75 − 32 = _____
```
  7 5
− 3 2
```

d 99 − 61 = _____
```
  9 9
− 6 1
```

e 57 − 14 = _____
```
  5 7
− 1 4
```

f 83 − 70 = _____
```
  8 3
− 7 0
```

3 Jo had 38 baby mice. She sold 15. How many did she have left? _____

4 Ali picked 49 apples. He gave 23 to his friend. How many did he keep? _____

Trial and error

Look at page 10. If you had $3, what toys would you buy?
How much change would you get? ☐

Problem solving

What's in a name?

Choose two friends and compare your names.

First name	Number of letters	Last name	Number of letters	Total

What is the total for: the longest name? the shortest? the difference between them?

_____

Now score each name if you made them with Scrabble tiles.

A₁ B₃ C₃ D₂ E₁ F₄
G₂ H₄ I₁ J₈ K₅ L₁
M₃ N₁ O₁ P₃ Q₁₀ R₁
S₁ T₁ U₁ V₄ W₄ X₈ Y₄ Z₁₀

First name	Score	Last name	Score	Total

What is the total for: the longest name? the shortest? the difference between them?

_____

Compare your results with other groups. Are their results the same as yours? _____

_____

Can you find someone whose name is double or half of yours? _____

Metres

Lab 3 basketball

Length

Elephant — Polar Bear — Gorilla — Giraffe — Tom — Dog — Brachiosaurus

1 Which animal is the tallest? _____
2 Which animal is the shortest? _____
3 How tall is the giraffe? _____
4 How tall is the elephant? _____
5 How much taller is the polar bear than Tom? _____
6 How much shorter is the gorilla than the elephant? _____
7 If Tom stood on the elephant's back how high would he be? _____
8 Are all dogs the same height? _____
9 Name a tall dog _____ and a short dog. _____
10 Write the animals in order from shortest to tallest.

_____

_____

ACMMG061 Using units of measurement • Measure, order and compare objects using familiar metric units of length, mass and capacity.

15

Measuring in metres and centimetres

Length

Estimate then measure the length of each item.

	Estimate	Measure
1 a length of board	about _____ m	about _____ m
b length of classroom	about _____ m	about _____ m
c length of school corridor	about _____ m	about _____ m

	Estimate	Measure
2 a length of this book	about _____ cm	about _____ cm
b length of your pencil	about _____ cm	about _____ cm
c length of your desk	about _____ cm	about _____ cm

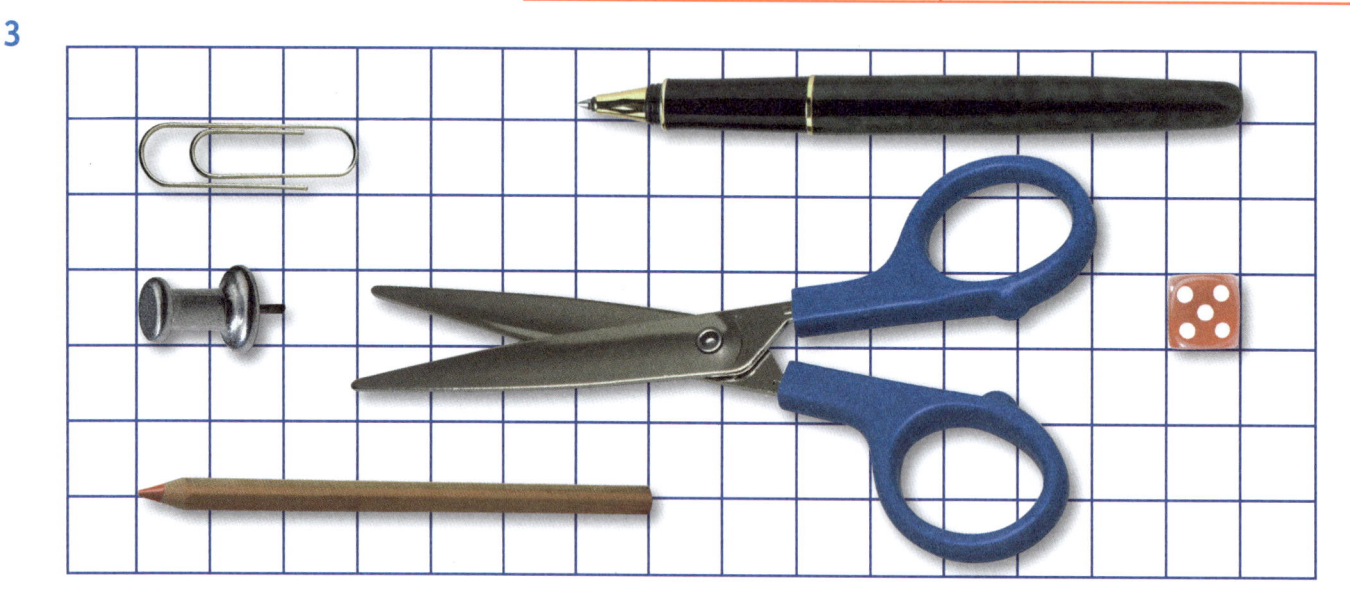

3

a What is the longest? _____
b What is the shortest? _____
c How long is the pen? _____
d How long is the paperclip? _____
e Which two items together are 5 cm? _____
f The pushpin is _____ cm longer than the die.
g The paperclip is _____ cm shorter than the scissors.

4 Find something in your classroom that is:

a 1 m _____
b 30 cm _____
c 2 m _____
d 10 cm _____
e 50 cm _____
f 80 cm _____

16

ACMMG061 Using units of measurement • Measure, order and compare objects using familiar metric units of length, mass and capacity.

Measuring and estimating length

Length

m = metre
cm = centimetre

1. Use the number bank to complete each sentence.

   Number Bank 1 2 4 10 30 180

   a The door is _____ m high.

   b The globe is _____ cm long.

   c The man is _____ cm tall.

   d The hen is _____ cm tall.

   e The car is _____ m long.

   f The wheelbarrow is _____ m long.

2. The bus stop sign is 1 m high.

   a How high is the bus? _____

   b How long is the bus? _____

3. Measure these lines.

   a
   b
   c
   d

   a _____ b _____ c _____ d _____

Challenge! How could you measure the length of this line?

How long is it? _____

ACMMG061 Using units of measurement • Measure, order and compare objects using familiar metric units of length, mass and capacity.

17

Fractions

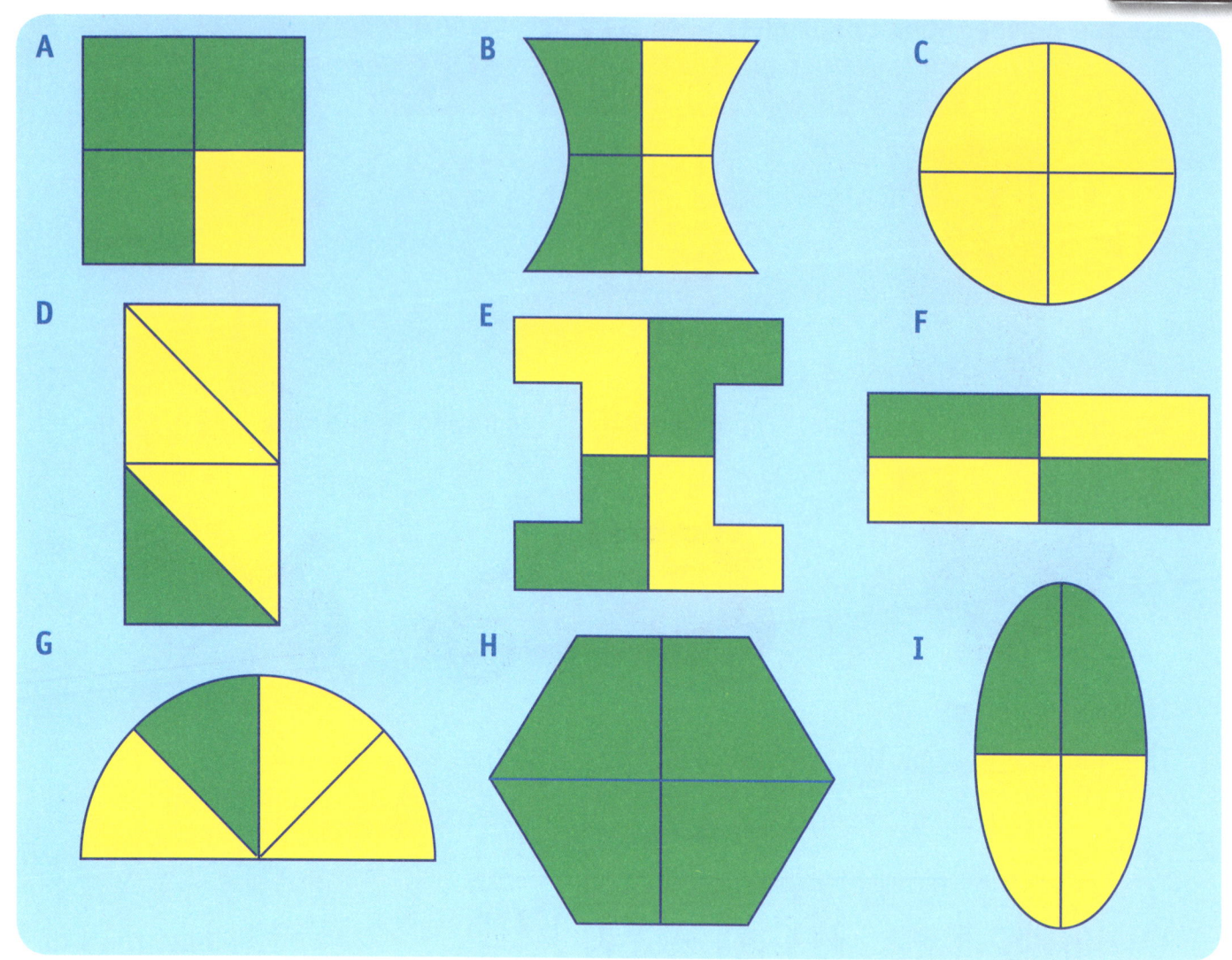

Lab 3 fraction 2

Halves and quarters

A B C
D E F
G H I

1. Which shapes are one quarter green? __D and__
2. Which shapes are one half yellow? _____
3. Which shapes show one whole? _____
4. Which shapes are one half green? _____
5. In F what fraction is yellow? _____
6. In G what fraction is green? _____
7. How many quarters are in one whole? _____
8. How many halves are in one whole? _____
9. How many quarters are in one half? _____
10. How many halves are in 2 wholes? _____
    3 wholes? _____

Quarters mean 4 equal parts.

ACMNA058 Fractions and decimals • Model and represent unit fractions including $\frac{1}{2}$, $\frac{1}{4}$, $\frac{1}{3}$, $\frac{1}{5}$ and their multiples to a complete whole.

Halves and quarters

1. Colour the letters that are cut in half.

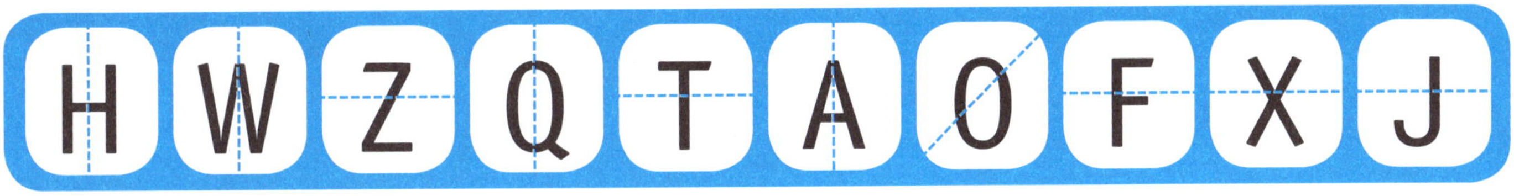

   H W Z Q T A O F X J

2. Draw a line to cut these letters in half.

   V B M C D

3. Circle the halves. Tick the quarters.

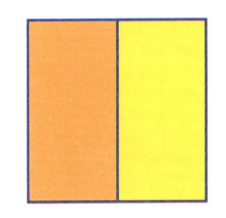

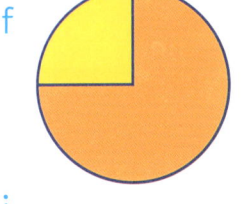

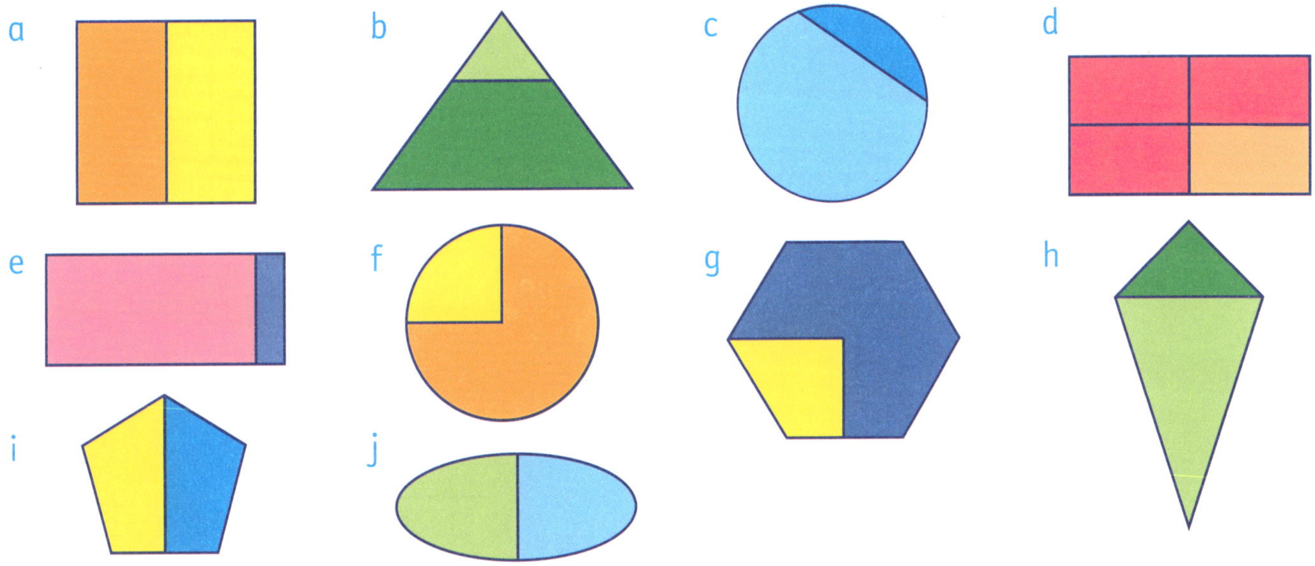

   a   b   c   d
   e   f   g   h
   i   j

4. Draw a line to cut each in half. Colour one half.

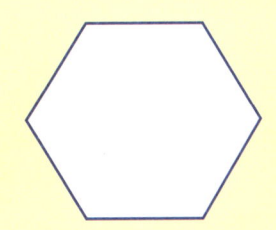

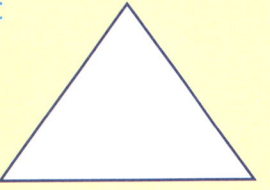

   a   b   c   d

5. Draw lines to cut each into quarters. Colour one quarter of each.

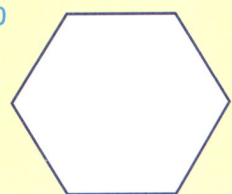

   a   b   c   d   e

ACMNA058 Fractions and decimals • Model and represent unit fractions including $\frac{1}{2}$, $\frac{1}{4}$, $\frac{1}{3}$, $\frac{1}{5}$ and their multiples to a complete whole.

19

Fractions as part of a whole

Working with fractions

1 Colour part of each shape to match the fraction.

a
1 out of 5
one fifth

b
1 out of 6
one sixth

c
1 out of 3
one third

d
1 out of 10
one tenth

e
1 out of five
one _____

f
1 out of two
one _____

g
1 out of four
one _____

h
1 out of five
one _____

2 Write the fraction for the coloured part.

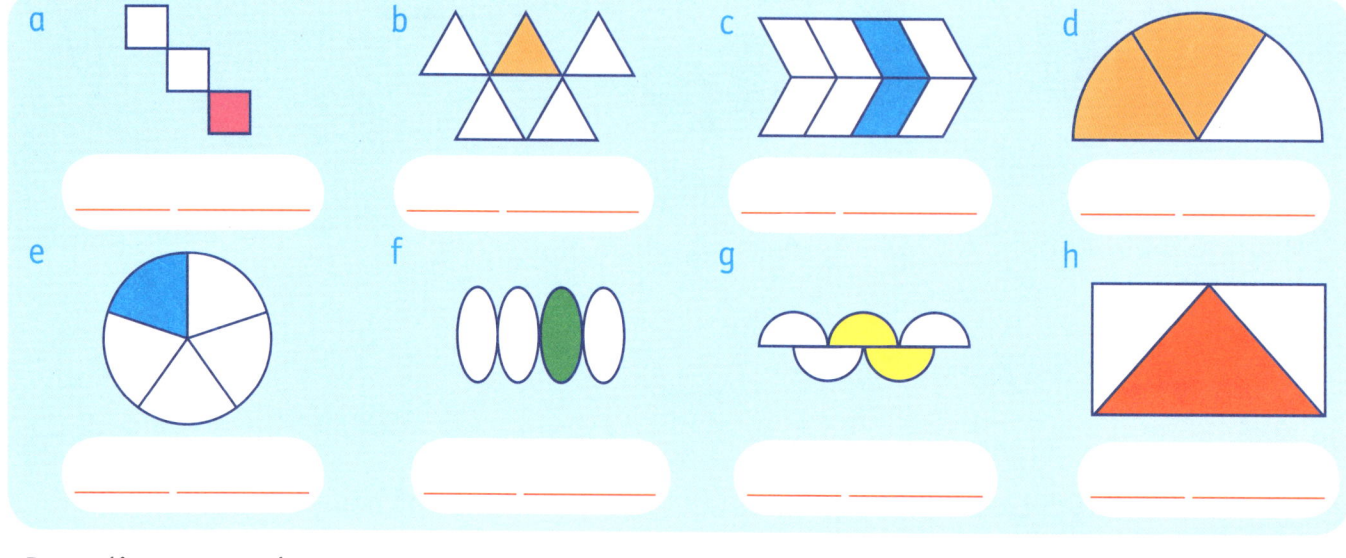

a   b   c   d

e   f   g   h

3 Draw lines to make equal parts. Colour and name a fraction you like.

a   b

ACMNA058 Fractions and decimals • Model and represent unit fractions including $\frac{1}{2}$, $\frac{1}{4}$, $\frac{1}{3}$, $\frac{1}{5}$ and their multiples to a complete whole.

Problem solving

Fraction rewards

1. As a reward each person in the red team got one piece of a Jolly Chew Bar. Colour the pieces each child received.

   a Nelly got one piece of a four piece bar.   b Feng got one piece of a three piece bar.

   c Sara got one piece of an eight piece bar.   d Mei got one piece of a six piece bar.

2. Write the names in order from smallest piece to largest piece.

   _____ _____ _____ _____

3. a Are these rewards fair? Why? _____

   b What would you have done? _____

4. How many different ways can you divide this Jolly Chew Bar into quarters to share with three other people and yourself?

Investigation 1 Measure length with people measures

Your classroom is getting new carpet. The principal needs the measurements of your room.

Estimate first. The room is _____ long and _____ wide.

How could you measure the room without using a tape measure?
_____

Draw your room here and show the different measurement tools you used.

Write what you found out.
_____
_____
_____
_____

Measure length with people measures — Investigation 1

Your teacher says you could rearrange the furniture in your classroom, so you have to measure it too. Do this with parts of your body: feet, hands, arms, forearms. Make a table to record the measurements. Explain how you measured the objects.

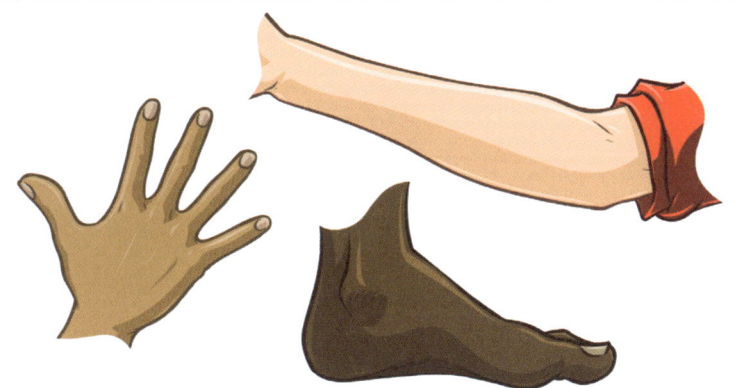

Why are people measures useful?

_____

_____

_____

To carry out these tasks I need to:
- ☐ estimate lengths.
- ☐ measure lengths with parts of my body.
- ☐ explain how I measure lengths.
- ☐ use a table to record lengths of different objects.
- ☐ work well in a group.

I enjoyed this task!
★★★★★

Revision

Shade one bubble.

1. Which number completes the pattern?

   278 268 258 248 ___

   228 282 238 283
   ○   ○   ○   ○

2. Which group shows 54?

   one / ten

   ○   ○   ○   ○

3. Huey had $1 to spend and bought this toy. 85c

   How much change did he get?

   5c   25c $1.15   15c
   ○   ○   ○   ○

4. A cake costs $13.
   How much for two cakes?

   $15 $23 $26 $25
   ○   ○   ○   ○

5. How much altogether?

   $100 $10 $100 $1 $1
   $100 $100 $10 $1 $100

   $523 $532 $343 $432
   ○   ○   ○   ○

24

Revision

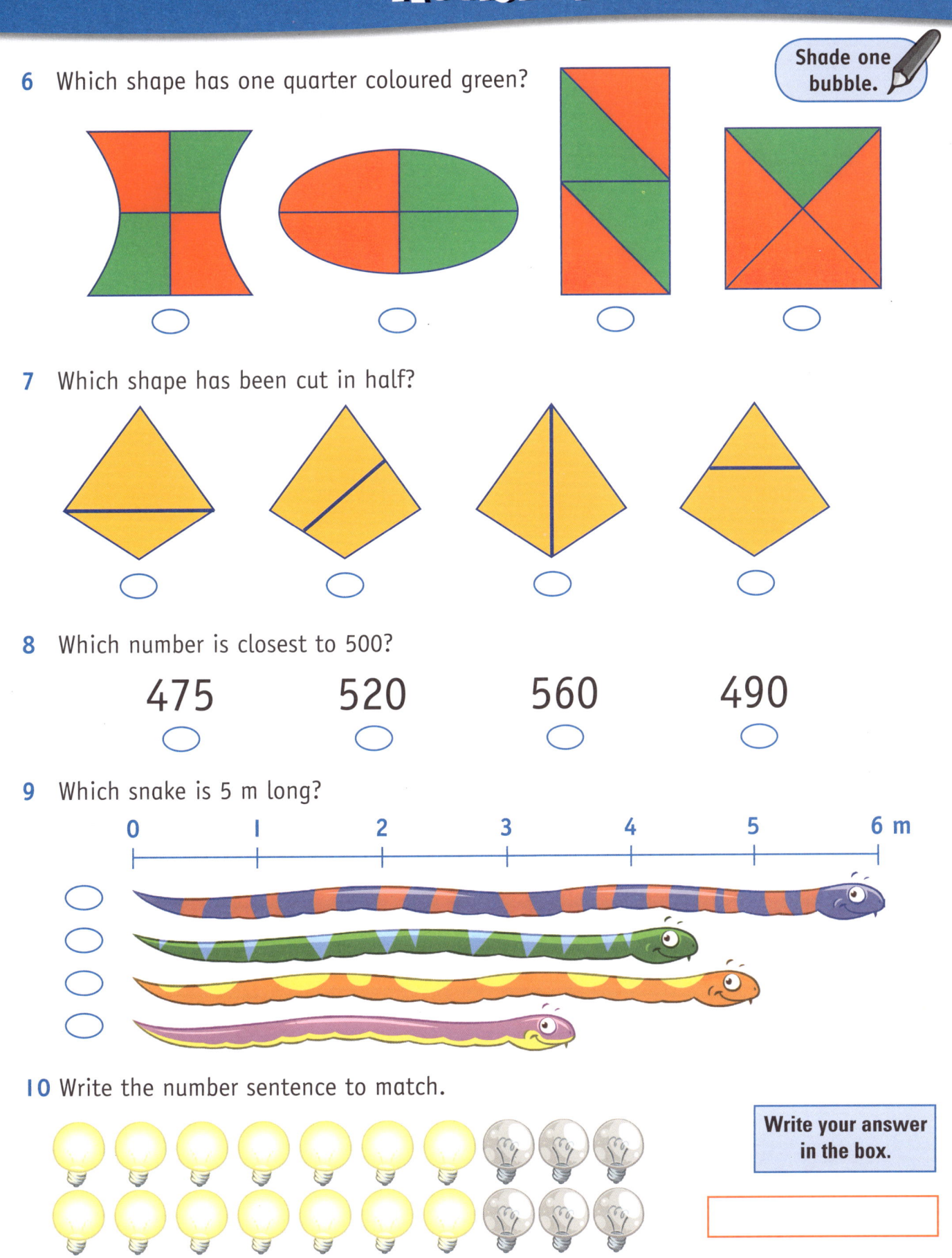

Shade one bubble.

6 Which shape has one quarter coloured green?

○　　　○　　　○　　　○

7 Which shape has been cut in half?

○　　　○　　　○　　　○

8 Which number is closest to 500?

475　　　520　　　560　　　490
○　　　○　　　○　　　○

9 Which snake is 5 m long?

0　　1　　2　　3　　4　　5　　6 m

○
○
○
○

10 Write the number sentence to match.

Write your answer in the box.

25

Number facts 2x, 5x, 10x

0x
0 × 2 = 0
0 × 5 = 0
0 × 10 = 0

1 Count backwards in:

   a **2s** from 20, ____, ____, ____, ____, ____, ____

   b **5s** from 30, ____, ____, ____, ____, ____, ____

   c **10s** from 100, ____, ____, ____, ____, ____, ____

2 How many:

   a wheels on 8 trikes? _____   on 3 trikes? _____
   b eyes on 9 owls? _____   on 5 owls? _____
   c 10c coins in $7? _____   in $4? _____
   d toes on 6 feet? _____   on 8 feet? _____
   e hands on 5 clocks? _____   on 10 clocks? _____
   f arms on 4 starfish? _____   on 9 starfish? _____
   g corners on 7 triangles? _____   on 4 triangles? _____
   h ears on 10 horses? _____   tails on 10 horses? _____

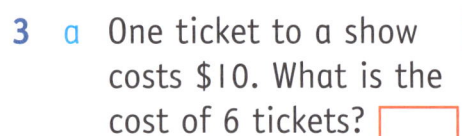

3 a One ticket to a show costs $10. What is the cost of 6 tickets? ☐

   b Ten children get 5 lollies each. How many lollies altogether? ☐

4 Complete these from memory.

a
×	3	0	5	7	9	6	8	2	4	10
2										

b
×	0	5	9	6	2	10	4	7	3	8
5										

c
×	7	5	1	8	4	10	0	6	2	9
10										

26 ACMNA056 Number and place value • Recall multiplication facts of two, three, five and ten and related division facts.

Odds and evens

1. Show by pairing circles that:

   a 14 is an even number.

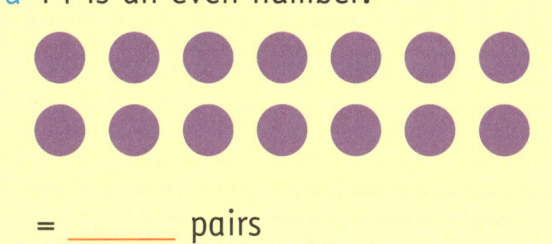

   = _____ pairs

   b 17 is an odd number.

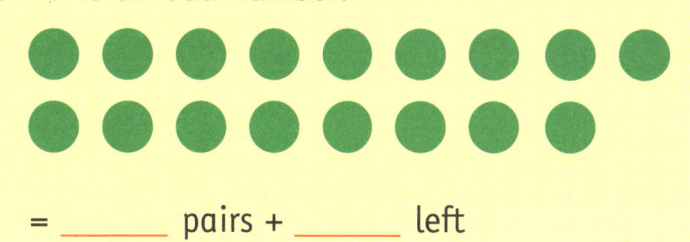

   = _____ pairs + _____ left

2. Circle the odd numbers.

   9, 15, 22, 100, 51, 352, 249, 150, 791

3. Write the next three numbers in the pattern.

   a 91, 89, 87 _____ _____ _____ odd or even? _____

   b 240, 242, 244 _____ _____ _____ odd or even? _____

4. a Odd numbers all end in _____ , _____ , _____ , _____ or 9.

   b Even numbers all end in 2, _____ , _____ , _____ or _____ .

5. Write 5 even numbers between 500 and 1000.

   _____

6. Circle all the sums with an odd number answer.

5 + 14	3 + 9	17 + 2	11 + 6	1 + 14
2 + 6	9 + 12	12 + 4	7 + 13	6 + 8
5 + 5	8 + 13	12 + 12	9 + 15	16 + 3

7. Answer odd or even.

   odd + odd = _____

   even + even = _____

   odd + even = _____

8. True or false?

   Numbers are odd or even. _____

   Only the ones digit tells us odd or even. _____

Challenge! Odd or even?

odd × odd = ☐   even × even = ☐   odd × even = ☐

Patterns

A 0 4 8 12 16 20

B

C 2 5 8 11 14 17

D

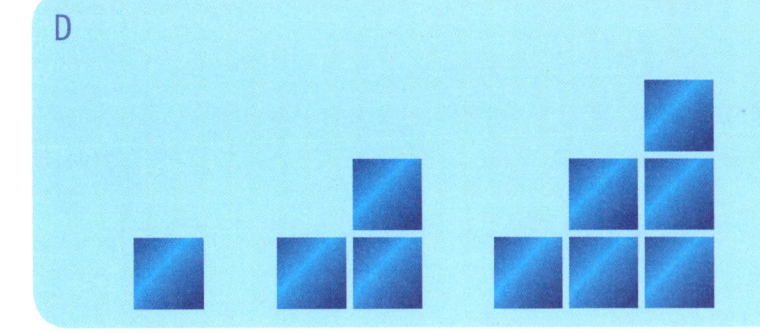

1. a How is pattern A made? _____
   b What are the next three numbers? _____ _____ _____
   c What will the 12th number be? _____

2. Draw the next term for B.

3. a What is the next number in C? _____
   b What is the pattern for C? _____
   c Will 27 be in C? _____ Why? _____

4. a How many squares will be in the next term for D? _____
   b Draw it.

28

ACMNA060 Patterns and algebra • Describe, continue, and create number patterns resulting from performing addition or subtraction.

Patterns using shapes and numbers

1 a Start at 2. Make a pattern by adding four.

      2

   b Start at 1. Make a pattern by adding four.

      1

   c 3 7 11 15 19 23

     How was this pattern made? _____

   d Each pattern rule is add 4. Why are the patterns different? _____
_____

Look at page 28.

2 a What is happening to change the terms in B? _____

   b Write the pattern in numbers? ____ ____ ____ ____

   c How many spots will there be in the 10th term? _____   14th term? _____

   d Draw another pattern like B using triangles.

3 a What shape is used for D? _____

   b Will the next term use a circle? _____

      Why? _____

Challenge! How many squares will be in the 10th shape for D? ☐

Patterns with numbers

1 Finish each pattern and write the rule.

a   2, 4, 6, 8   ____, ____, ____   Rule _____
b   10, 13, 16, 19   ____, ____, ____   Rule _____
c   30c, 25c, 20c, 15c   ____, ____, ____   Rule _____
d   20 cm, 30 cm, 40 cm, 50 cm   ____, ____, ____   Rule _____
e   1, 10, 19, 28   ____, ____, ____   Rule _____
f   1, 2, 4, 8   ____, ____, ____   Rule _____
g   48, 42, 36, 30   ____, ____, ____   Rule _____
h   2, 9, 16, 23   ____, ____, ____   Rule _____
i $\frac{1}{5}$, $\frac{2}{5}$, $\frac{3}{5}$, $\frac{4}{5}$ ____, ____, ____   Rule _____
j   39, 35, 31, 27   ____, ____, ____   Rule _____

2 a Start with 20. Make a pattern by adding 3.
   20, ___, ___, ___, ___

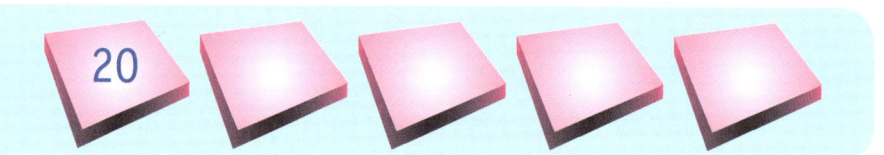

   b Start with 86. Make a pattern by taking away 10.
   86, ___, ___, ___, ___

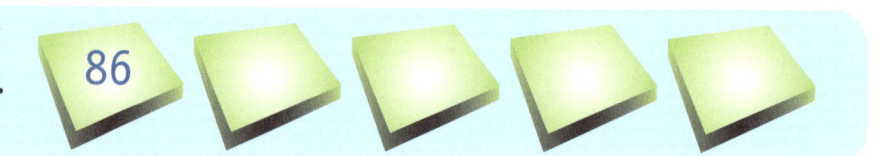

   c Start with 5. Make a pattern by doubling.
   5, ___, ___, ___, ___

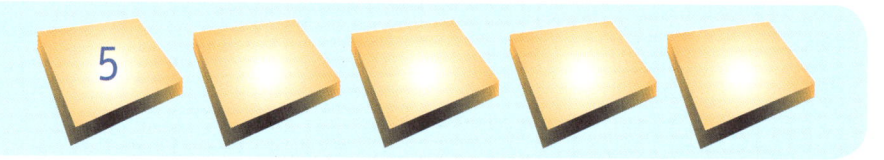

   d Write the instructions for this pattern. _____
   0, 11, 22, 33, 44

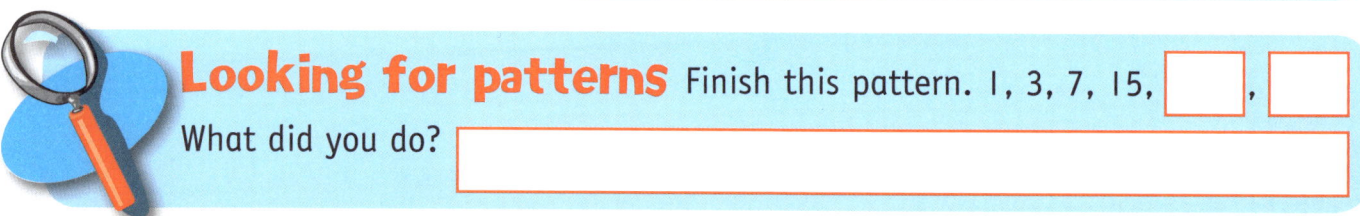

Looking for patterns Finish this pattern. 1, 3, 7, 15, ☐, ☐

What did you do? _____

30

ACMNA060 Patterns and algebra • Describe, continue, and create number patterns resulting from performing addition or subtraction.

Problem solving

Frog Jumps

Froggy jumps by twos to visit Ducky. He jumps to lily pad 2, then 4 and so on until he gets there.

Froggy's jumps: 2, 4, 6 _____ How many jumps? _____

From Ducky, Froggy jumps by threes to the flies for a snack, starting at 12.

Froggy's jumps: 12 _____ How many jumps? _____

From the flies, Froggy jumps by fives to visit his mum, starting at 5.

Froggy's jumps: 5 _____ How many jumps? _____

Make up your own pattern for Froggy to jump. Add a home for him to jump to.

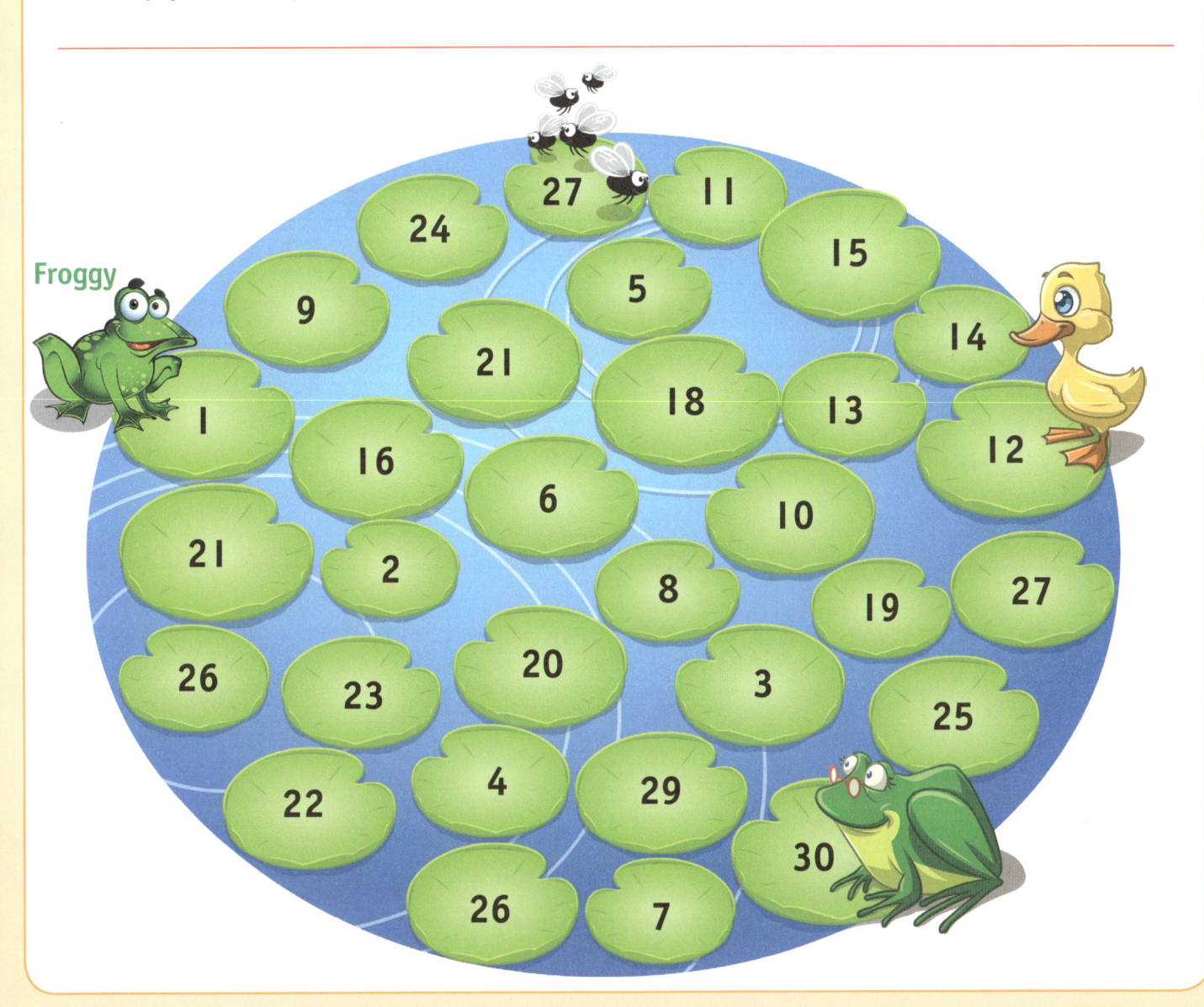

_____

ACMNA060 Patterns and algebra • Describe, continue, and create number patterns resulting from performing addition or subtraction.

Lab 3 — time quiz
Half hours and quarter hours

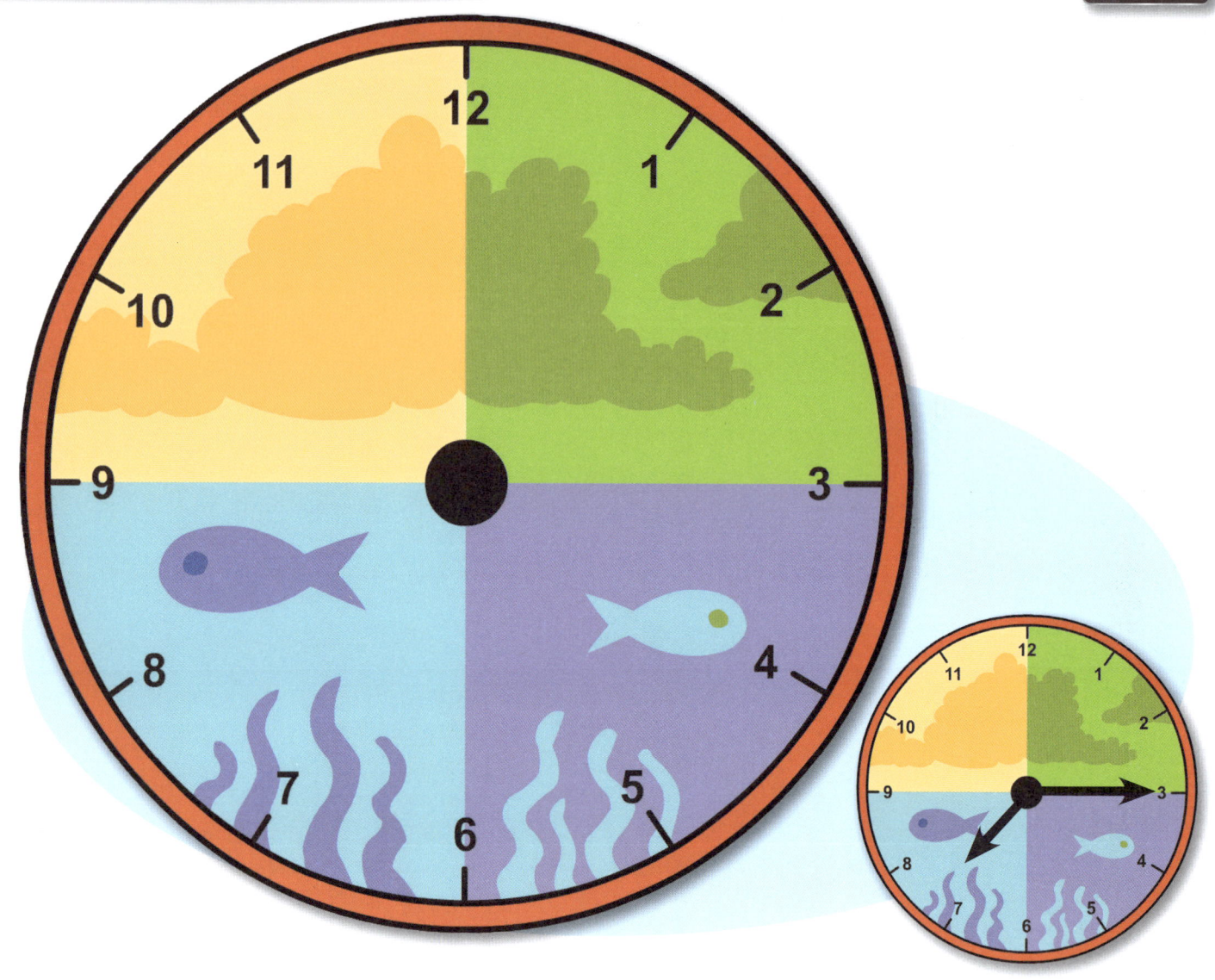

1 With your sticks show: a 4 o'clock   b 7 o'clock   c 10 o'clock
   d Where is the minute hand each time? _____
   e Where is the hour hand at 4 o'clock? _____

2 With your sticks show: a $\frac{1}{2}$ past 8   b $\frac{1}{2}$ past 11   c $\frac{1}{2}$ past 5
   d Where is the minute hand each time? _____
   e Where is the hour hand at $\frac{1}{2}$ past 8? _____

3 a What is the time on the small clock? _____
   b Why is the minute hand on 3? _____
   c Where is the hour hand? _____

4 With your sticks show: a $\frac{1}{4}$ past 9   b $\frac{1}{4}$ past 2   c $\frac{1}{4}$ past 10
                            d $\frac{1}{4}$ to 5   e $\frac{1}{4}$ to 3   f $\frac{1}{4}$ to 12

ACMMG062 Using units of measurement • Tell time to the minute and investigate the relationship between units of time.

5 minute intervals

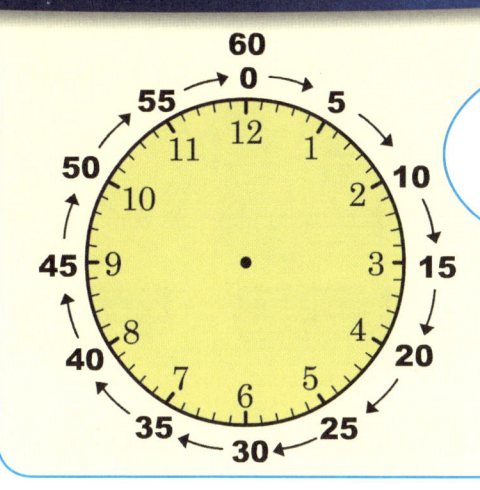

Between each number on the clock face there are 5 minutes.

short hand tells the hour
long hand tells the minute
60 minutes = 1 hour

1 How many minutes pass as the minute hand moves from:

a 12 to 1 _____   b 12 to 3 _____   c 12 to 6 _____
d 12 to 9 _____   e 12 to 7 _____   f 12 to 2 _____
g 12 to 12 _____ h 12 to 11 _____ i 12 to 4 _____
j 12 to 10 _____ k 12 to 5 _____   l 12 to 8 _____

2

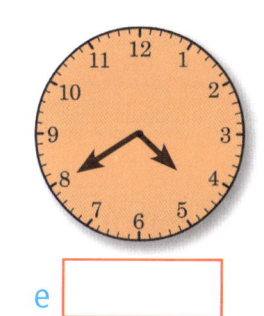

a 3:25   b ____   c ____   d ____   e ____

3 Use 'past' and 'to' to tell these times, eg $\frac{1}{4}$ to 5.

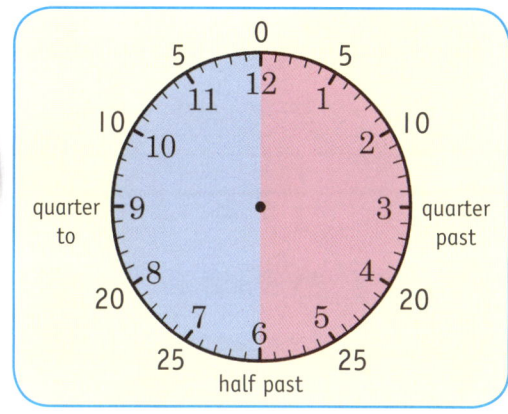

a ____   b ____   c ____

quarter to | quarter past
half past

4 Draw these times.

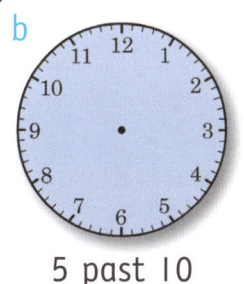

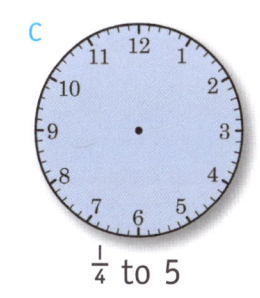

a 25 to 5   b 5 past 10   c $\frac{1}{4}$ to 5   d 20 past 12   e 10 past 7

Analogue and digital times

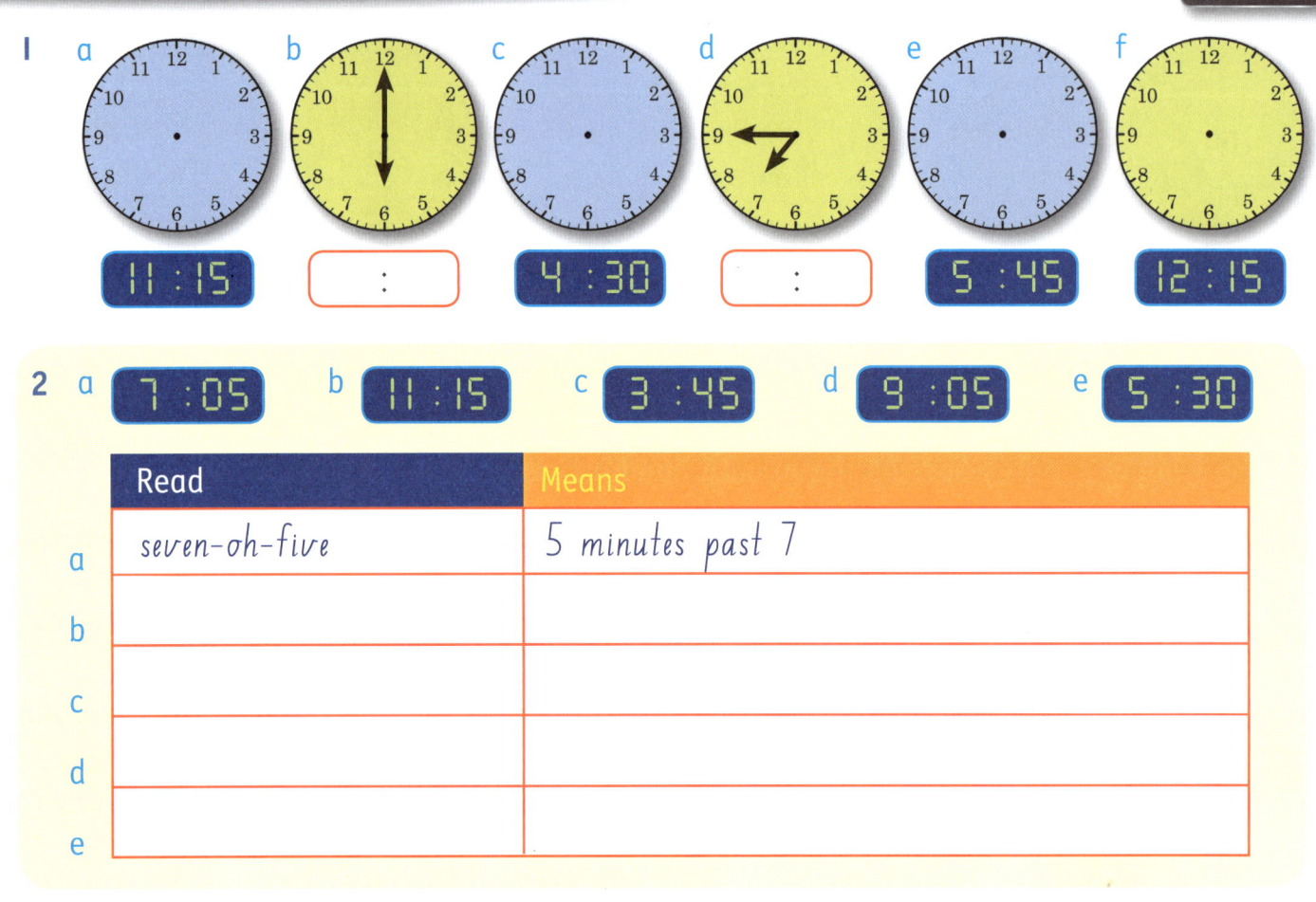

1 a `11:15`   b `  :  `   c `4:30`   d `  :  `   e `5:45`   f `12:15`

2 a `7:05`   b `11:15`   c `3:45`   d `9:05`   e `5:30`

	Read	Means
a	seven-oh-five	5 minutes past 7
b		
c		
d		
e		

3 Match the time to the correct clock.

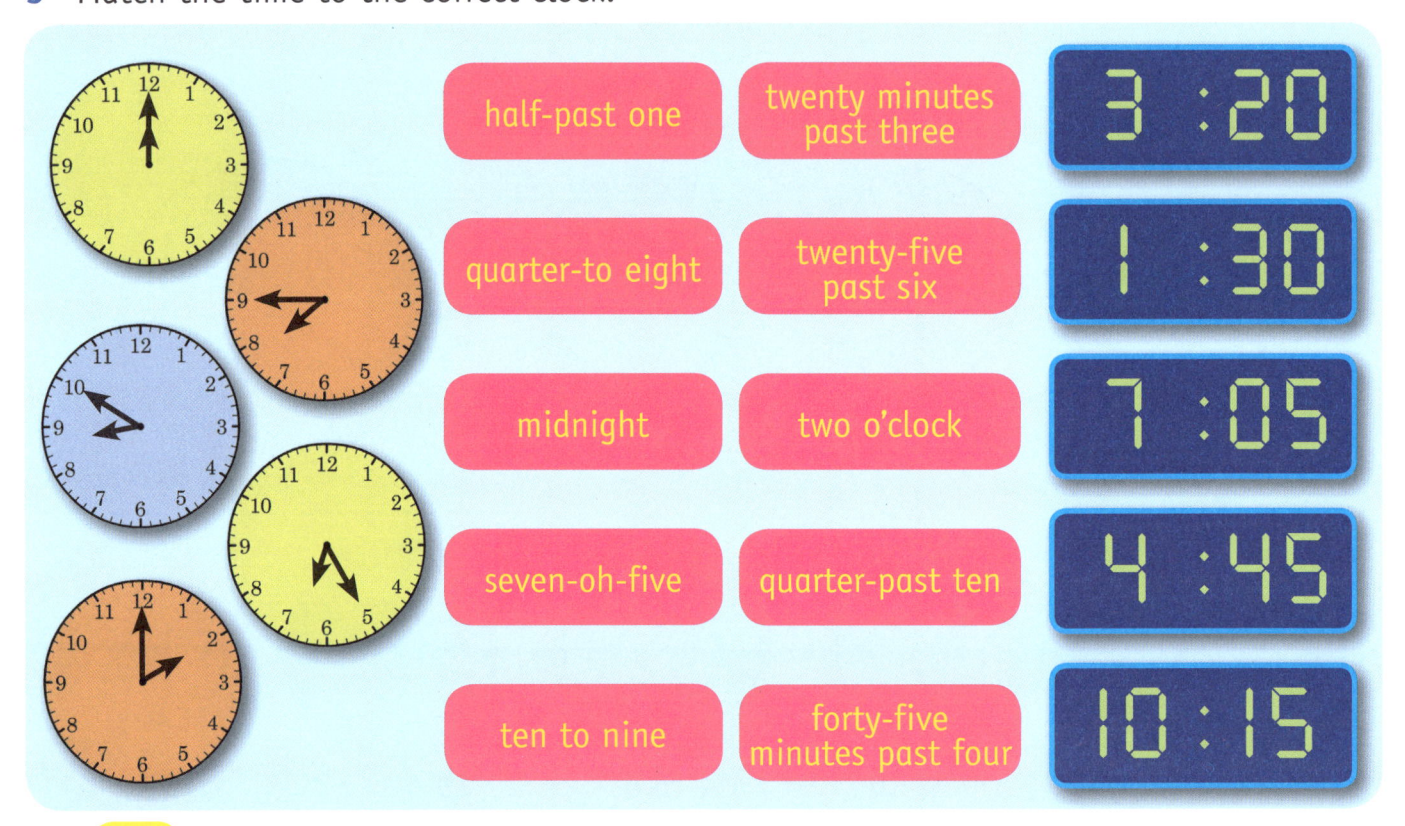

half-past one	twenty minutes past three	`3:20`
quarter-to eight	twenty-five past six	`1:30`
midnight	two o'clock	`7:05`
seven-oh-five	quarter-past ten	`4:45`
ten to nine	forty-five minutes past four	`10:15`

34 ACMMG062 Using units of measurement • Tell time to the minute and investigate the relationship between units of time.

Lab 3 — Prisms

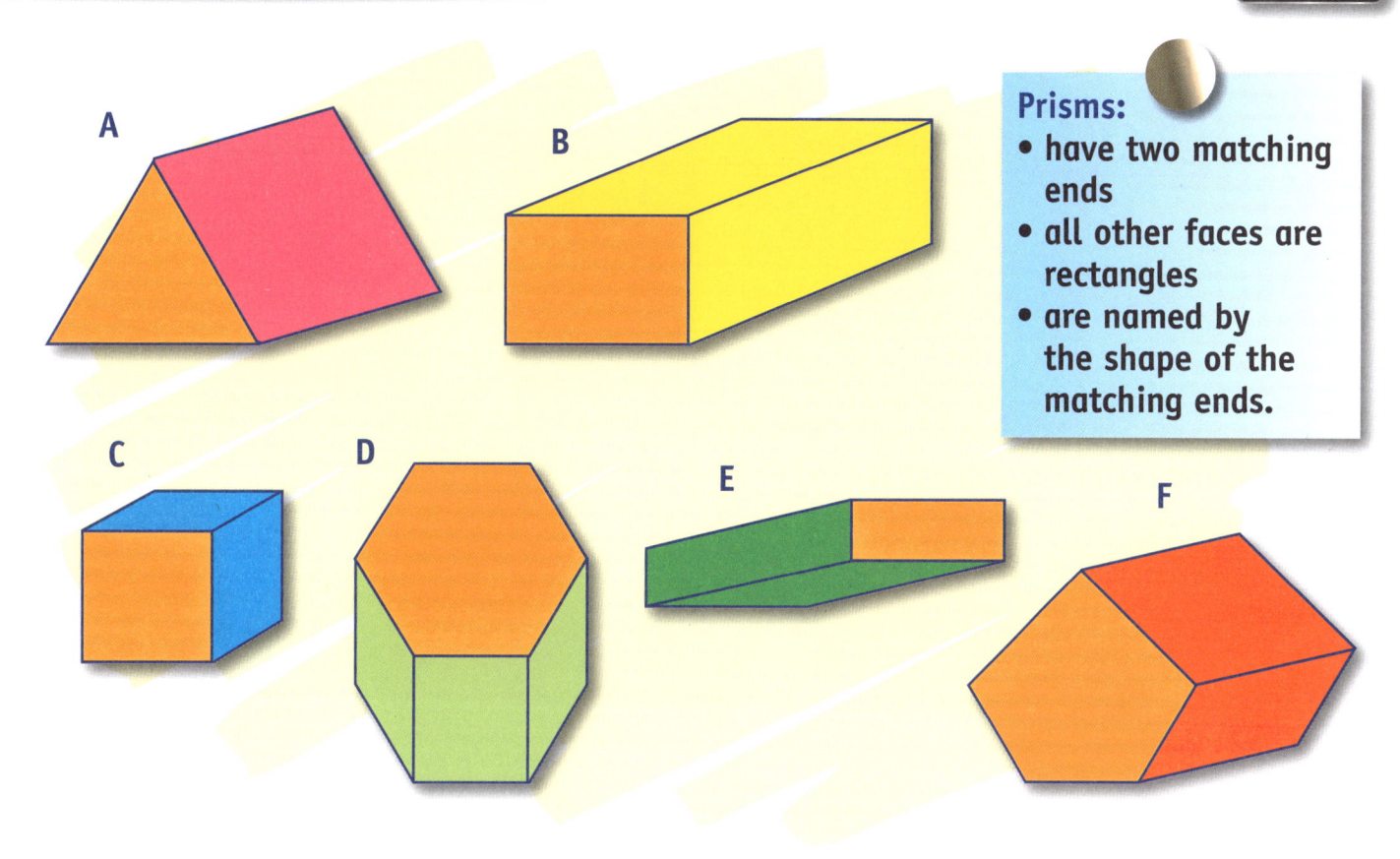

Prisms:
- have two matching ends
- all other faces are rectangles
- are named by the shape of the matching ends.

1. Name the shape of each orange face.
   A _____   B _____
   C _____   D _____
   E _____   F _____

2. Use the face name to name each prism.
   A *Triangular prism*   B _____
   C _____   D _____
   E _____   F _____

3. How many faces has each prism? Remember that you can't see them all.
   A _____   B _____   C _____
   D _____   E _____   F _____

4. What shape are all the faces that aren't ends? _____

5. What is a prism? _____
   _____

ACMMG063 Shape • Make models of three-dimensional objects and describe key features.

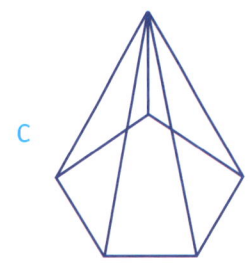

Pyramids

1 Name these pyramids.

   a   b   c

   _____   _____   _____
   _____   _____   _____

Pyramids:
- have one base.
- all other faces are triangles.
- are named by the shape of the base.

2 Circle the pyramids. Draw a square around the prisms.

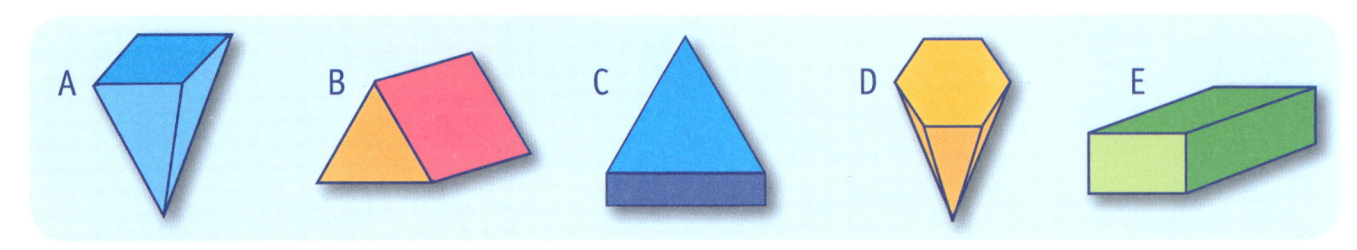

   A   B   C   D   E

   a How many faces has shape D? _____   b shape A? _____
   c Which picture shows a square pyramid? _____
   d Which picture shows a rectangular prism? _____

3 Draw each face.

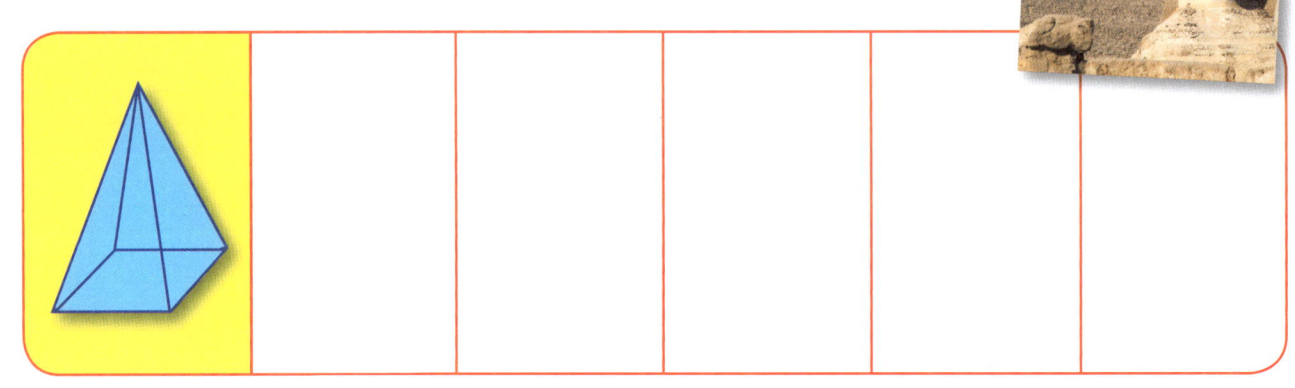

Challenge! How many everyday items can you name that are pyramid-shaped or triangular prisms?

Cones, cylinders and spheres

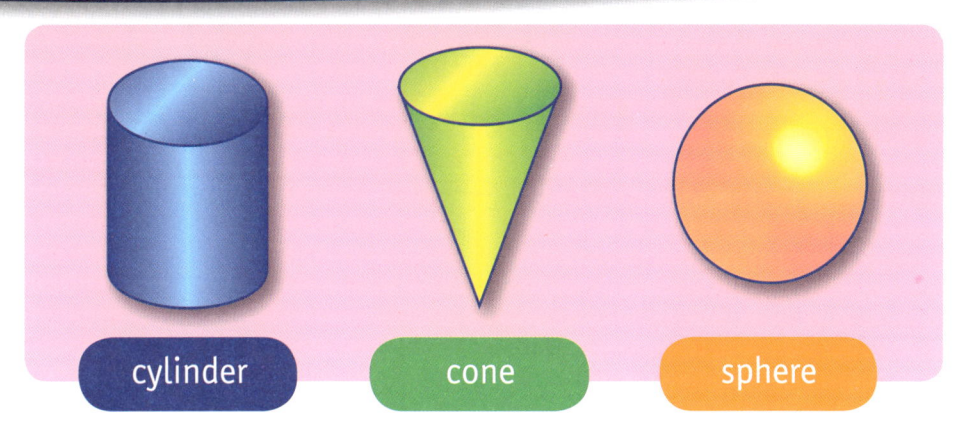

cylinder   cone   sphere

1 Name three things that are cylinders.
   a _____ b _____ c _____

2 Name three things that are cones.
   a _____ b _____ c _____

3 Name three things that are spheres.
   a _____ b _____ c _____

4 Which object above can be most easily stacked? _____
   Why? _____

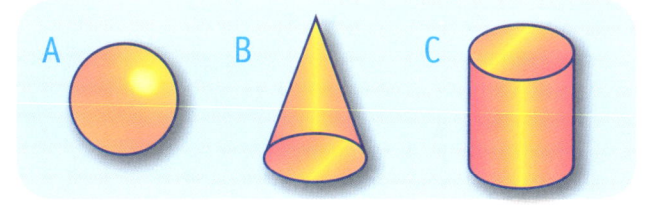

5 A   B   C

   Am I A, B or C?
   a I have one curved surface and 1 flat surface. _____
   b I have only one surface. _____
   c I have 2 flat surfaces and 1 curved surface. _____

6 How many surfaces has A? _____ B? _____ C? _____

7 Draw the view from the:

Top			Side		
A	B	C	A	B	C

ACMMG063 Shape • Make models of three-dimensional objects and describe key features.   37

Problem solving

How can you make prisms?

1. Write the time when you start this page, using 'to' or 'past'. _____

2. Make a prism. Choose from the following ways.
   Use pattern blocks.
   Use paper.
   Use clay or another solid material.

3. Describe what you did and how you did it. Draw it.

   _____
   _____
   _____
   _____
   _____
   _____

4. Draw your prism from a different view.

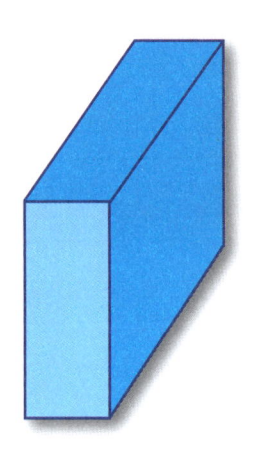

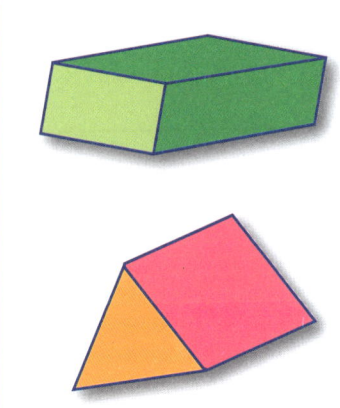

5. What did you find out about prisms?

   _____
   _____

6. Write the time when you finished working on this page. _____

   How long were you working on this page? _____

38   ACMMG063 Shape • Make models of three-dimensional objects and describe key features.

Graphs

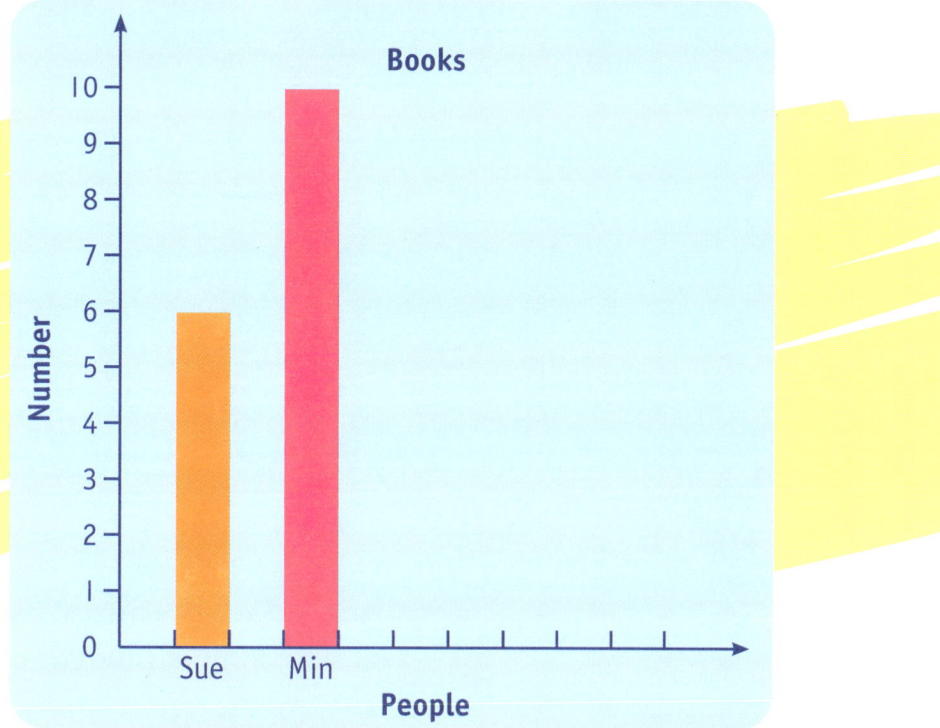

Lab 3 — jetpack jenny

1. Complete the column graph. Write the children's names under the columns.
2. What is this graph telling us? _____
3. Who has: a the most books? _____ b the least books? _____
4. Who has two less books than Amy? _____
5. Which two children together have 9 books? _____
6. How many books do the children have altogether? _____
7. If John gives half his books to Min, how many will he now have? _____
8. Does the graph tell us who likes reading most? Why or why not?

_____

_____

_____

ACMSP069 & ACMSP070 Data representation and interpretation • Collect data, organise into categories and create displays using lists, tables, picture graphs and simple column graphs, with and without the use of digital technologies. • Interpret and compare data displays.

Column graph

At the beginning of the year Mr Wright gave the students in his class new pencils.

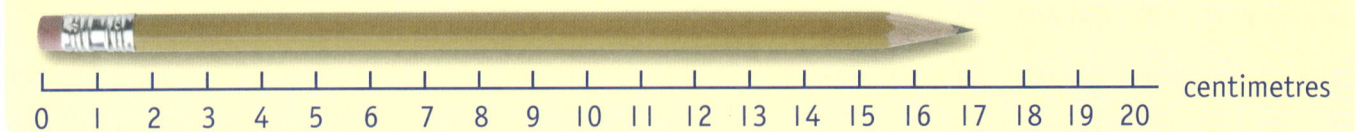

```
|—|—|—|—|—|—|—|—|—|—|—|—|—|—|—|—|—|—|—|—|—| centimetres
0  1  2  3  4  5  6  7  8  9  10 11 12 13 14 15 16 17 18 19 20
```

1 How long were the pencils? _____

One month later Mr Wright asked some students how long their pencils were now. He graphed the results.

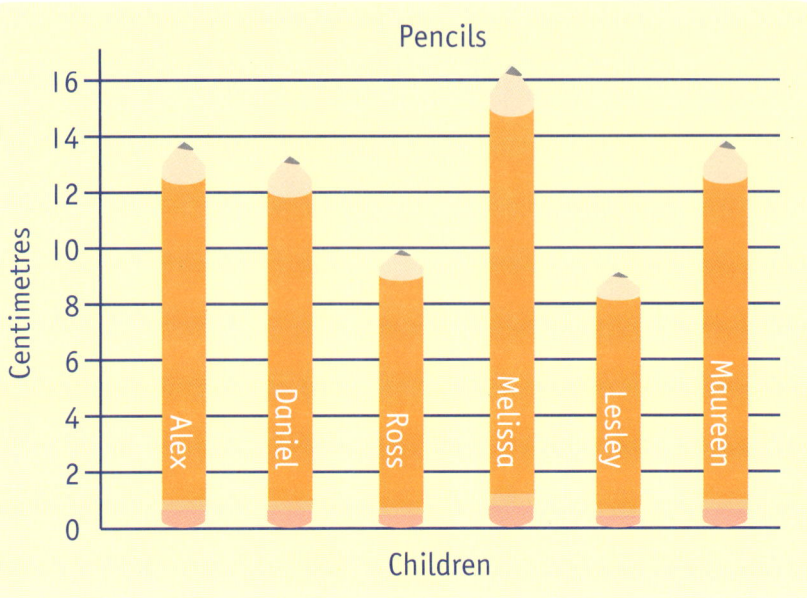

Pencils

Column graph showing pencil lengths in centimetres:
- Alex: 12.5
- Daniel: 12
- Ross: 9
- Melissa: 15
- Lesley: 8
- Maureen: 12.5

(Y-axis: Centimetres, 0–16; X-axis: Children)

2 How long is Alex's pencil? _____

3 How long is Daniel's pencil? _____

4 Who has the longest pencil? _____

5 Whose pencil is the shortest? _____

6 a How long is Lesley's pencil? _____

b How much shorter is it now than when she got it? _____

7 How much shorter is Ross's pencil now than when Mr Wright gave it to him? _____

8 Give one reason why Lesley's pencil is so short.

_____

9 Why do you think Melissa's pencil is so long?

_____

10 Why did Mr Wright measure pencils? _____

Draw a diagram

Show this information in a different way. Make sure you label your work clearly.

ACMSP070 Data representation and interpretation • Interpret and compare data displays. • Compare data representations and describe their similarities and differences.

Problem solving

Class favourites survey

Find out about your class. Survey the class about a topic: Sports, Food or Games. What questions will you ask?

Carry out a survey.

Tally

Show your results as a picture graph or column graph.

What did you find out?

Certain, likely, unlikely, impossible

1. Write *certain*, *likely*, *unlikely* or *impossible*.

   a The sky will be green tomorrow. _____

   b The sun will rise in the morning. _____

   c I may not be able to go to the party. _____

   d I will grow taller than a giraffe. _____

   e It might rain tonight. _____

   f We will have a holiday this year. _____

2. There are 6 red, 4 green and 2 yellow balls in the bag.

   Without looking what is your chance of choosing a:

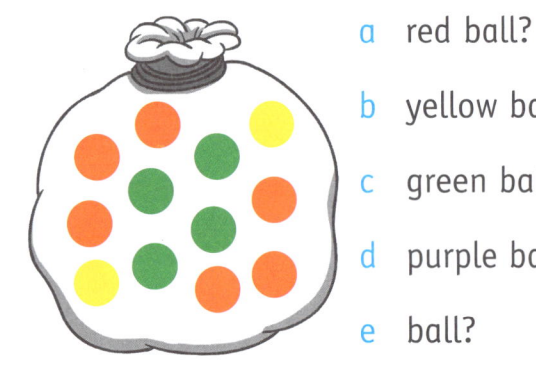

   a red ball?   50-50   likely   unlikely   impossible

   b yellow ball?   50-50   likely   unlikely   impossible

   c green ball?   50-50   likely   unlikely   impossible

   d purple ball?   50-50   likely   unlikely   impossible

   e ball?   50-50   likely   unlikely   impossible

3. Colour the flowers so that it would be likely you choose purple, unlikely you choose orange, impossible to choose white.

4. Colour the marbles so you have an equal chance of choosing red or blue.

Chance outcomes

The different ways a thing can happen are called outcomes.

1. A coin is tossed.
   a What two ways can it fall? _____ _____
   b How many outcomes can there be? _____

2. a What colours show on traffic lights? _____
   b How many are there? _____
   c How many possible outcomes are there? _____

3. a How many faces are on this die? _____
   b If you toss the die what are the possible outcomes?
   _____ _____ _____ _____ _____
   c How many possible outcomes are there? _____

4. This basket contains two apples and two oranges. Without looking, you pick out one piece of fruit.
   a What could it be? _____
   b How many possible outcomes are there? _____

5. Write something where:
   a the outcome is certain. _____
   b the outcome is impossible. _____
   c the outcome is likely. _____
   d the outcome is unlikely. _____

Challenge! Work with a partner. Throw a die 10 times. Record the outcomes. There are 6 possible outcomes. Does each outcome occur the same number of times? Why or why not?

ACMSP067 Chance • Conduct chance experiments, identify and describe possible outcomes and recognise variation in results.

Revision Term 1

1 Write the number: p 2

   a 10 more than 115 _____

   b 100 less than 810 _____

   c an even number larger than 135

   _____

2 Write in numerals: p 5

   a three hundred and seventy-one

   _____

   b five hundred and six _____

   c two hundred and forty _____

3 Write in words: p 5

   a 98 _____

   b 613 _____

   c 480 _____

4 Write in the missing numbers.   p 7

   a 95 90 ___ 80 75 ___

   b 59 ___ 39 ___ 19

   c 19 17 ___ ___ 11 9

5 Double: a 7 ___   b 19 ___   p 8

6 a 17 − 9 = ___   b 15 − 8 = ___   p 11

   c 20 − 13 = ___   d 16 − 7 = ___

7 Use the number lines.   p 13

   a 32 − 17 = ___

   b 53 − 25 = ___

8   p 11

Write a story and a number sentence.

_____

_____

_____

9 Circle the correct answer.   p 16

   a A door is about 2 cm 2 m high.

   b A book cover is about 20 cm 1 m wide.

   c A bedroom is about 50 m 4 m long.

10 Measure these lines.   p 17

   a ____ b ____

11 What part has been shaded?   p 18

   a ____   b ____

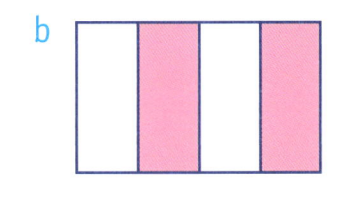

   c ____

   d Draw lines to cut this into quarters. Shade $\frac{1}{2}$.   p 19

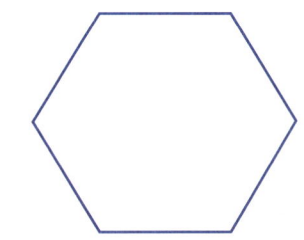

44

Revision Term 1

12 Write a fraction for the coloured part.

a

b

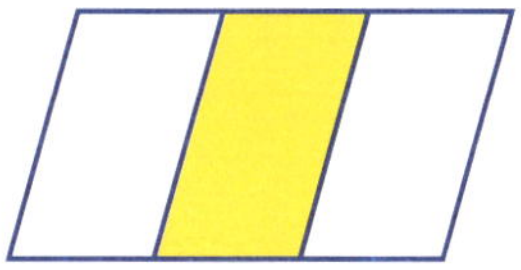

c

d

13

×	6	8	0	9	5	3	7	4
2								

14 Write the next two terms and the rule.

a 5   8   11   14   17   _____   _____

Rule _____

b 20   25   30   35   _____   _____

Rule _____

c 63   58   53   48   _____   _____

Rule _____

15

1	2	3	4	5
6	7	8	9	10
11	12	13	14	15
16	17	18	19	20
21	22	23	24	25

Make your own pattern on the grid. Write the rule.

16 What is the time?

a

b

17 Name these shapes.

a 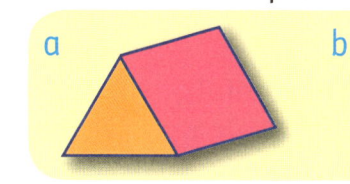   b

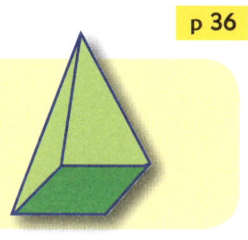

_____   _____

18 How many faces has:

a a cube?   b a triangular pyramid?

_____   _____

19 Draw the top view of:

a cone	a cylinder

20 What am I?

a I have one curved surface only.

_____

b I have 4 triangular faces.

_____

21 Write one thing for tomorrow:

a that is certain to happen.

_____

b that is unlikely to happen.

_____

c that is impossible.

_____

22 a How many possible outcomes are there if you throw a die? _____

b What are they? _____

45

NAPLAN* practice

This is a test to see how well you understand what you have learnt.

Instructions

Read each question carefully. There are three different ways to show your answer:
- Shade the bubble next to the correct answer.
- Write a word in a box.
- Write a number in a box.

Use a pencil. DO NOT use a pen. If you make a mistake, rub it out and try again.

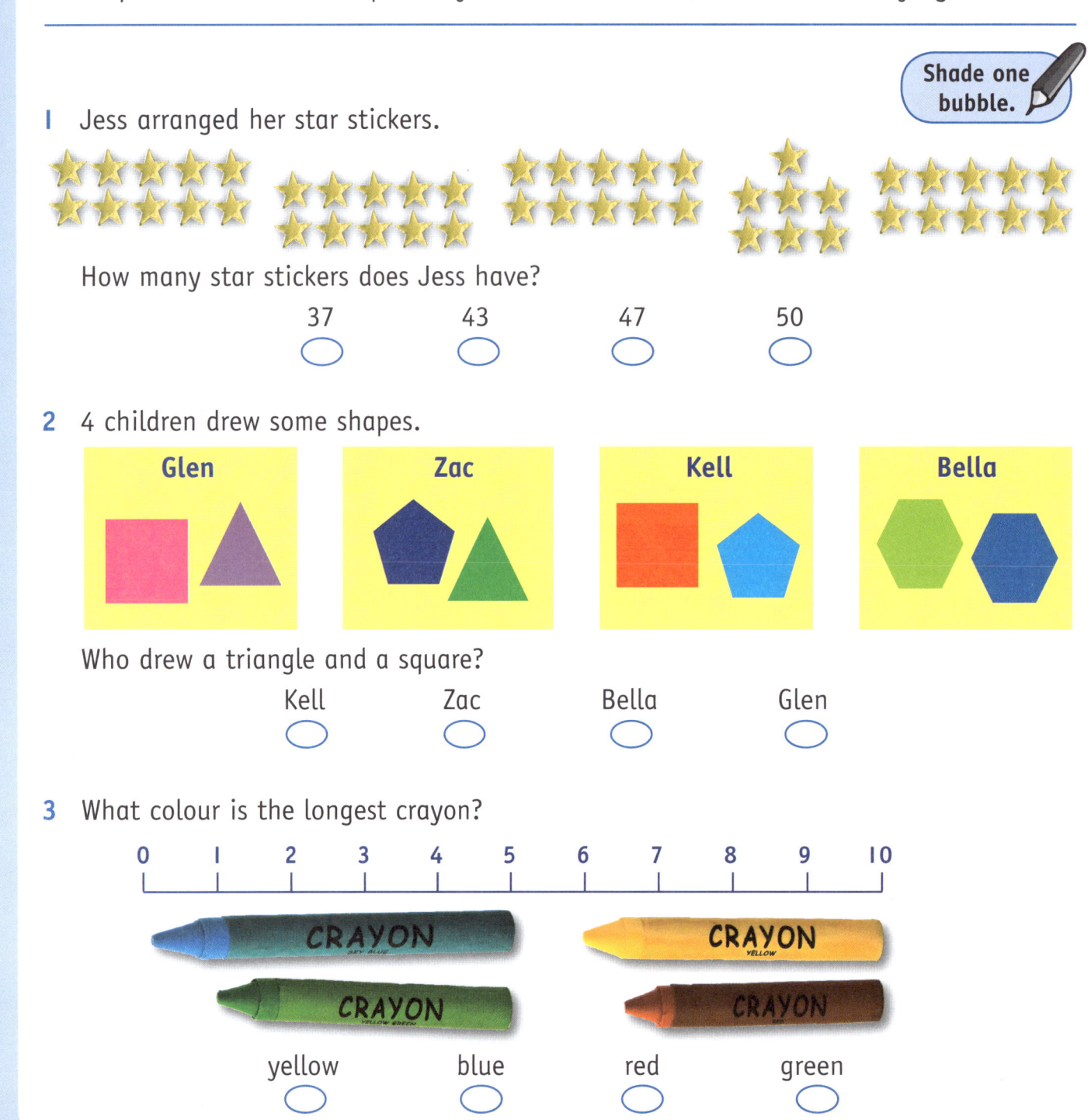

Shade one bubble.

1 Jess arranged her star stickers.

How many star stickers does Jess have?

    37   43   47   50
    ○   ○   ○   ○

2 4 children drew some shapes.

| Glen | Zac | Kell | Bella |

Who drew a triangle and a square?

    Kell   Zac   Bella   Glen
    ○   ○   ○   ○

3 What colour is the longest crayon?

0 1 2 3 4 5 6 7 8 9 10

    yellow   blue   red   green
    ○   ○   ○   ○

* This is not an officially endorsed publication of the NAPLAN program and is produced by Pascal Press independently of Australian governments.

Test practice

4 Here are four numbers.

$$85 \quad 805 \quad 588 \quad 815$$

What is the second largest number?

    85   805   588   815
    ◯   ◯   ◯   ◯

Shade one bubble.

5 28 + 9 = ☐

Write your answer in the box.

6 Double 9 and add 4. ☐

7 Which letter has one line of symmetry?

    H   K   B   F
    ◯   ◯   ◯   ◯

Shade one bubble.

8 If we count by threes, what will we say after 24?

    25   26   27   28
    ◯   ◯   ◯   ◯

9 How many wheels on 4 cars?

    5 + 4 + 4 + 4 =   5 × 4 =   4 + 4 + 4 + 4 =   5 + 4 =
    ◯   ◯   ◯   ◯

10 Jimmy's shape has a right angle. Which is Jimmy's shape?

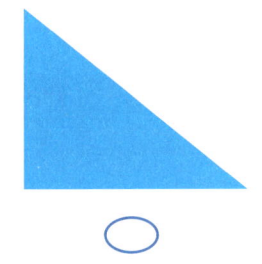

Test practice

11 Gary has 8 more fish than mice. Which statement is true?

There are less mice than fish. ○

There are the same numbers of fish and mice. ○

There are less fish than mice. ○

Mice plus fish is more than fish plus mice. ○

Shade one bubble.

12 Nan has 20 metres of ribbon and cuts off 5 metres for Nadeem, then another 5 metres for Stacey.

How much does she have left? ☐

Write your answer in the box.

13 47 − 34 = ☐

14 There was 2 L of juice in this bottle. How much did I pour out?

○ one litre
○ half a litre
○ 750 mL
○ 2 litres

Shade one bubble.

15 If this Friday is 9th April, what is the date next Friday? ☐

Write your answer in the box.

Test practice

16 This is a counting pattern.

38, 35, 32, △, 26, 23, ◯

Shade one bubble.

What numbers go in the shapes?

26 and 23　　30 and 29　　31 and 30　　29 and 20
　◯　　　　　　◯　　　　　　◯　　　　　　◯

17 Which pattern has one quarter coloured?

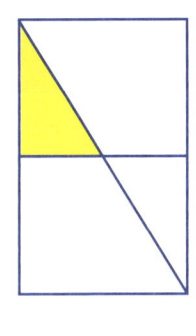

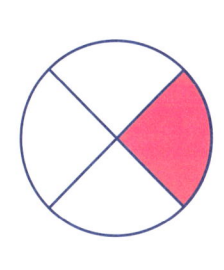

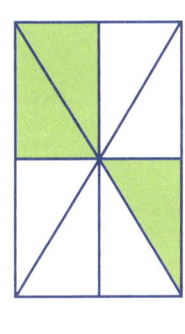

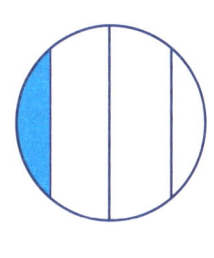

◯　　　◯　　　◯　　　◯

18 What is the top view of this object?

◯　　　◯　　　◯　　　◯

49

Test practice

Shade one bubble.

19 This is a symmetrical shape with a piece missing.

Which piece is missing?

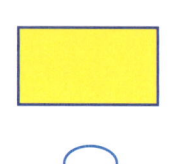

○   ○   ○   ○

20 This graph shows runs scored by 5 children.

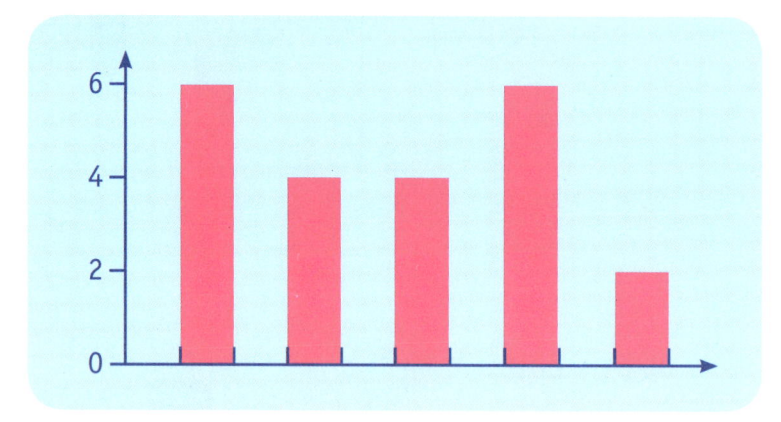

How many children scored 6 runs?

1   6   2   5
○   ○   ○   ○

21 This arrow shows how many metres a snail has travelled.

200 ←――――――――――→ 300 m

How many metres has the snail travelled?

250   280   207   290
○   ○   ○   ○

50

Test practice

22 Which clock is showing a quarter to 4?

Shade one bubble.

○   ○   ○   ○

23 Talya has 24 stickers to share equally. If she has 8 friends, how many stickers can she give each friend? ▢

Write your answer in the box.

24 To be certain of pulling out a red ball from a bag of six balls, what should be in the bag?

Shade one bubble.

3 red 3 blue   5 red 1 blue   4 red 2 blue   6 red
○   ○   ○   ○

25 Cow needs 25 squares. Horse needs 30 squares. Pig needs 18 squares. Sheep needs 17 squares. Which paddock does the sheep live in?

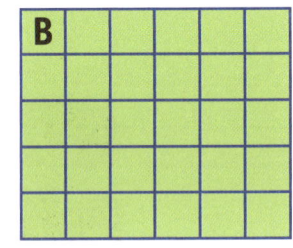

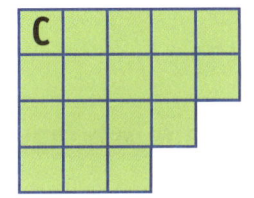

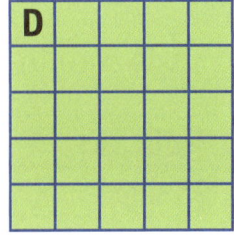

A   B   C   D
○   ○   ○   ○

26 We spent $4.80 on biscuits and $3.95 on drinks. How much more did we spend on biscuits than drinks?

$0.85 $1.05 $0.90 $1.15
○   ○   ○   ○

51

Test practice

27 The cow is heavier than the pig, the pig is heavier than the cat, but the cat is lighter than the dog. Which animal is lightest?

Shade one bubble.

the dog	the cow	the cat	the pig
○	○	○	○

28

$100 $100 $100 $100 $100 $1 $1 $1

How much money do I have?

$530	$511	$503	$500
○	○	○	○

29 Kerry built a cube from straws. She used one straw for each edge. How many straws did she use?

12	8	21	24
○	○	○	○

30 This is a train timetable.

Train to:	Time leaving:
Banker	10:00
Havely	10:10
Spickle	10:15
Kenso	10:40

Which train is leaving at a quarter past ten?

Banker	Havely	Spickle	Kenso
○	○	○	○

52

Test practice

31 Some friends had 10 strawberries to share equally. There was 1 left over. How many friends were there?

        3   4   5   2
        ○   ○   ○   ○

Shade one bubble.

32 This is a map of Jackie's town.

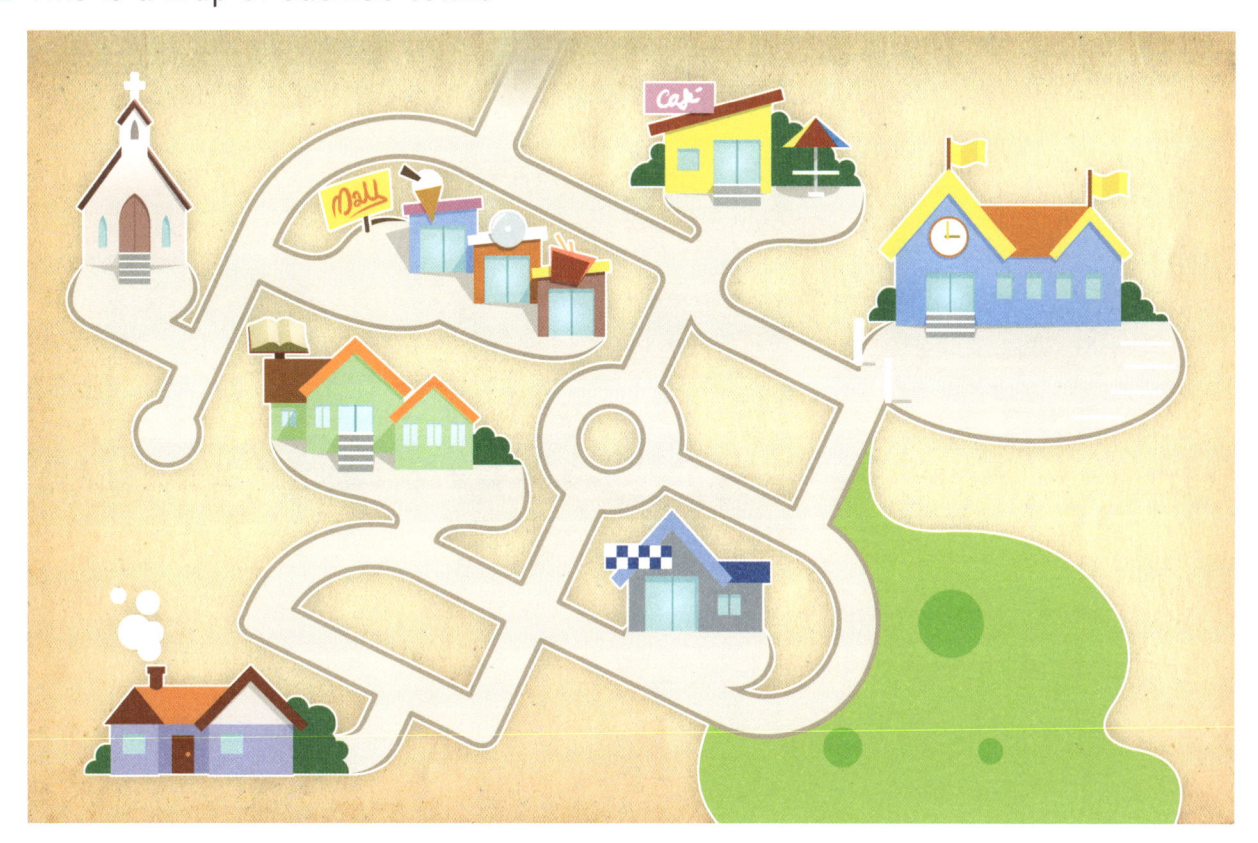

On her way to the Library after school, what does Jackie walk past?

- ○ the Café and home
- ○ the field and the Police Station
- ○ the Café and the Church
- ○ the field and the Mall

33 To make this number pattern, what is the rule?

7, 11, 15, 19, 23

- ○ all odd numbers to 20
- ○ double and add 1
- ○ add 5
- ○ add 4

53

Lab 3 — ordering numbers

Bridging 1000

Numbers to 1000

A $946
B $75
C $608
D $1261
E $1035
F $1197
G $2413

1 Which wallet holds the most money? _____

2 Which wallet holds the least money? _____

3 Order the wallets from holds least to holds most.

   ☐ ☐ ☐ ☐ ☐ ☐ ☐

4 Add $10 to:

   a B _____   b C _____   c D _____   d G _____   e A _____

5 Take $100 from:

   a A _____   b C _____   c F _____   d G _____   e E _____

6 Which wallet holds: a closest to $100? _____   b closest to $1000? _____

7 A TV costs $980. Which wallets could you use? _____
   Why? _____

54   ACMNA052 & ACMNA053 Number and place value • Recognise, model represent and order numbers to at least 10 000. • Apply place value to partition, rearrange and regroup numbers to at least 10 000 to assist calculations and solve problems.

Thousands

0 1000 2000 3000 4000 5000 6000 7000 8000 9000 10 000

1. Write the number 1000 more than:
   a 2000. _____   b 5000. _____   c 7000. _____   d 3000. _____

2. Write the number 1000 less than:
   a 10 000. _____   b 5000. _____   c 9000. _____   d 2000. _____

3. What number is halfway between:
   a 0 and 1000? _____
   b 6000 and 7000? _____
   c 3000 and 4000? _____
   d 9000 and 10 000? _____
   e 1000 and 2000? _____
   f 8000 and 9000? _____

4. Fill in the missing numbers.

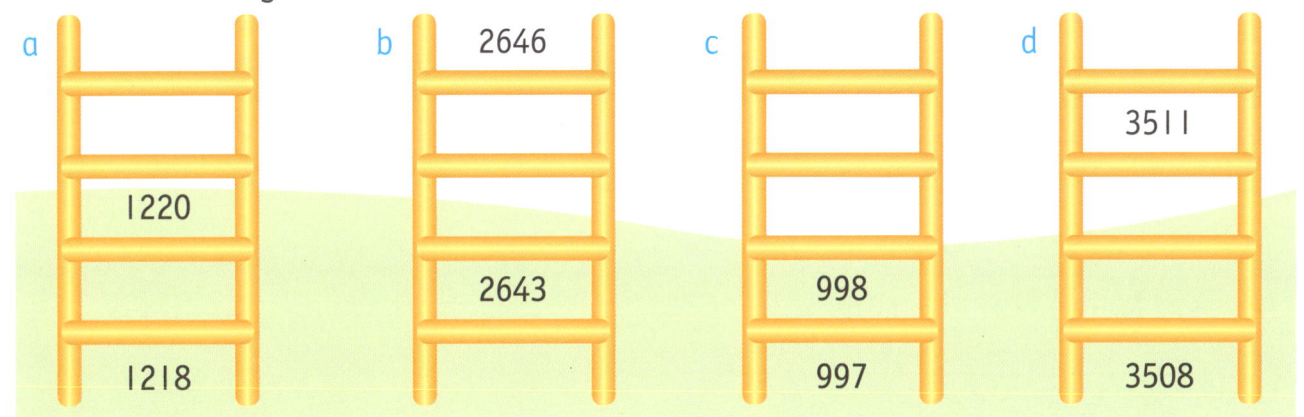

   a
   1220
   1218

   b 2646
   2643

   c
   998
   997

   d 3511
   3508

5. Write the number for:
   a two hundred and forty-eight. _____
   b eight hundred and eleven. _____
   c four hundred and fifty. _____
   d seven hundred and nine. _____
   e one thousand three hundred and sixty-five. _____
   f two thousand one hundred and ninety-seven. _____
   g four thousand five hundred and eighteen. _____
   h seven thousand six hundred and twenty. _____

Challenge! What is my number?

a My ones digit is 4, my hundreds digit is 7, my tens digit is 5 and my thousands digit is 9. ☐

b My tens digit is 8 and my thousands digit is 2. ☐

Numbers to 10 000

1 Write the number shown.

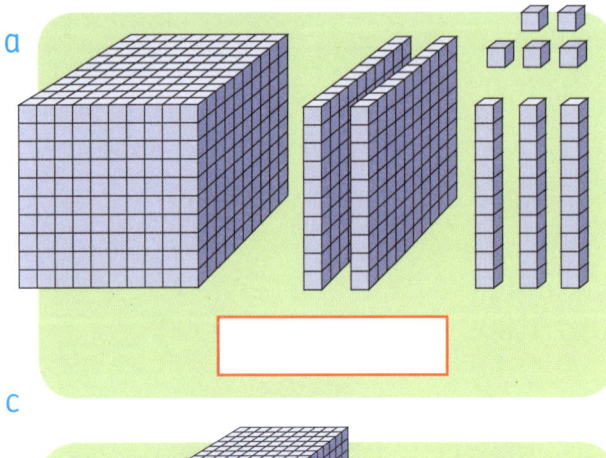

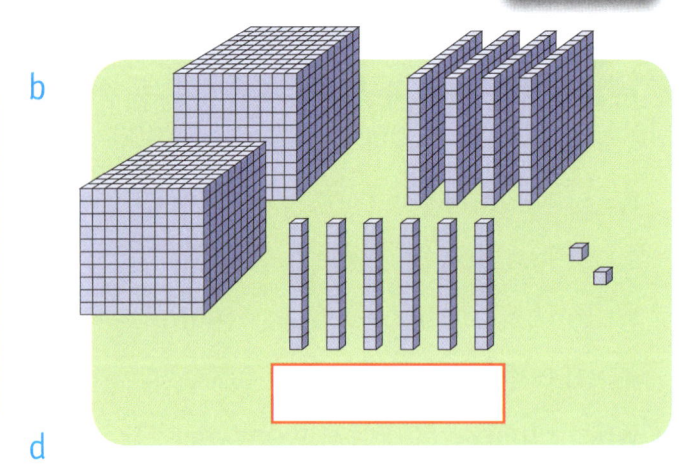

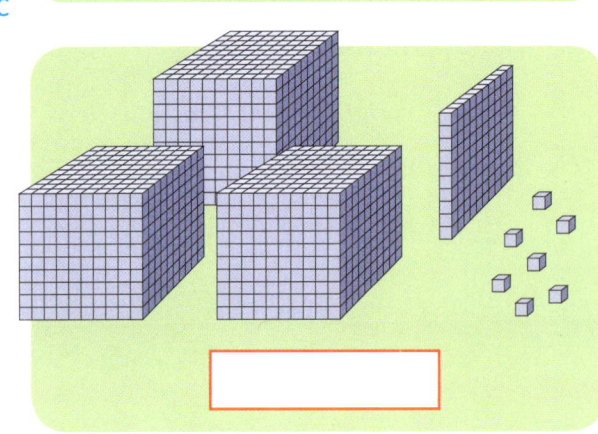

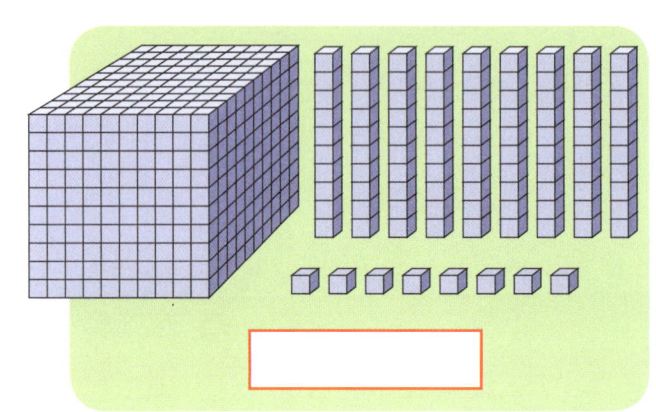

a

b

c

d

2 Write the numbers from question 1 in words.

a _____

b _____

c _____

d _____

3 Circle the larger number.

a 690   609   b 937   793   c 2985   2002

d 4157   5147   e 8061   6810   f 2594   2954

4 Join the numeral to its name.

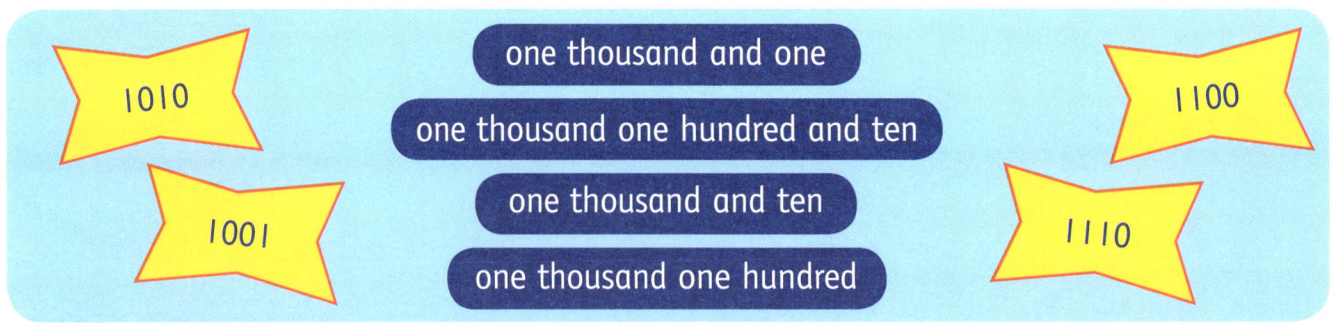

1010

1001

one thousand and one

one thousand one hundred and ten

one thousand and ten

one thousand one hundred

1100

1110

56 ACMNA052 & ACMNA053 Number and place value • Recognise, model represent and order numbers to at least 10 000. • Apply place value to partition, rearrange and regroup numbers to at least 10 000 to assist calculations and solve problems.

Place value

1 Complete.

   a 9526 = 9000 + 500 + _____ + _____

   b 3749 = _____ + _____ + _____ + _____

   c 5618 = _____ + _____ + _____ + _____

   d 7293 = _____ + _____ + _____ + _____

   e 6054 = _____ + _____ + _____ + _____

> **3648**
> 3000 + 600 + 40 + 8
> **The value**
> of the 3 is 3000
> of the 6 is 600
> of the 4 is 40
> of the 8 is 8

2 Write the number.

   a 2000 + 800 + 10 + 7 = _____   b 8000 + 400 + 60 + 1 = _____

   c 4000 + 900 + 70 + 2 = _____   d 1000 + 300 + 80 + 5 = _____

   e 3000 + 40 + 8 = _____   f 7000 + 200 + 6 = _____

3 What is the value of the underlined numeral?

   a 26_1_8 _____   b 15_8_4 _____   c _6_372 _____   d 949_3_ _____

   e _3_265 _____   f _7_726 _____   g 1_5_9 _____   h 50_8_7 _____

   i 4_9_03 _____   j 2_6_00 _____   k _7_008 _____   l 30_4_ _____

4 [6] [1] [8] [5]

   Use the cards to make four numbers with the:

   a 5 in the thousands place.   _____ _____ _____ _____

   b 5 in the hundreds place.   _____ _____ _____ _____

   c 5 in the tens place.   _____ _____ _____ _____

   d 5 in the ones place.   _____ _____ _____ _____

5 Write these in ascending order.

   a 8420   2048   3915   _____ _____ _____

   b 7506   983   9375   _____ _____ _____

   c 5130   5301   5013   _____ _____ _____

Challenge! Use these numerals to write as many different four-digit numbers as you can.
How many could you find? _____

[2] [9] [0] [3]

3× table

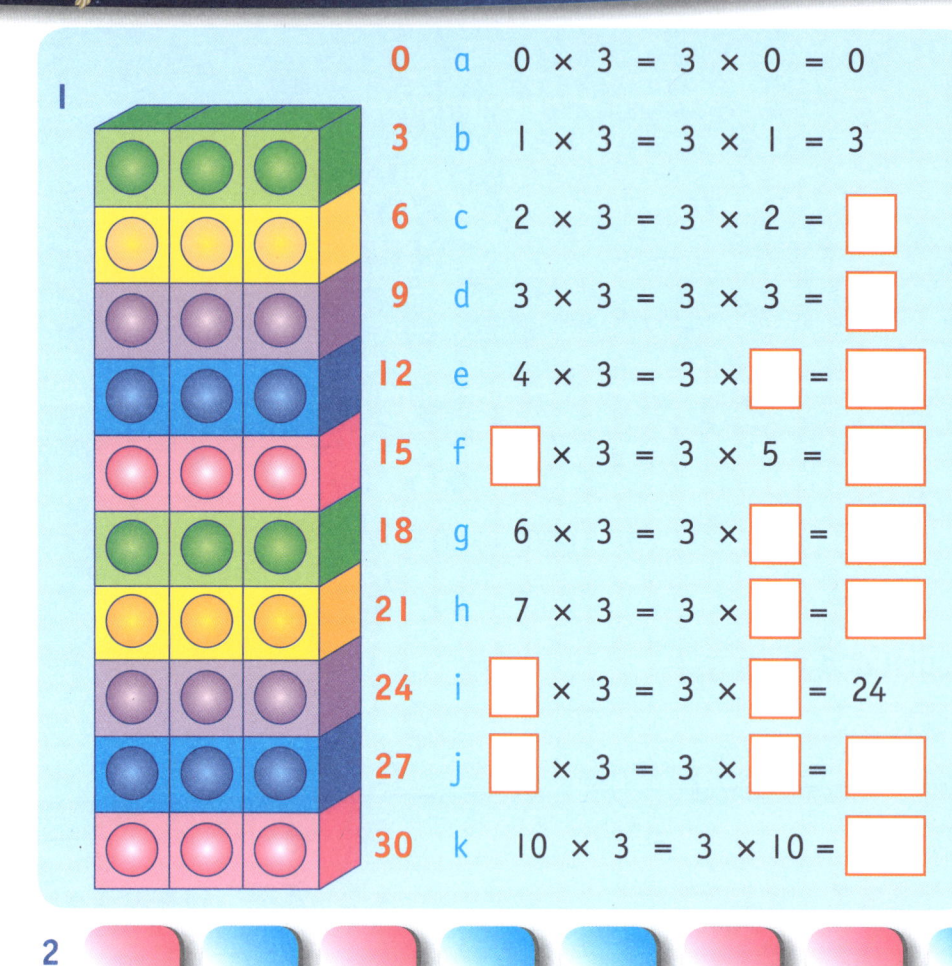

Lab 3 tables tennis

NOTICE! Memorise the 3× table.

1.
- 0 a 0 × 3 = 3 × 0 = 0
- 3 b 1 × 3 = 3 × 1 = 3
- 6 c 2 × 3 = 3 × 2 = ☐
- 9 d 3 × 3 = 3 × 3 = ☐
- 12 e 4 × 3 = 3 × ☐ = ☐
- 15 f ☐ × 3 = 3 × 5 = ☐
- 18 g 6 × 3 = 3 × ☐ = ☐
- 21 h 7 × 3 = 3 × ☐ = ☐
- 24 i ☐ × 3 = 3 × ☐ = 24
- 27 j ☐ × 3 = 3 × ☐ = ☐
- 30 k 10 × 3 = 3 × 10 = ☐

Count by threes.

2. 30 • ☐ • 24 • ☐ • ☐ • 15 • 12 • ☐ • 6 • ☐ • ☐

3. Pick ③ and another number from the bag. Multiply them. Colour the two numbers in the bag and the answer in the rhombus the same colour.

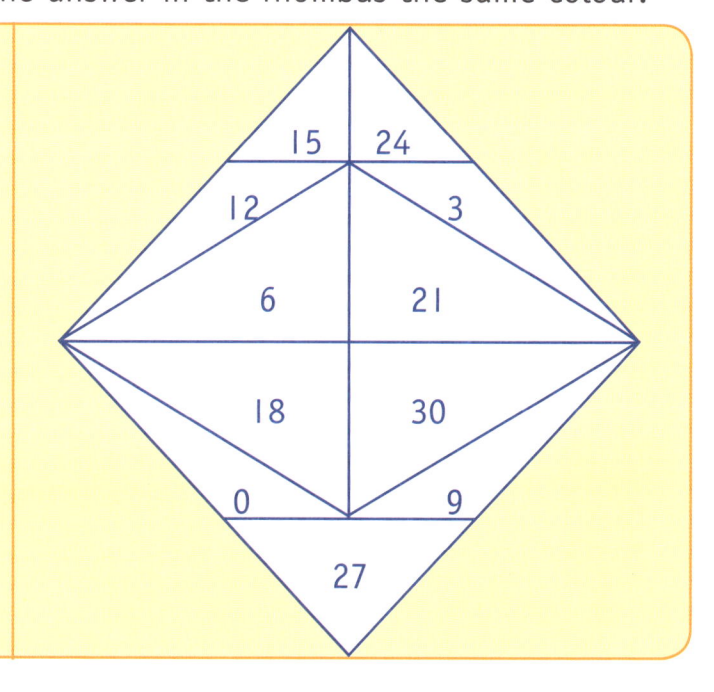

Bag numbers: 3, 3, 3, 3, 8, 0, 6, 5, 3, 3, 9, 3, 3, 4, 1, 10, 2, 3, 3, 3, 3, 7

Rhombus: 15, 24, 12, 3, 6, 21, 18, 30, 0, 9, 27

ACMNA056 & ACMNA057 Number and place value • Recall multiplication facts of two, three, five and ten and related division facts. • Represent and solve problems involving multiplication.

5x, 0x

5, 10 tables

1 How many petals on:

a 1 flower? _____ b 7 flowers? _____
c 3 flowers? _____ d 10 flowers? _____
e 2 flowers? _____ f 4 flowers? _____
g 9 flowers? _____ h 6 flowers? _____
i 5 flowers? _____ j 8 flowers? _____
k How many petals on no flowers? _____
l 11 × 5 = _____   m 12 × 5 = _____

Any number times zero is always equal to zero.

2 a 0 × 6 = ☐ b 3 × 0 = ☐ c 2 × 0 = ☐ d 0 × 8 = ☐
e 9 × 0 = ☐ f 0 × 4 = ☐ g 66 × 0 = ☐ h 999 × 0 = ☐

3 Count by 5s.

50, 55, 60, ...

4

1	2	3	4	5	6	7	8	9	10
11	12	13	14	15	16	17	18	19	20
21	22	23	24	25	26	27	28	29	30
31	32	33	34	35	36	37	38	39	40
41	42	43	44	45	46	47	48	49	50
51	52	53	54	55	56	57	58	59	60

a Colour the ×3 numbers yellow.
b Colour the ×5 numbers blue.
c Which numbers turn green?

ACMNA056 & ACMNA057 Number and place value • Recall multiplication facts of two, three, five and ten and related division facts. • Represent and solve problems involving multiplication.

Lab 3 estimation
Subtraction facts to 20

Subtract to 20

1. Ronnie made a pile of cans for target practice.
   a How many cans are there? _____

   How many would be left if she knocked down:
   b 6? _____   c 11? _____   d 15? _____   e 2? _____   f 13? _____
   g the top row? _____   h the top two rows? _____
   i the top three rows? _____   j the top four rows? _____
   k all the cans? _____

2. How many would she need to rebuild if these were left?
   a 7 _____   b 12 _____   c 19 _____   d 4 _____   e 9 _____

3. She rebuilds only the bottom three rows. How many are left if she knocks down:
   a 6? _____   b 9? _____   c 13? _____   d 7? _____   e 3? _____

4. She doesn't put up the top row. How many are left if she knocks down:
   a 18? _____   b 11? _____   c 6? _____   d 13? _____   e 4? _____

ACMNA053 & **ACMNA055** Number and place value • Apply place value to partition, rearrange and regroup numbers to at least 10 000 to assist calculations and solve problems.
• Recall addition facts for single-digit numbers and related subtraction facts to develop increasingly efficient mental strategies for computation.

Subtraction linked with addition

1 Write three more related facts.

a 20 − 6 = 14   20 − 14 = 6   6 + 14 = 20   14 + 6 = 20

b 20 − 13 = ___   _____   _____   _____

c 20 − 9 = ___   _____   _____   _____

d 20 − 16 = ___   _____   _____   _____

e 20 − 5 = ___   _____   _____   _____

f 20 − 12 = ___   _____   _____   _____

2 Complete these puzzles.

−			−			−			−	
18	6		20	9		19	7		16	8
14	3		15	7		11	4		9	5

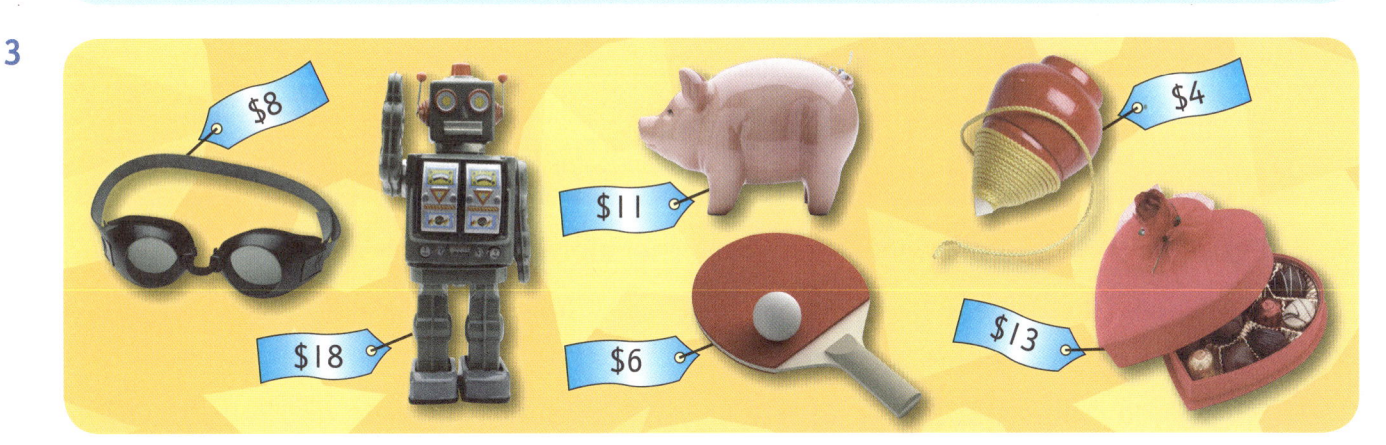

3

Price tags: goggles $8, robot $18, piggy bank $11, table tennis bat $6, top $4, chocolates $13.

Jay has $20. How much change would she get if she bought the:

a top? _____   b piggy bank? _____   c robot? _____   d goggles? _____

e top and chocolates? _____   f table tennis bat and goggles? _____

4 Vinny has $16. What item can't he buy? _____

5 True or false.

a Jay could buy three items. _____

b Why? _____

c Vinny bought the goggles and has $8 left. _____

d Why? _____

Counting on

**subtract
minus
less than
take from
take away
difference**

Difference and patterns

1 a 16 take away 9 _____   b 11 minus 7 _____
   c 19 subtract 12 _____   d take 8 from 12 _____
   e 80 subtract 10 _____   f 7 less than 47 _____
   g 15 minus 10 _____   h 39 less than 40 _____   i take 0 from 18 _____

We sometimes find the difference by counting on.

20, 21, 22, 23, 24, 25. That's 6 more!

2 Count on to complete.

a | 39 | 43 | 40 | 42 | 46 | 45
−37 | | | | | |

b | 62 | 68 | 60 | 66 | 64 | 61
−59 | | | | | |

c | 26 | 21 | 25 | 20 | 23 | 28
−18 | | | | | |

d | 80 | 87 | 89 | 83 | 90 | 84
−76 | | | | | |

3 Count on to find the answers. Then write the subtraction.

a Carl had 19 marbles.
   Ingrid had 24 marbles.
   How many more did Ingrid have? _____
   ☐ − ☐ = ☐

b Bella had 37 Smarties.
   Bill had 29 Smarties.
   How many more did Bella have? _____
   ☐ − ☐ = ☐

c Shona ate 53 cherries.
   Seb ate 61 cherries.
   How many more did Seb eat? _____
   ☐ − ☐ = ☐

d Nicole read 48 pages.
   Ned read 39 pages.
   How many more did Nicole read? _____
   ☐ − ☐ = ☐

Look for patterns

What is the pattern? Make up another subtraction pattern.

	11	61	81	31	51	91	21	71
−7								

Two-digit subtraction

Jump strategy

1 Quick practice.

a	b	c	d	e	f	g
16	20	18	14	13	15	12
− 7	− 12	− 13	− 9	− 6	− 8	− 5

Sometimes we take small jumps.

Sometimes we take big jumps.

2 Use the number line.

a 37 minus 23

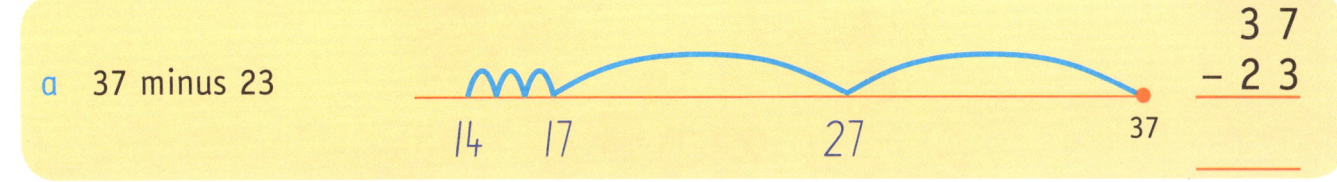

14 17 27 37

37
− 23
___

b 52 take away 34

52

52
−
___

c subtract 15 from 61

61

61
−
___

d 94 less 47

94

−
___

e difference between 72 and 23

−
___

Draw a diagram

Jay's ant farm had 96 ants. 47 escaped and 25 died. How many are left? ☐

Hint: Draw a number line.

Lab 3 place value

Subtraction strategies

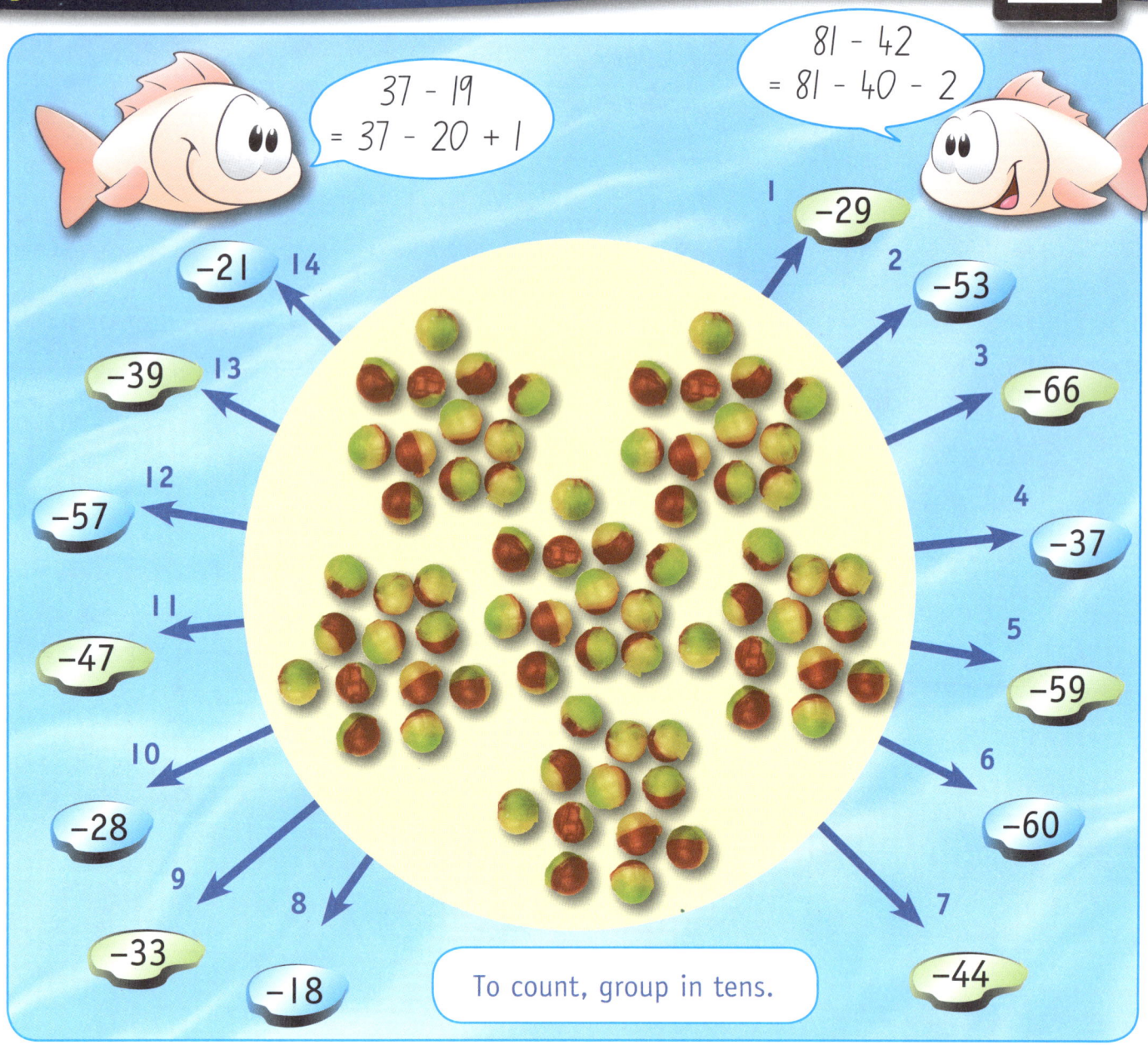

Subtract to 100

37 – 19
= 37 – 20 + 1

81 – 42
= 81 – 40 – 2

1 –29
2 –53
3 –66
4 –37
5 –59
6 –60
7 –44
8 –18
9 –33
10 –28
11 –47
12 –57
13 –39
14 –21

To count, group in tens.

1 72 – 30 + 1 = _____   ☐ – ☐ = ☐
2 72 – 50 – 3 = _____   ☐ – ☐ = ☐
3 _____ = _____   ☐ – ☐ = ☐
4 _____ = _____   ☐ – ☐ = ☐
5 _____ = _____   ☐ – ☐ = ☐
6 _____ = _____   ☐ – ☐ = ☐
7 _____ = _____   ☐ – ☐ = ☐
8 _____ = _____   ☐ – ☐ = ☐
9 _____ = _____   ☐ – ☐ = ☐
10 _____ = _____   ☐ – ☐ = ☐
11 _____ = _____   ☐ – ☐ = ☐
12 _____ = _____   ☐ – ☐ = ☐
13 _____ = _____   ☐ – ☐ = ☐
14 _____ = _____   ☐ – ☐ = ☐

ACMNA053 & ACMNA055 Number and place value • Apply place value to partition, rearrange and regroup numbers to at least 10 000 to assist calculations and solve problems. • Recall addition facts for single-digit numbers and related subtraction facts to develop increasingly efficient mental strategies for computation.

Two-digit subtraction

1 Write stories.

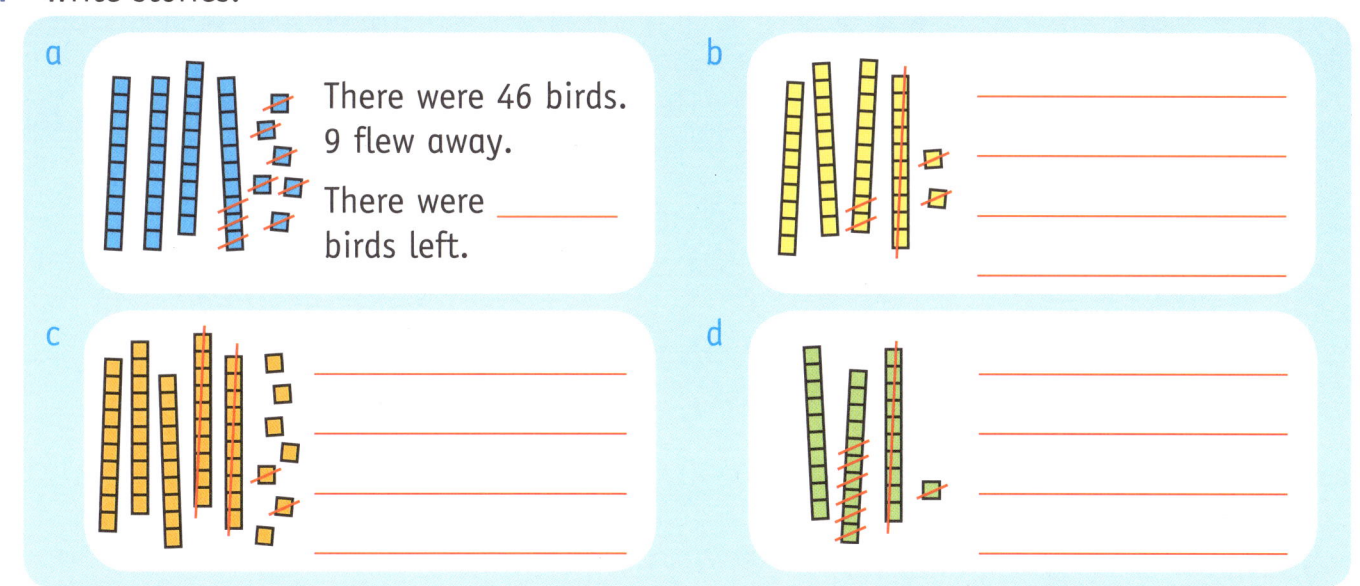

a There were 46 birds. 9 flew away. There were ___ birds left.

b

c

d

2 Use the blocks to find the answers.

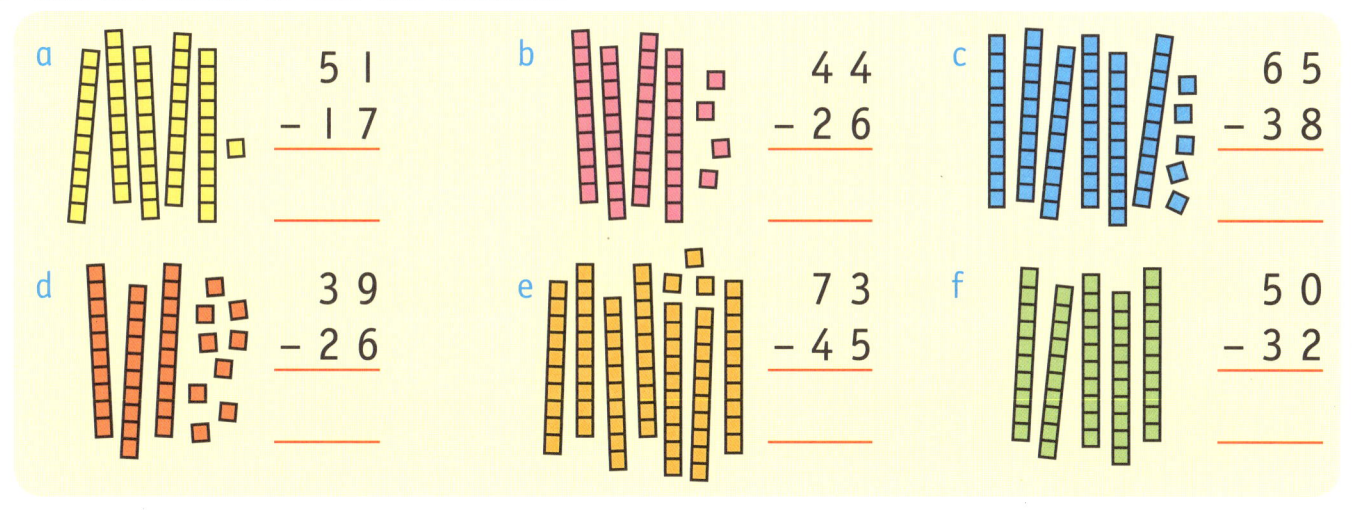

a) 51 − 17

b) 44 − 26

c) 65 − 38

d) 39 − 26

e) 73 − 45

f) 50 − 32

3 Use Base 10 blocks if you need help.

a) 78 − 35

b) 64 − 21

c) 96 − 34

d) 39 − 15

e) 47 − 23

f) 28 − 17

g) 85 − 35

h) 55 − 13

i) 49 − 36

j) 88 − 54

k) 97 − 75

l) 57 − 22

m) 68 − 38

n) 35 − 20

Challenge! Find 4 pairs of numbers with a difference of 27.

Subtraction stories

1
a Find pairs of numbers the same colour.
b Work out the difference for each pair.
c Write one subtraction sentence and one addition sentence for each pair.

74	−	3	=	
	+		=	

2
a Tom threw the basketball 25 m and kicked the soccerball 67 m. Write the difference in metres.

b The red balloon drifted 39 m and the blue balloon drifted 24 m. Write the difference in metres.

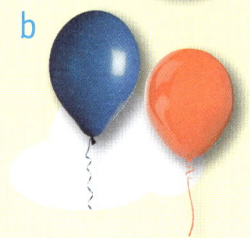

c The green lollipop lasted 58 minutes and the yellow lollipop lasted 35 minutes. What is the difference in minutes?

d Sal jumped 44 cm and Sue jumped 66 cm. Write the difference in centimetres.

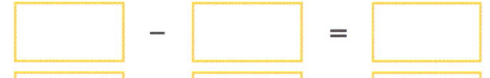

Problem solving

Work backwards

1. Three children ran a race. Jack ran the race 3 seconds faster than Dave. Dave ran 2 seconds slower than Jerry. Jerry took 14 seconds. What was Jack's time?

   Working:

   Jerry 14 secs   Dave 14 + 2 = 16   Jack 16 − 3 = 13

   Dave 16 secs   Jack's time was _____

2. Four children joined the 'Read-a-thon' to improve their reading rate. Toby read 4 books more than Koli. Koli read 5 books less than Troy, who read 16. How many books did Toby read?

   Working:

   Troy _____   Koli _____   Toby _____

   Troy read _____   Koli read _____   Toby read _____

Write your own *work backwards* problems and show the solution.

3. The answer is 50 stickers. What might the problem be?

   _____
   _____
   _____
   _____

   Working: _____
   _____

4. Write your own.

   _____
   _____
   _____
   _____

   Working: _____
   _____

Fractions in a line

Thirds: $\frac{1}{3}$, $\frac{2}{3}$, $\frac{3}{3}$

Quarters: $\frac{1}{4}$, $\frac{2}{4}$, $\frac{2}{3}$, $\frac{4}{4}$

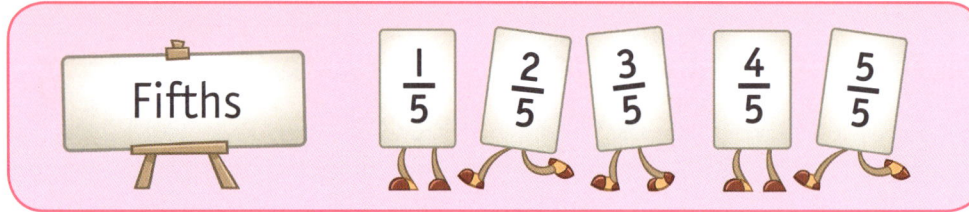

Fifths: $\frac{1}{5}$, $\frac{2}{5}$, $\frac{3}{5}$, $\frac{4}{5}$, $\frac{5}{5}$

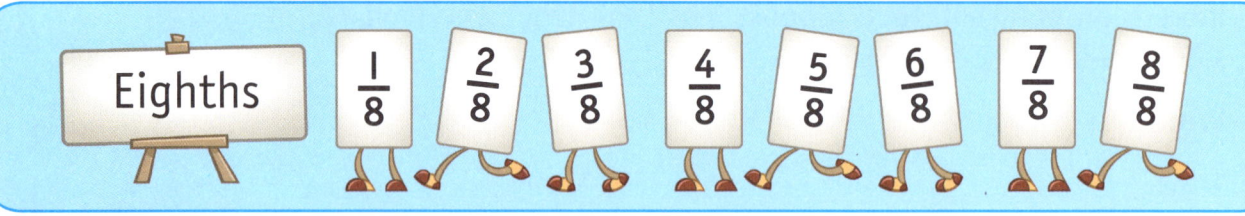

Eighths: $\frac{1}{8}$, $\frac{2}{8}$, $\frac{3}{8}$, $\frac{4}{8}$, $\frac{5}{8}$, $\frac{6}{8}$, $\frac{7}{8}$, $\frac{8}{8}$

1 Write each set of fractions in order, smallest to largest.

a $\frac{1}{4}$, $\frac{3}{4}$, $\frac{2}{4}$, $\frac{4}{4}$

b $\frac{3}{3}$, $\frac{1}{3}$, $\frac{2}{3}$

c $\frac{1}{5}$, $\frac{2}{5}$, $\frac{3}{5}$, $\frac{5}{5}$, $\frac{4}{5}$

d $\frac{1}{8}$, $\frac{3}{8}$, $\frac{2}{8}$, $\frac{4}{8}$, $\frac{5}{8}$, $\frac{6}{8}$, $\frac{7}{8}$, $\frac{8}{8}$

e $\frac{3}{5}$, $\frac{2}{5}$, $\frac{1}{5}$, $\frac{4}{5}$

f $\frac{3}{6}$, $\frac{2}{6}$, $\frac{4}{6}$, $\frac{5}{6}$, $\frac{1}{6}$, $\frac{6}{6}$

2 Colour the fraction. Write and colour a smaller fraction.

a $\frac{4}{5}$

b $\frac{5}{8}$

c $\frac{3}{4}$

Count with fractions

Thirds, sixths, fourths, eighths

1 Count by quarters up to 1.

0 _____ _____ _____ _____

2 Count by fifths up to 1.

0 _____ _____ _____ _____ _____

3 Count by eighths up to 1.

0 $\frac{1}{8}$ _____ _____ _____ _____ _____ _____ _____

4 a Four boys get 2 slices each.   b Three girls get 2 slices each.

How much pizza did each boy get?   How much pizza did each girl get?

_____   _____

Challenge! I cut a pizza into ten slices to share between five people.
How many pieces does each person get? _____
What fraction of the pizza is that? _____

ACMNA058 Fractions and decimals • Model and represent unit fractions including $\frac{1}{2}$, $\frac{1}{4}$, $\frac{1}{3}$, $\frac{1}{5}$ and their multiples to a complete whole.

Mixed numbers

> A mixed number is a whole number and a fraction. $1\frac{1}{2}$ = one and a half.

1 Colour the whole number and a fraction.

a $1\frac{1}{2}$

b $1\frac{1}{4}$

c $2\frac{1}{2}$

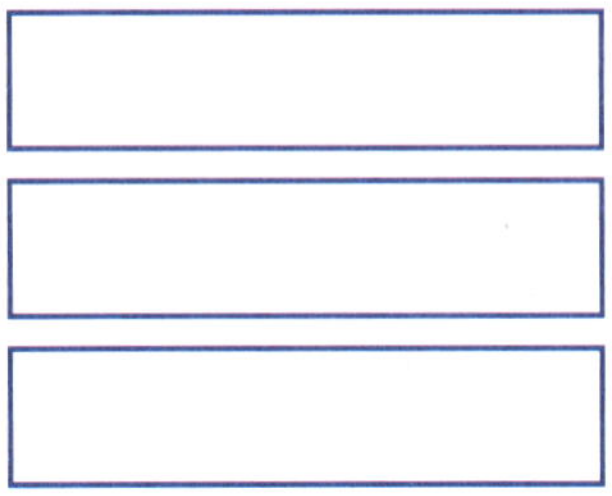

d $1\frac{3}{4}$

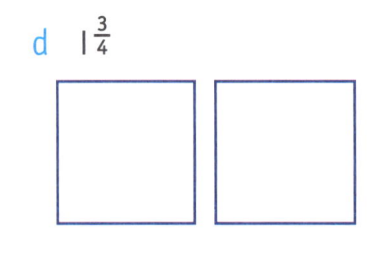

e $2\frac{1}{4}$

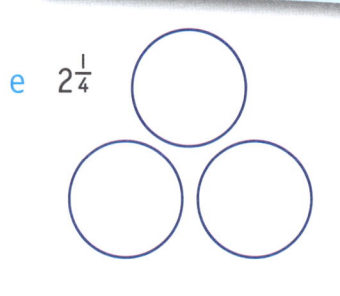

2 Place these fractions and mixed numbers on the number lines.

a $0, \frac{1}{2}, 1, 1\frac{1}{2}, 2$

b $0, \frac{1}{4}, \frac{1}{2}, \frac{3}{4}, 1, 1\frac{1}{4}, 1\frac{1}{2}$

c $0, \frac{1}{3}, \frac{2}{3}, 1, 1\frac{1}{3}, 1\frac{2}{3}, 2$

3 Put these mixed numbers in order.

a $1, \frac{1}{2}, 1\frac{1}{2}, 0$ _____

b $\frac{1}{4}, 1\frac{1}{4}, 1, 1\frac{1}{2}$ _____

c $1\frac{1}{2}, \frac{1}{2}, 2, 1,$ _____

d $3\frac{1}{5}, 1\frac{1}{5}, 4\frac{1}{5}, 2\frac{1}{5}$ _____

Challenge! Share 10 apples evenly between 4 rabbits. How much apple does each rabbit get?

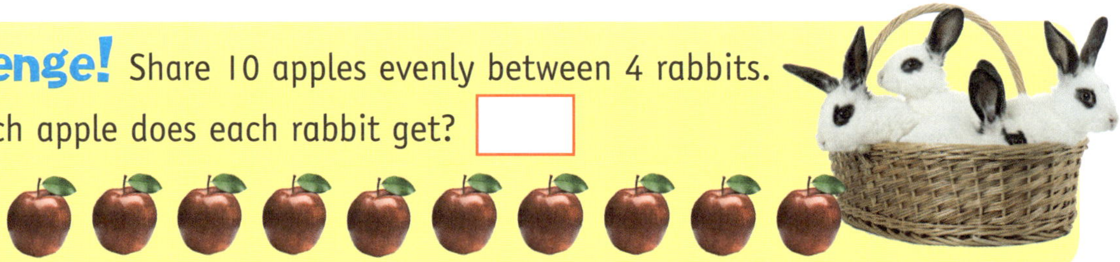

Fractions of a group

$\frac{1}{4}$ means one of four equal parts. We can make a fractional part of a group.
Find $\frac{1}{4}$ of a group by dividing it into 4.
eg $\frac{1}{4}$ of 8 is the same as 8 divided by 4.

$\frac{1}{4}$ of 8 is 2

1 One half of 8 is 8 divided into 2 equal parts.

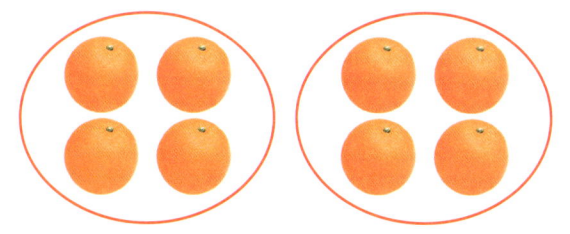

$\frac{1}{2}$ of 8 is _____

2 Look at the number 12 and circle fractions of 12.

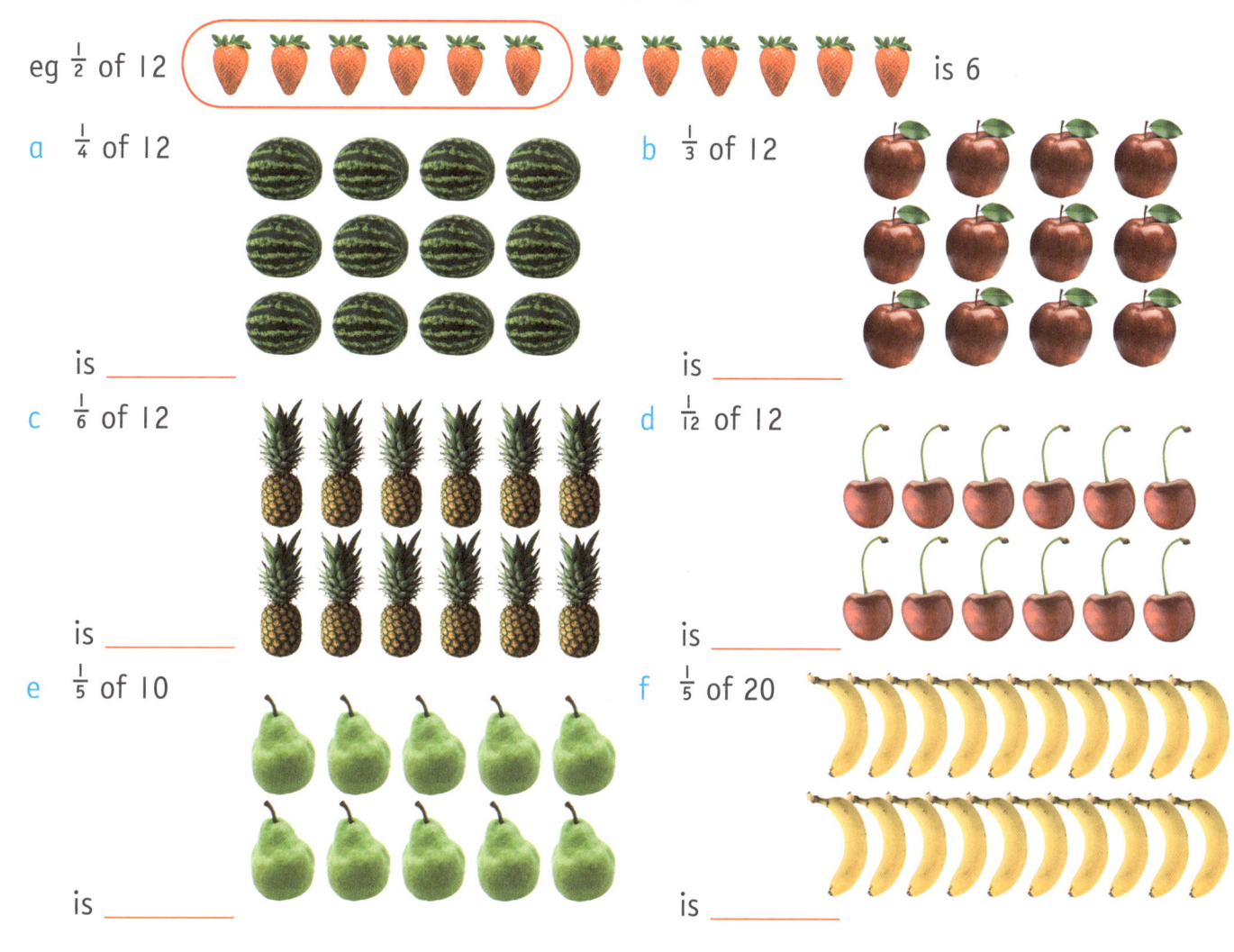

eg $\frac{1}{2}$ of 12 is 6

a $\frac{1}{4}$ of 12

is _____

b $\frac{1}{3}$ of 12

is _____

c $\frac{1}{6}$ of 12

is _____

d $\frac{1}{12}$ of 12

is _____

e $\frac{1}{5}$ of 10

is _____

f $\frac{1}{5}$ of 20

is _____

ACMNA058 Fractions and decimals • Model and represent unit fractions including $\frac{1}{2}$, $\frac{1}{4}$, $\frac{1}{3}$, $\frac{1}{5}$ and their multiples to a complete whole.

Investigation 2

Cakes and Biscuits

Parents are coming to visit your class and you have to make morning tea. You will need 50 muffins. This recipe makes 20 muffins.

Ingredients:
- 3 cups self-raising flour
- 1 cup of butter
- 1 cup of sugar
- 2 large eggs
- 1 cup of milk
- vanilla essence to taste
- some choc-bits, diced apple or banana

Method:

Place dry ingredients in a bowl. Mix in wet ingredients. Add choc-bits, apple or banana.

Pour into regular muffin tins and cook for 10-15 minutes at 160°C.

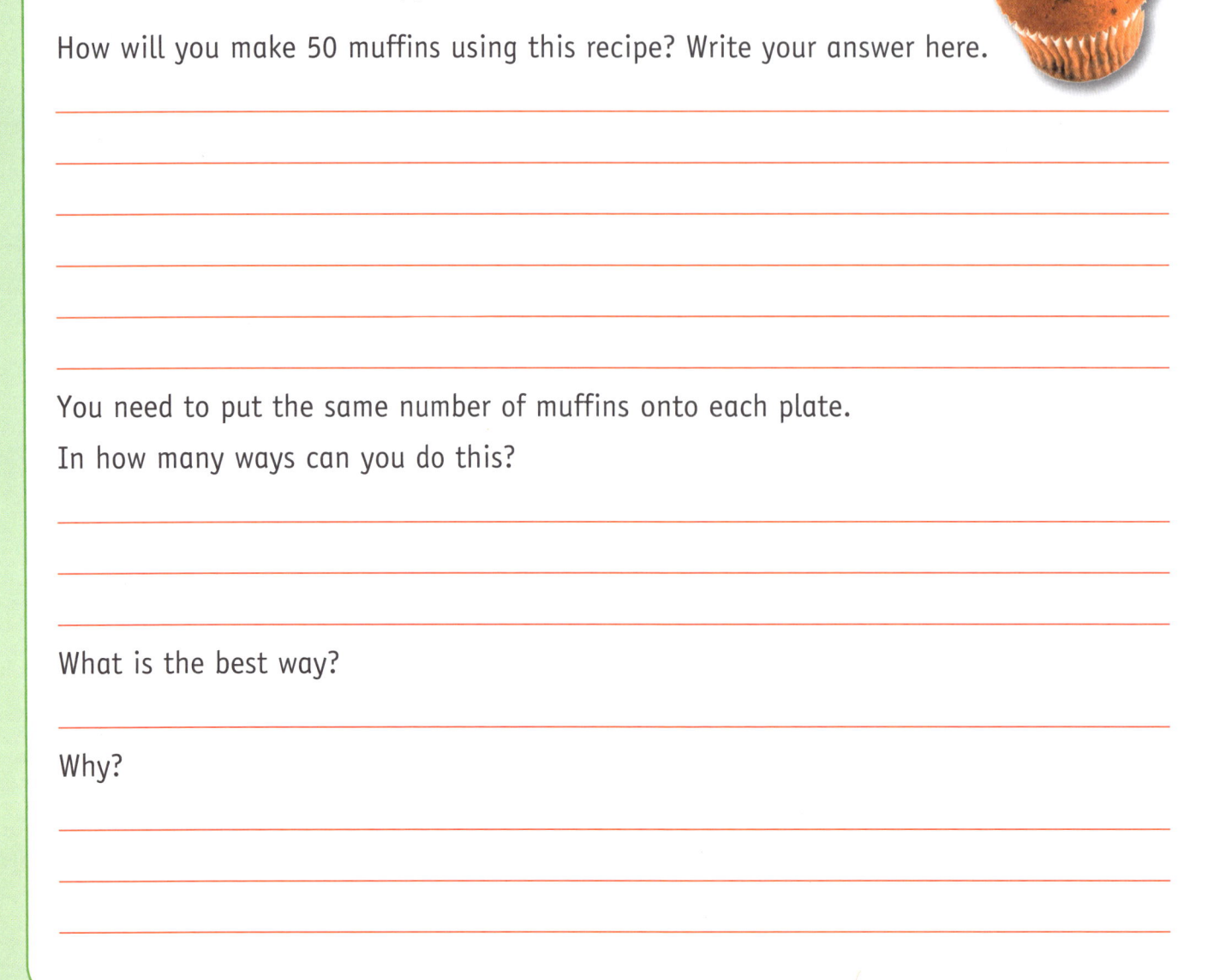

How will you make 50 muffins using this recipe? Write your answer here.

You need to put the same number of muffins onto each plate.
In how many ways can you do this?

What is the best way?

Why?

Cakes and Biscuits

Investigation 2

The Fete is coming and your class has the biscuit stall. Use one of these ingredient lists to work out how much money you can make selling 120 biscuits.

Ingredients — 20 biscuits in a batch
- 1 cup sugar
- 125 g butter, melted
- 1 teaspoon vanilla
- 1 cup plain flour
- 1 cup self-raising flour
- 1 egg, lightly beaten
- sprinkles and decorations

Cost of ingredients $5

Ingredients — 24 biscuits in a batch
- 125 g butter
- $\frac{1}{2}$ cup sugar
- $\frac{1}{2}$ cup brown sugar
- 1 egg
- $\frac{1}{2}$ tsp vanilla essence
- $\frac{1}{4}$ tsp salt
- $1\frac{3}{4}$ cups self-raising flour
- 150 g milk choc chips

Cost of ingredients $5.50

How will you make 120 biscuits?

_____
_____
_____
_____
_____
_____
_____
_____
_____
_____

How much will you charge for each biscuit? _____

Money spent _____   Money raised _____

To carry out these tasks I need to:
- ☐ use doubling to multiply ingredients.
- ☐ calculate how many batches to make.
- ☐ calculate how to put biscuits onto trays evenly.
- ☐ calculate how much money is spent and raised.
- ☐ explain how I solve the problem.

I enjoyed this task!
★★★★

Revision

1 How many minutes have passed when the minute hand moves from 5 to 8?

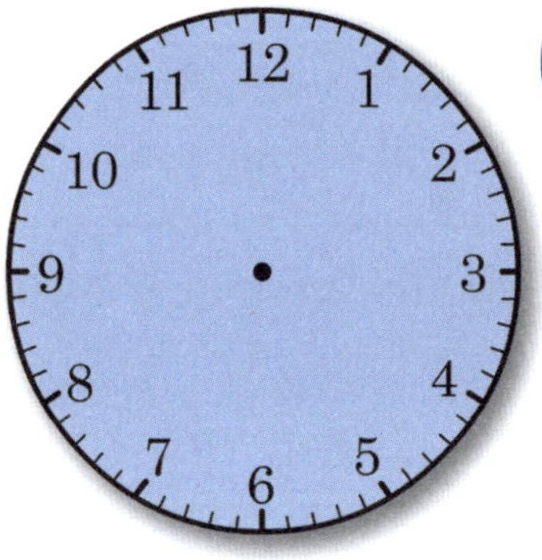

   5   8   15   20
   ○   ○   ○   ○

   Shade one bubble.

2 Which object is a pyramid?

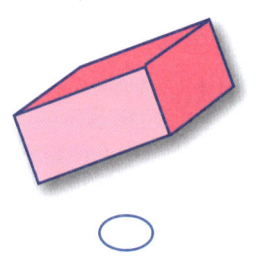

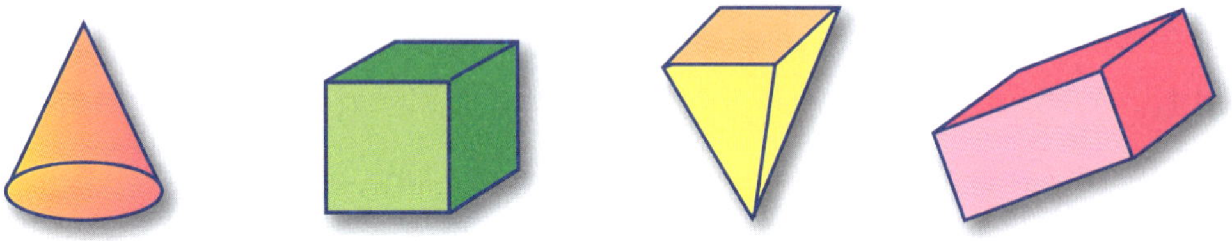

   ○   ○   ○   ○

3 Using only three cards, what is the largest number you can make?

   4   0   7   1

   714   471   741   704
   ○   ○   ○   ○

4 Which operation does this number line show?

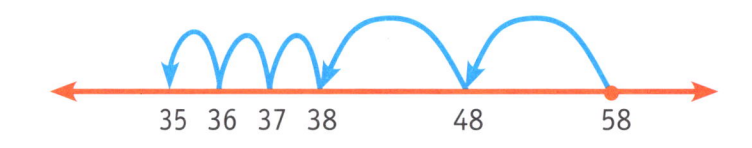

   35 36 37 38   48   58

   58 + 23   35 − 23   58 − 23   38 − 3
   ○   ○   ○   ○

5 Write the next number in this pattern.

   63   50   37   24   ?

   Write your answer in the box.

Revision

6 Which label is missing?

Shade one bubble.

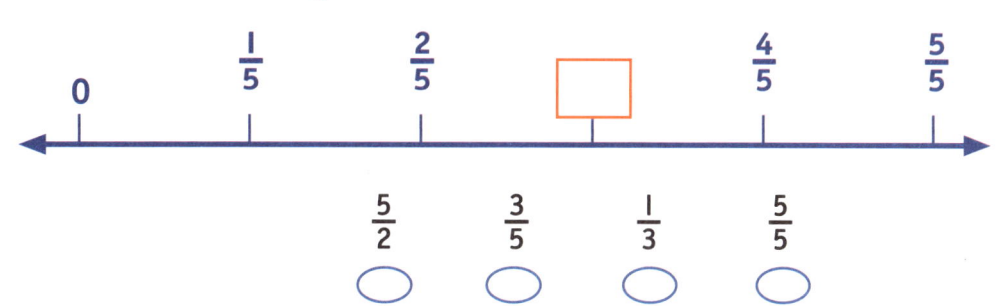

0, 1/5, 2/5, ▢, 4/5, 5/5

- 5/2
- 3/5
- 1/3
- 5/5

7 Which diagram shows $2\frac{1}{4}$?

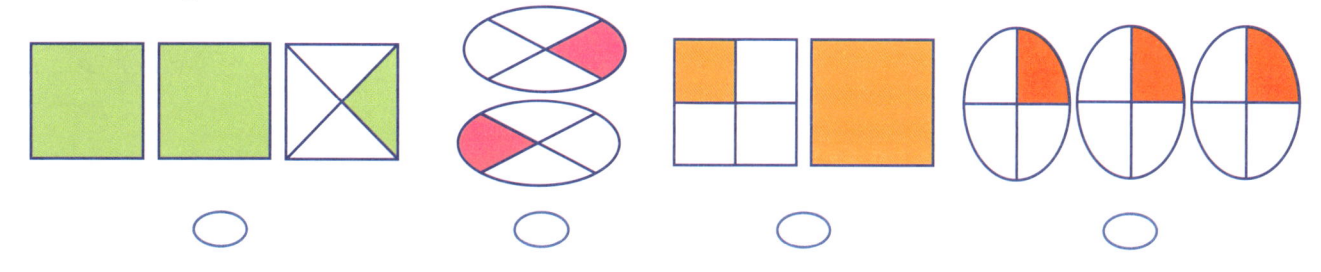

○   ○   ○   ○

8 18 bunnies are in a row, if 11 hop away how many are left?

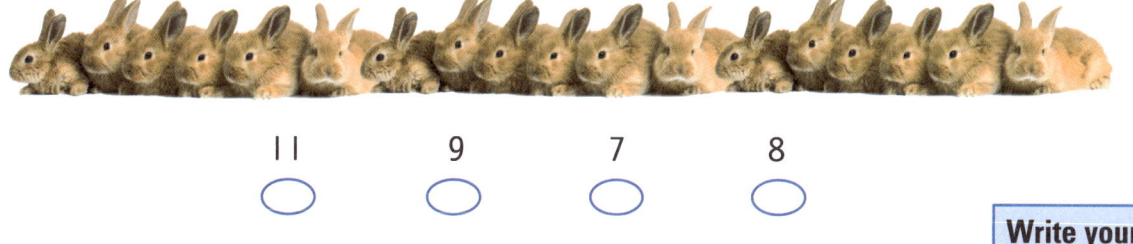

- 11
- 9
- 7
- 8

Write your answer in the box.

9 Sam started his homework at 4:35 pm and finished at 5:05 pm.

How long did it take him? ▢ minutes

10 How many working dogs do they have altogether?

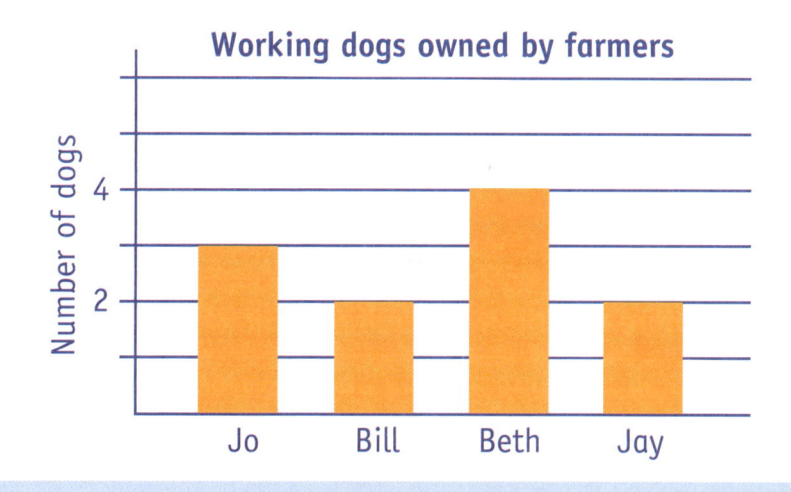

▢

Working dogs owned by farmers

Jo: 3, Bill: 2, Beth: 4, Jay: 2

75

Eating in Japan

Menu

- sushi ¥200 each
- spring rolls ¥500 for 3
- soup ¥350
- yakitori ¥600 for 2
- green tea ¥100
- rice pancakes ¥450 for 4
- stir fry noodles ¥800

1. Which items cost less than ¥500?

2. Which items cost betwen ¥500 and ¥1000?

3. What three items could I buy for a total less than ¥1000?

4. If I bought the yakitori, the stir fry and a green tea, what change would I get from ¥5000?

5. What notes and coins would my change contain?

6. If you had ¥2000, what would you buy? What is the total price of your choice?

7. Answer true or false.
    a. You pay more yen than Australian dollars for food in Japan. _____
    b. This menu shows that food in Japan is more expensive than in Australia.

Notes

1 Match.

$5

$10

$20

$50

$100

2 Circle the coins to make the amount.

a $1.10	
b $3.45	
c $5.80	
d $0.95	

Money

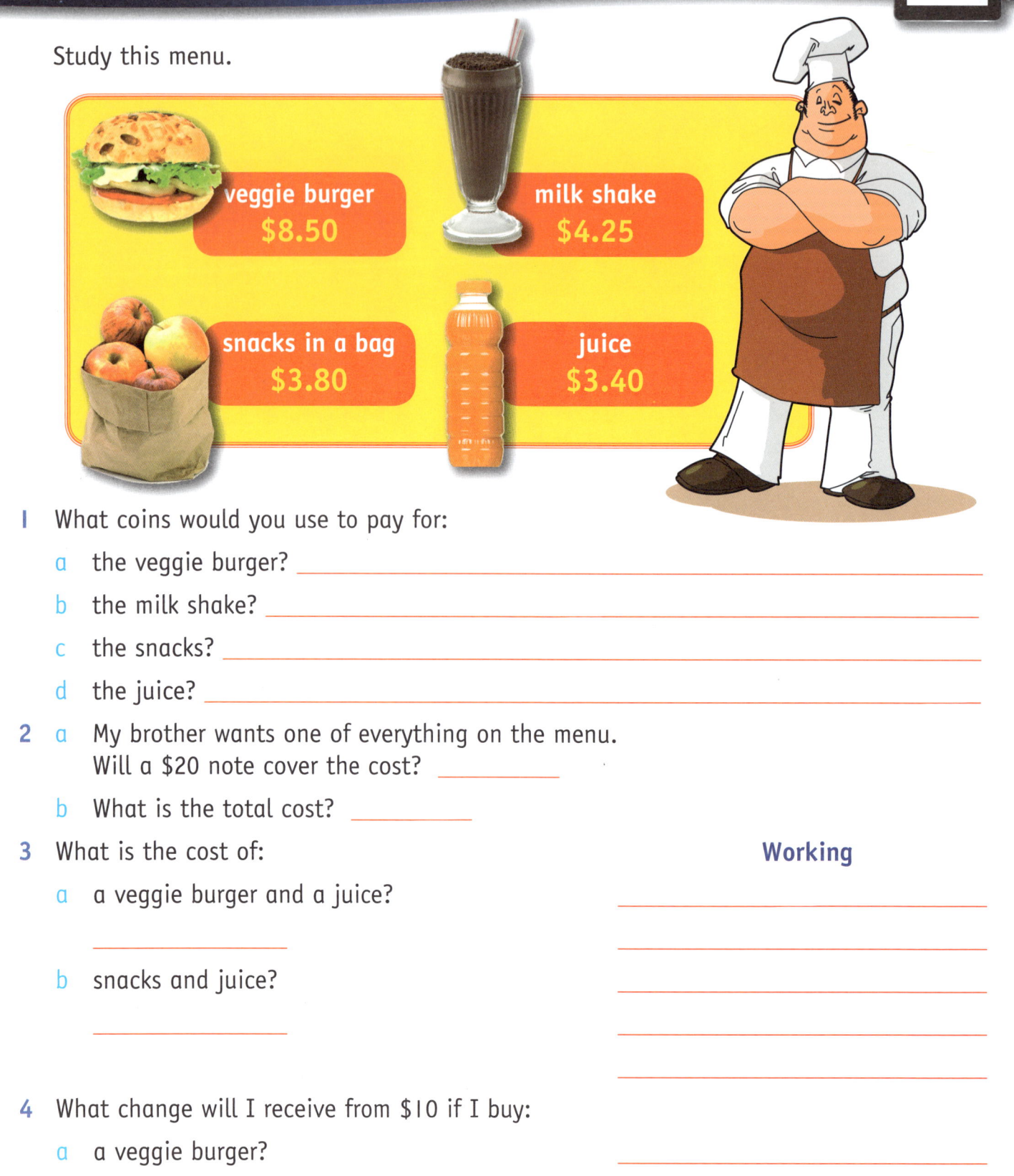

Study this menu.

- veggie burger $8.50
- milk shake $4.25
- snacks in a bag $3.80
- juice $3.40

1 What coins would you use to pay for:

a the veggie burger? _____

b the milk shake? _____

c the snacks? _____

d the juice? _____

2 a My brother wants one of everything on the menu. Will a $20 note cover the cost? _____

b What is the total cost? _____

3 What is the cost of: **Working**

a a veggie burger and a juice?

_____

b snacks and juice?

_____

4 What change will I receive from $10 if I buy:

a a veggie burger?

_____

b both drinks?

_____

Addition and subtraction of money

1. a 10c + 10c + 10c + 20c = _____
   b 50c + 10c + 5c + 5c = _____
   c 50c + 50c + 50c = _____
   d 5c + 10c + 20c + 50c = _____
   e 20c + 20c + 20c + 50c = _____
   f 10c + 50c + 20c + 5c + 5c = _____
   g $10 + $5 + $20 + $5 = _____
   h $100 + $50 + $20 + $10 = _____

2. a $10 − $7 = _____
   b $20 − $12 = _____
   c $10 − $4 = _____
   d $20 − $13 = _____
   e $50 − $30 = _____
   f $100 − $50 = _____
   g $5 − $4.50 = _____
   h $5 − $1.50 = _____
   i $10 − $5.50 = _____

3. Complete.

   a

+	$5	$36	$19	$1.50	$2.80
$7					

   b

+	50c	25c	$2	$18	$1.45
35c					

   c

−	$20	$31	$17	$6.50	$8.25
$4					

   d

−	$1	$4	$6.80	$13.90	$10.10
80c					

4. Round these to the closest 5c.
   a 31c _____   b 68c _____   c 42c _____   d 89c _____   e 57c _____

5. Round these to the closest dollar.
   a $6.10 _____   b $2.35 _____   c $8.70 _____   d $3.65 _____   e $1.45 _____

6. Jay had $5 pocket money. He spent $2 on sweets and $1 on a drink. How much did he have left? ☐

7. For her birthday Kay was given $5. She already had $7.60. How much does she now have? ☐

8. Bozo's owner paid $35 at the vet and $17 for a new lead. How much did he spend? ☐

9. I bought an ice-cream for $2 and a sandwich for $4.40. How much change did I get from $10? ☐

Number patterns

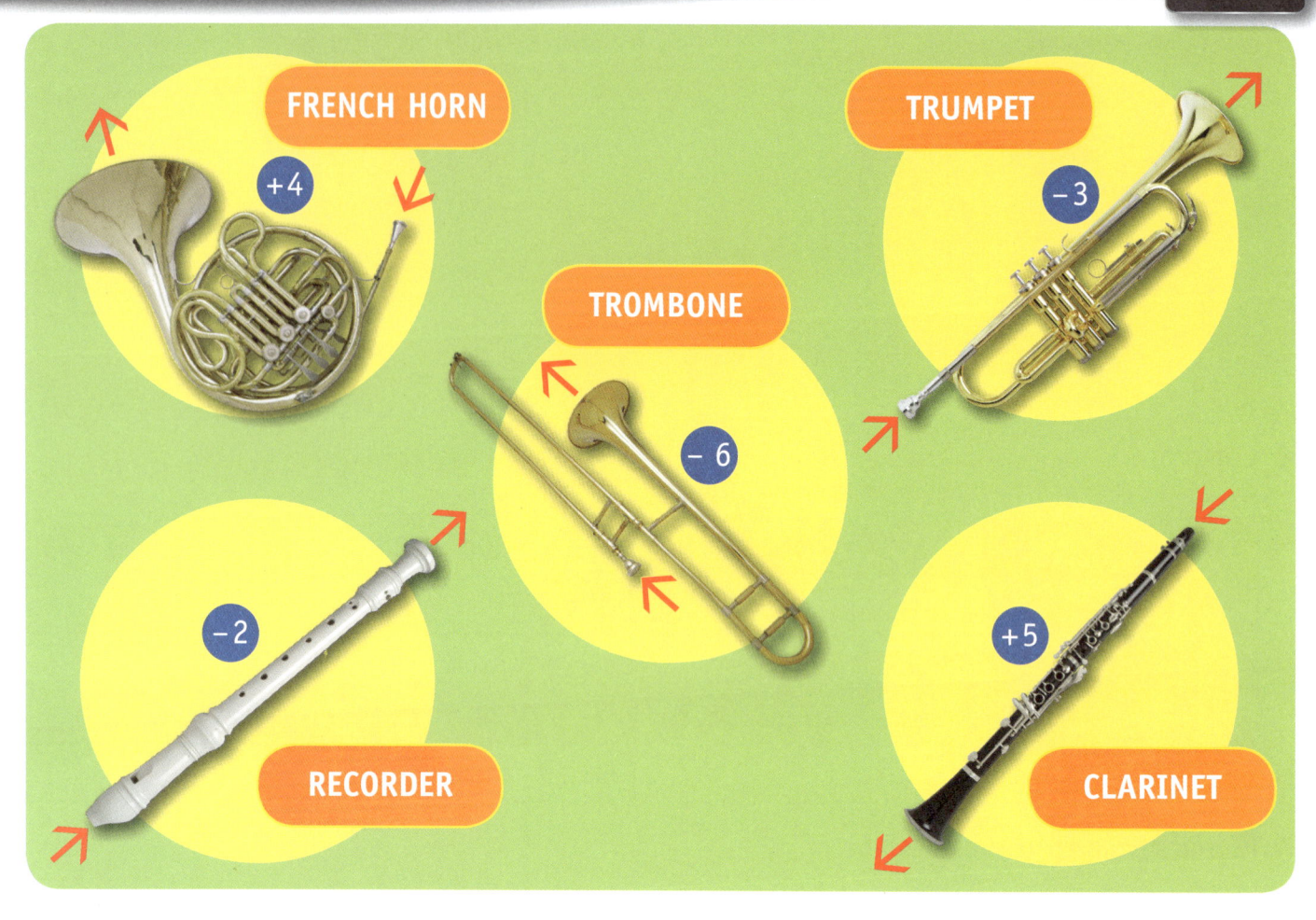

Lab 3 patterns 2

Sequences

[Instruments shown: FRENCH HORN +4, TRUMPET −3, TROMBONE −6, RECORDER −2, CLARINET +5]

These are magical instruments.

When a number is blown in one end, it changes four times and all four numbers come out the other end. Each instrument has its own rule for making number patterns.

1 What numbers come out of the French horn if 7 is put in?

    _____   _____   _____   _____

2 What numbers come out of the trombone if 34 is put in?

    _____   _____   _____   _____

3 What happens to a 14 in a:

    a trumpet? _____   _____   _____   _____

    b clarinet? _____   _____   _____   _____

    c recorder? _____   _____   _____   _____

4 What must be put in the clarinet for 40 to come out at the end of 4 changes?

    _____

80 ACMNA060 Patterns and algebra • Describe, continue, and create number patterns resulting from performing addition or subtraction.

Pattern rules

1 Look at page 80. Complete these:

   a for the trumpet.   Start with 18. _____ _____ _____ _____

      Rule = _____   Start with 25. _____ _____ _____ _____

   b for the clarinet.   Start with 18. _____ _____ _____ _____

      Rule = _____   Start with 23. _____ _____ _____ _____

   c for the recorder.   Start with 18. _____ _____ _____ _____

      Rule = _____   Start with 15. _____ _____ _____ _____

   d for the French horn.   Start with 16. _____ _____ _____ _____

      Rule = _____   Start with 11. _____ _____ _____ _____

   e for the trombone.   Start with 24. _____ _____ _____ _____

      Rule = _____   Start with 29. _____ _____ _____ _____

2 This is your kazoo. Decide how it changes numbers and how many changes it makes before it runs out of puff.

KAZOO

3 Use your kazoo.

   a Start with 84. _____ _____ _____ _____

   b Start with 110. _____ _____ _____ _____

4 Invent a musical instrument and make it add and subtract numbers.

   a Instrument name

   b Changes it makes

   c Use your instrument.

      Start at 92.

Draw it here.

ACMNA060 Patterns and algebra • Describe, continue, and create number patterns resulting from performing addition or subtraction.

Number Patterns

1 Write the next three rows.

a
| 4 + 9 = 13 |
| 14 + 9 = 23 |
| 24 + 9 = 33 |

b
| 8 + 7 = 15 |
| 18 + 7 = 25 |
| 28 + 7 = 35 |

c
| 9 + 7 = 16 |
| 19 + 7 = 26 |
| 29 + 7 = 36 |

d
| 46 − 12 = 34 |
| 56 − 12 = 44 |
| 66 − 12 = 54 |

e
| 89 − 5 = 84 |
| 89 − 15 = 74 |
| 89 − 25 = 64 |

f
| 6 + 6 + 6 = 18 |
| 7 + 7 + 7 = 21 |
| 8 + 8 + 8 = 24 |

2 Start at 3. Use a straight line to join it to the next multiple of 3. Continue until you have reached 15. What shape have you made?

_____

Colour this shape.

(Circle with numbers 1–15 around it, line drawn from 3 to 15)

3 Follow the patterns.

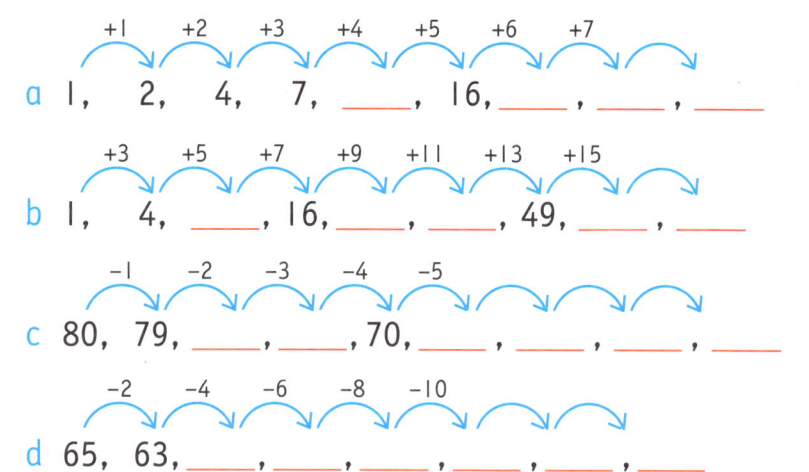

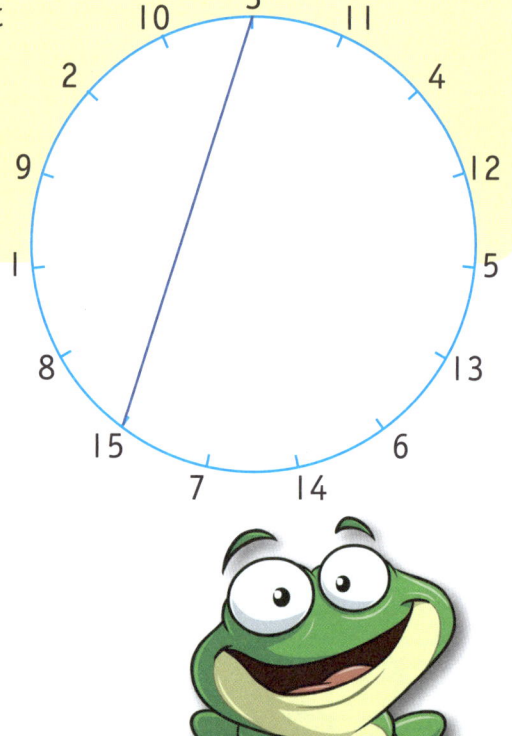

+1 +2 +3 +4 +5 +6 +7

a 1, 2, 4, 7, ____, 16, ____, ____, ____

+3 +5 +7 +9 +11 +13 +15

b 1, 4, ____, 16, ____, ____, 49, ____, ____

−1 −2 −3 −4 −5

c 80, 79, ____, ____, 70, ____, ____, ____, ____

−2 −4 −6 −8 −10

d 65, 63, ____, ____, ____, ____, ____

Problem solving

Patterns using multiples

Look for the patterns in tables.

1. Complete this multiplication square neatly in pencil.

×	1	2	3	4	5	6	7	8	9	10	11	12
1												
2		4										
3									27			
4												
5					25							
6												
7								56				
8												
9				36								
10										100		
11							77					
12												

2. Colour the multiples of 3.
3. Describe the pattern you coloured.

_____

_____

4. Use different colours, make some different patterns. Try colouring different patterns, using the multiples of 4 and 5.
5. What patterns did you find?

_____

Polygons

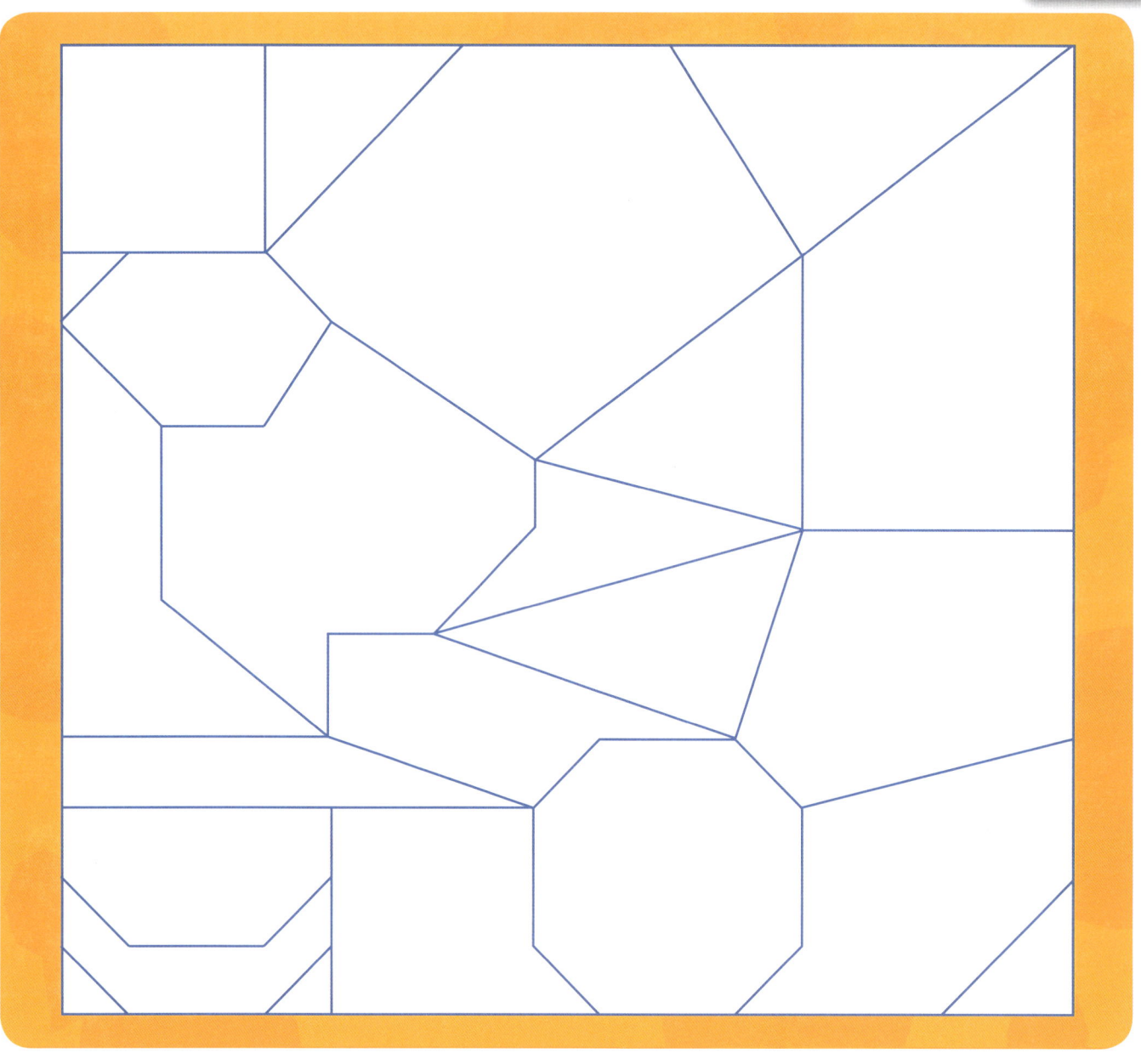

2D shapes

1 How many sides?

   a triangle ☐   b quadrilateral ☐

   c pentagon ☐   d hexagon ☐

   e octagon ☐

2 Colour:

   a the triangles green.   b the quadrilaterals blue.

   c the pentagons yellow.   d the hexagons red.

   e the octagons purple.

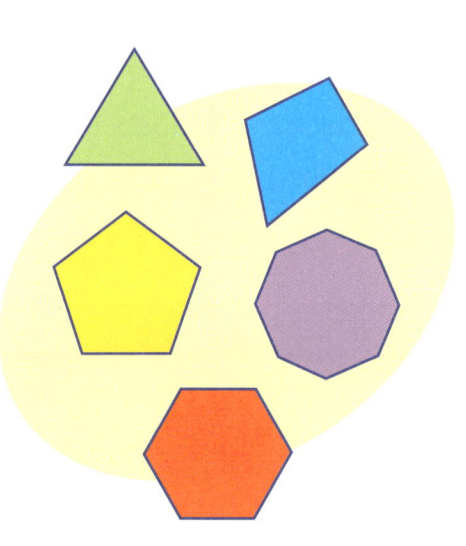

84

Revise: **ACMMG042** Shape • Describe and draw two-dimensional shapes, with and without digital technologies.

Sides and angles

2D shapes

2D Shapes
- 3 sides – triangle
- 4 sides – quadrilateral
- 5 sides – pentagon
- 6 sides – hexagon
- 7 sides – heptagon
- 8 sides – octagon

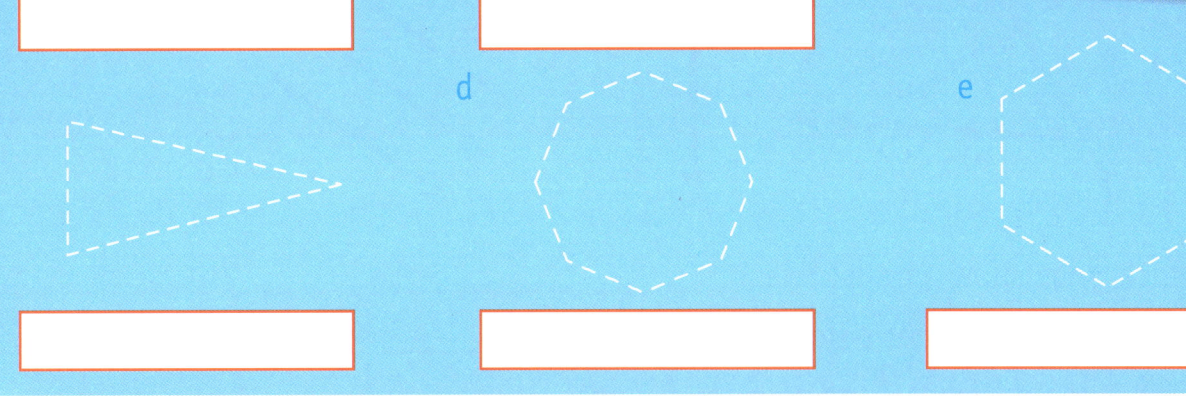

1 Trace and name these shapes.

a
b
c
d
e

2

	Draw the shape	Name	Number of sides	Number of angles
a		triangle		
b		pentagon		
c		quadrilateral		
d		octagon		
e		hexagon		

Challenge! How many:
circles? ☐ squares? ☐
rectangles? ☐ triangles? ☐

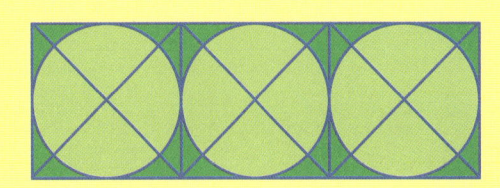

Revise: **ACMMG042** Shape • Describe and draw two-dimensional shapes, with and without digital technologies.

Parallelograms and trapeziums

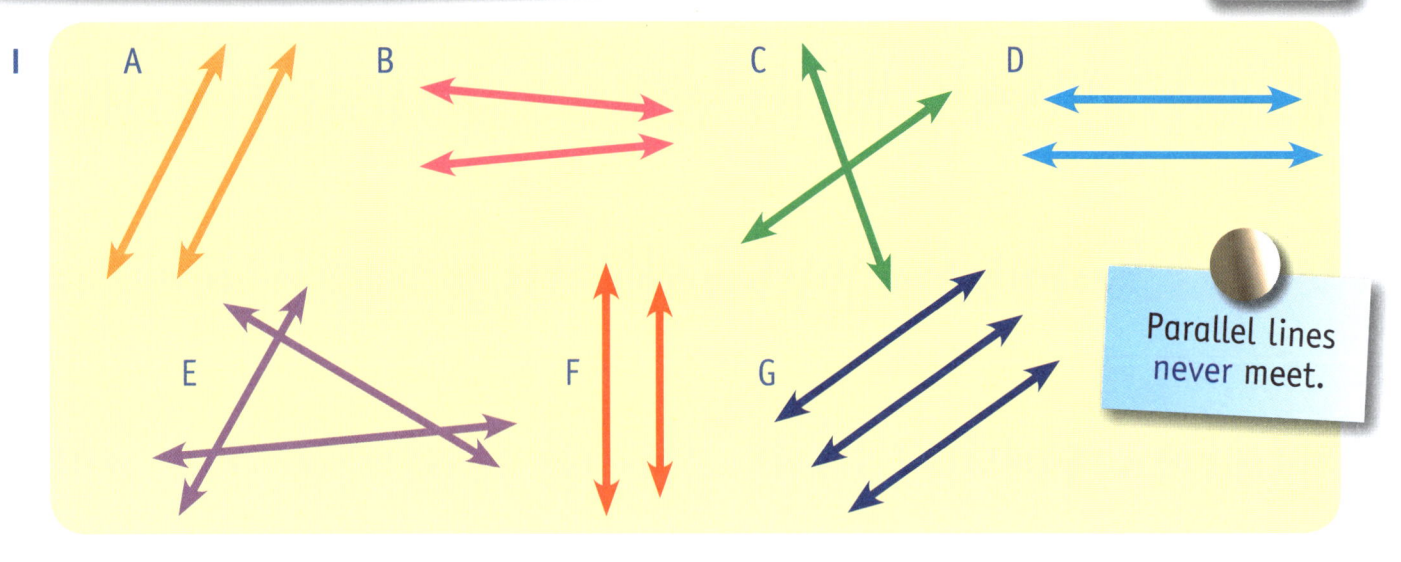

1

A   B   C   D

E   F   G

Parallel lines never meet.

a Which ones show parallel lines? _____

b The lines in C are not parallel. Why? _____

c Draw three different pairs of parallel lines.

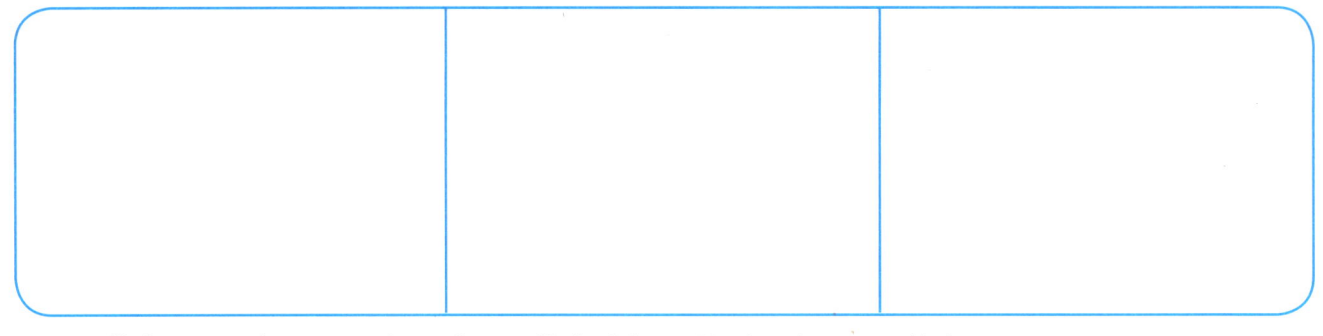

2 A parallelogram has 2 pairs of parallel sides. Circle the parallelograms.

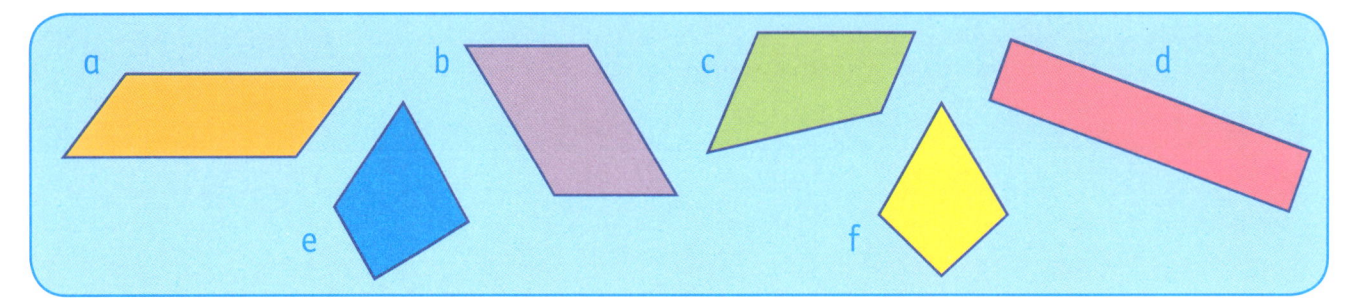

a   b   c   d   e   f

3 A trapezium has 1 pair of parallel sides. Draw a cross on the parallel sides.

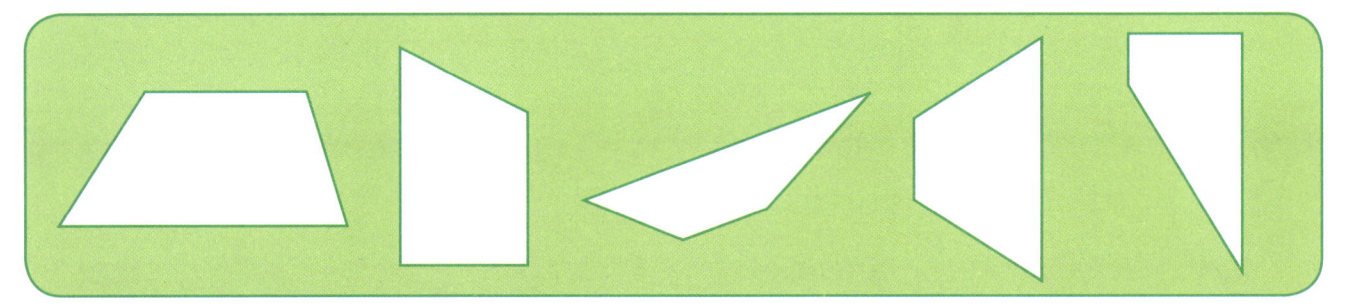

Drawing shapes

2D shapes

1 Circle the shape that is different.

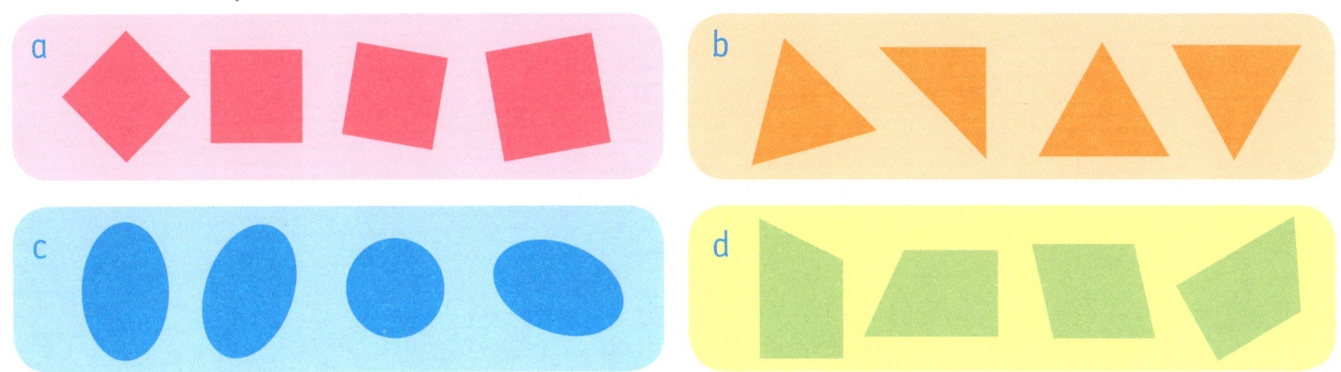

a

b

c

d

2 On the dot paper draw and label:
   a a parallelogram.
   b a trapezium.
   c a pentagon.
   d a hexagon.
   e an octagon.
   f a square.

3 Which was hardest? _____ Why? _____

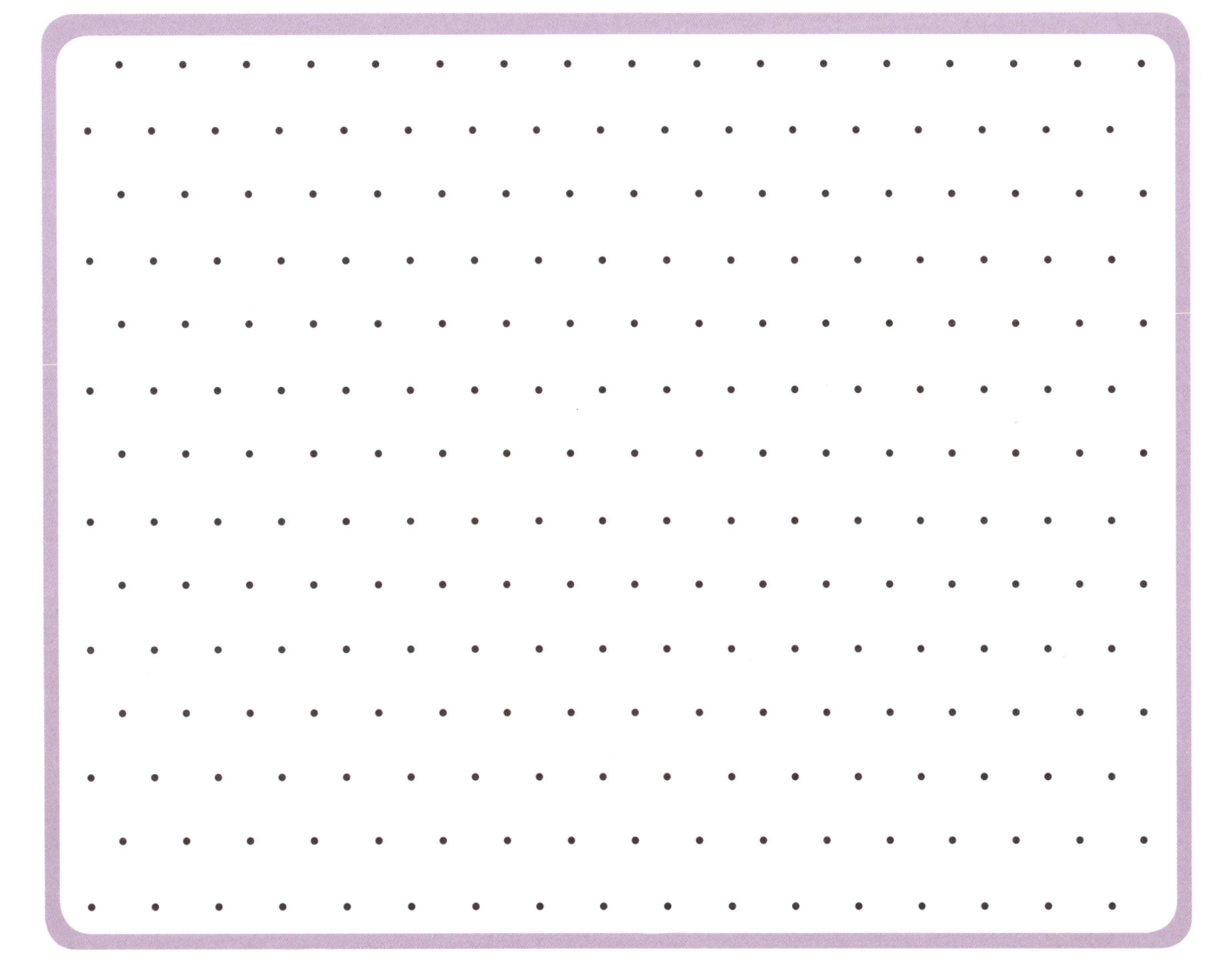

Revise: **ACMMG042** Shape • Describe and draw two-dimensional shapes, with and without digital technologies.

87

Capacity

A   B   C   D   E   F   G

1. Which container holds the most? _____
2. Which container holds the least? _____
3. Name two containers that hold about the same amount? _____
4. Name two containers which hold more than any of these. _____
_____
5. Name two containers which hold less than any of these. _____
_____
6. About how many cups (E) would be needed to fill:
   a B? _____   b D? _____   c A? _____   d F? _____
7. Write the containers in order from holds least to holds most.
_____

8. Get an empty plastic soft drink bottle and a plastic cup.
   a How many cups does the bottle hold? _____
   b Does every one in the class get the same answer? _____
   c Why or why not? _____

ACMMG061 Using units of measurement • Measure, order and compare objects using familiar metric units of length, mass and capacity.

The litre

Capacity

1   Ali used a plastic cup to fill coloured containers with water.

L stands for litre.
5 L is 5 litres.

Container	Number of cups needed
Blue	5 cups
Green	7 cups
Yellow	10 cups
Red	8 cups
Orange	8½ cups
Pink	7½ cups

a How many cups does the green container hold? _____

b Which container holds the most? _____

c Which container holds the least? _____

d How many cups did the orange one hold? _____

e Which two held about the same?
_____

2   Lucy used a different cup. She needed 8 cups to fill the green container.

a Is her cup bigger or smaller than Ali's cup? _____

b About how many of her cups will fill the yellow container? _____

c Is a plastic cup a good measure? _____
   Give a reason. _____

3   a How much milk was in the carton? ☐
    b How much does the jug hold? ☐

4   Fill an empty 1 litre container with water. Pour it into some empty cups. How many cups does it fill? ☐

5   Use water and your 1 litre container to find things that hold:

less than 1 litre	about 1 litre	more than 1 litre

ACMMG061 Using units of measurement • Measure, order and compare objects using familiar metric units of length, mass and capacity.

89

Millilitres

These containers measure millilitres.

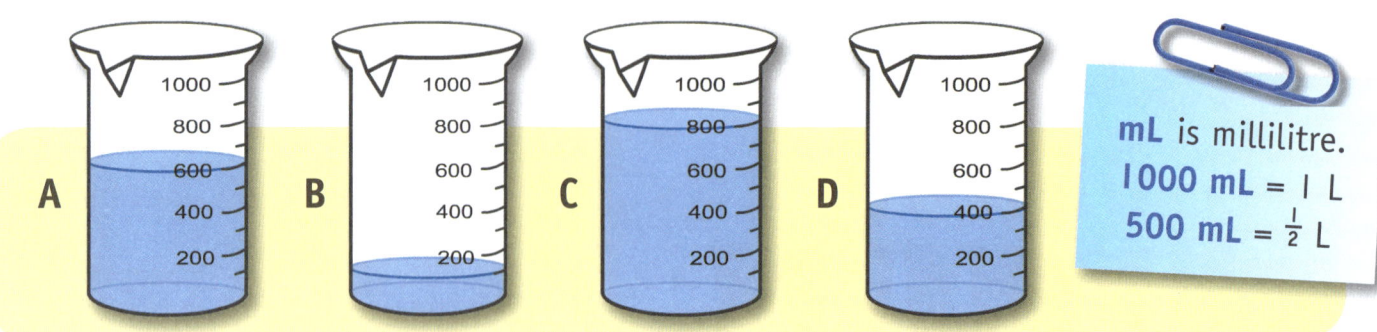

A 600 mL   **B** 200 mL   **C** 800 mL   **D** 400 mL

mL is millilitre.
1000 mL = 1 L
500 mL = $\frac{1}{2}$ L

1 How much water is in:
  a A? _____   b B? _____   c C? _____   d D? _____

2 How much more is in: a A than B? _____   b C than D? _____

3 How much must be added to:
  a B to make 1 L? _____   b C to make 1 L? _____

4 Which container is closest to: a 1 L? _____   b $\frac{1}{2}$ L? _____

5 Name 6 things which could be measured in millilitres.

6 a What is the capacity of A? ☐
  b What is the capacity of B? ☐
  c Which container holds more? ☐
  d How much more does it hold? ☐

A MOTOR OIL 2L   B DISHWASHING LIQUID 5L

7 True (T) or false (F).
  a A dose of medicine is 5 L. ____   b A car can hold 40 L of petrol. ____
  c A glass holds about 250 mL. ____   d The capacity of a cup is 200 L. ____
  e My dog drank 1 mL of water today. ____   f The tall vase can hold 1 L of water. ____

Challenge! On a large plastic bottle place an elastic band to show where you think $\frac{1}{2}$ L is. Check. Try with different containers.

Problem solving

Drinks for all

There will be 40 people at a party and you need to buy drinks for them all.
A 2 litre bottle holds 8 cups and a 3 litre bottle holds 12 cups.
How many bottles do you need to buy so that everyone can have two cups?
Find 3 different ways to buy enough bottles of drink.

A	B	C

If 2 litre bottles are $2 and 3 litre bottles are $3, what is the cheapest option?

How many mL in each drink? _____

Lab 3 — am and pm
time quiz

am is ante meridiem – before midday
pm is post meridiem – before midnight

1. Write am or pm.

   a go to bed _____   b eat breakfast _____
   c wake up _____   d finish school _____
   e get dressed _____   f morning recess _____
   g do homework _____   h eat afternoon tea _____

2. Write the above activities in the order you do them.

   a _____   b _____
   c _____   d _____
   e _____   f _____
   g _____   h _____

3. Name two things which take you:

   a about one hour to do. _____
   b about 10 minutes to do. _____
   c about 2 minutes to do. _____
   d only a few seconds to do. _____

4. Number these from shortest time (1) to longest time (6).

   Watch one TV show. ☐
   Clean my shoes. ☐
   Feed the dog. ☐
   Clean my teeth. ☐
   Eat my lunch. ☐
   Drink a glass of water. ☐

5. Circle the shortest time and cross the longest time.

   a 1 week   1 month   1 hour   1 day
   b 1 day   1 second   1 hour   1 week
   c 1 month   1 year   1 fortnight   1 week

ACMMG062 Using units of measurement • Tell time to the minute and investigate the relationship between units of time.

Time facts

1 Write the days of the week in order.

a Sunday   b _____   c _____   d _____

e _____   f _____   g _____

2 How many:

a days in 1 week? _____   b hours in 1 day? _____

c minutes in 1 hour? _____   d seconds in 1 minute? _____

e minutes in $\frac{1}{2}$ hour? _____   f days in 3 weeks? _____

g seconds in 5 minutes? _____   h hours between noon and 3pm? _____

i seconds between 9:00 and 9:01? _____   j minutes in $\frac{3}{4}$ hour? _____

3 a Draw a circle around the earliest time.

   10:31 pm   3:10 am   1:30 pm   10:30 am

b Draw a circle around the latest time.

   2:45 am   6:40 pm   11:30 pm   11:50 am

4 Number these times in order from earliest to latest.

   5:10 pm   12:00 noon   7:45 am   1:10 am   9:30 pm

5 Complete.

$\frac{1}{4}$ past 7	get dressed	7:15
	go to school	:
	start school	:
	have lunch	:
	eat dinner	:

Lab 3 — jetpack jenny
Presenting data

Tallies and graphs

1 Some friends drew a picture graph of the fish they caught.

   a How many people went fishing? _____
   b How many fish did Julio catch? _____
   c Who caught the most fish? _____
   d Who caught twice as many fish as Arthur? _____
   e How many fish were caught altogether? _____
   f Who said this? "I caught more fish than Julio, but fewer than Mary." _____

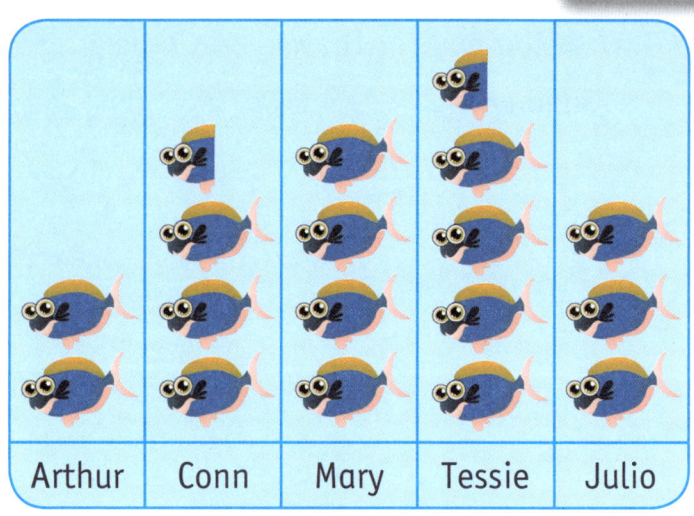

   Arthur | Conn | Mary | Tessie | Julio

   Key: 🐟 = 2 fish

2 Mary decided to show the information as a column graph. She drew this.

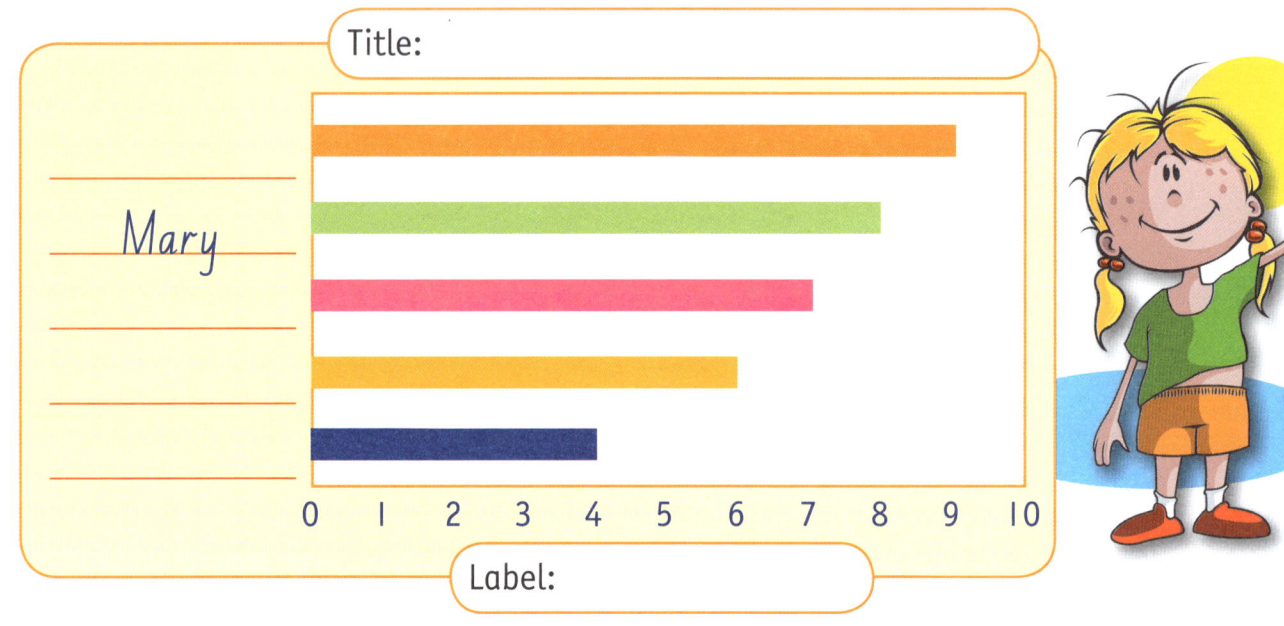

   Title: _____

   Mary

   0 1 2 3 4 5 6 7 8 9 10

   Label: _____

   a Complete the column graph by writing the name of each person.
   b Write a title on the graph.
   c Write the missing label.

3 Conn said he would write a table for the information.

   a Complete the table for Conn.
   b In which order did he write the names of the people who went fishing? _____

Name	Number of fish caught
Arthur	
Julio	
Conn	7
Mary	
Tessie	

94   ACMSP070 Data representation and interpretation • Interpret and compare data displays. • Compare data representations and describe similarities and differences.

Drawing a column graph

1 Eight children have heavy school bags. Their teacher weighs each bag using books.

Amanda's bag (A)	= 8 books
Bruce's bag (B)	= 12 books
Roger's bag (R)	= 10 books
Jan's bag (S)	= 14 books
Peter's bag (P)	= 7 books
George's bag (G)	= 9 books
Michelle's bag (M)	= 8 books
Timothy's bag (T)	= 15 books

a How heavy is Roger's bag? _____ books

b Who has the heaviest bag? _____

c Who has the lightest bag? _____

d Which two bags have the same mass? _____ and _____

e Write the three students with the heaviest bags from lightest to heaviest.

_____ , _____ , _____

f Whose bag is heavier than George's, but lighter than Bruce's? _____

g What is the mass, in books, of Peter's bag and Roger's bag together? _____

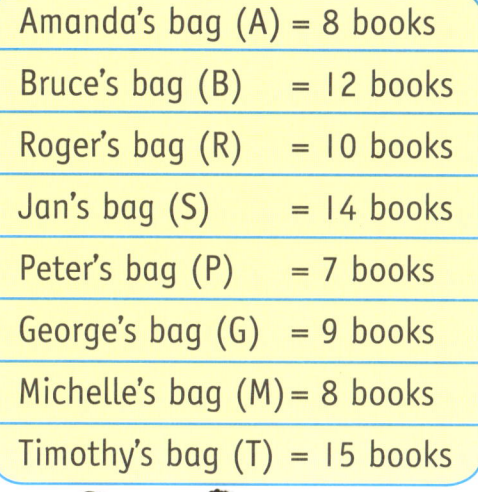

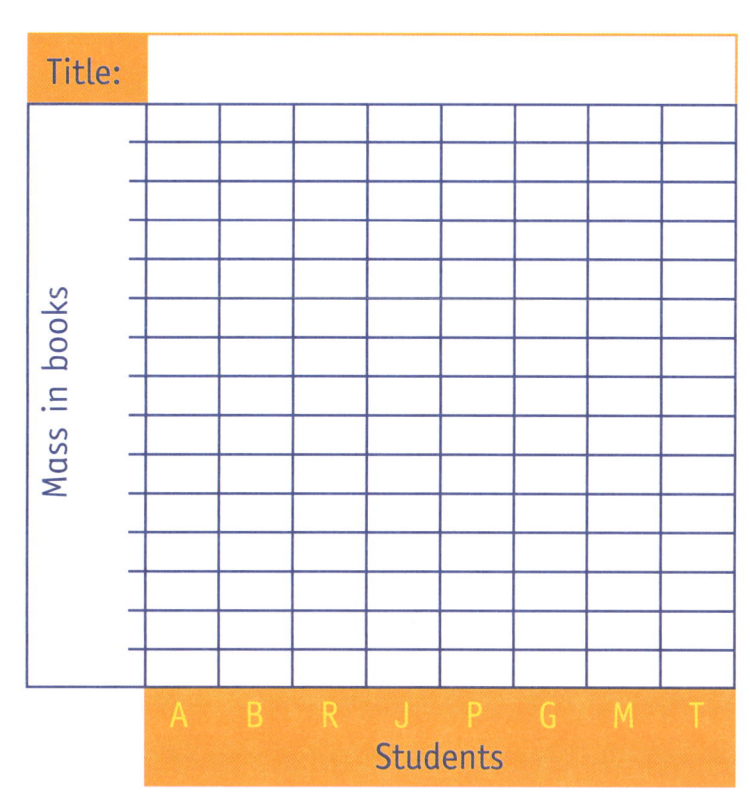

Title: _____

Mass in books

Students: A B R J P G M T

2 a Make a column graph by colouring the spaces.

b Write in the vertical scale.

c Write a title for your graph.

3 True or False?

a Jan's bag is twice as heavy as Peter's bag. _____

b Roger's bag is lighter than George's bag. _____

c Timothy's bag has the same mass as Michelle's bag and Peter's bag together. _____

d Three students have bags lighter than Roger's bag. _____

4 Amanda complained that girls' bags are heavier than boys' bags.

a Is this true? _____   b Explain. _____

Draw a diagram Find another way to present this information.

Revision Term 2

1 Order from smallest to largest.   p 54

9390 9309 9399 9319 9380 9331

____ ____ ____ ____ ____ ____

2 What is the value of the underlined number?   p 57

a 57_8_2 _____

b _9_603 _____

3 Use the numerals 6, 7, 8, 9 to write a number with: p 57

a 6 in the hundreds place. _____

b 9 in the ones place. _____

c 7 in the thousands place. _____

4   p 59

(wheel with ×5 in center; outer numbers: 6, 8, 0, 9, 5, 4, 7, 3)

5 Write three more facts.   p 61

20 − 13 = 7

____ − ____ = ____

____ + ____ = ____

____ + ____ = ____

6 Count on to complete: p 62

49	53	50	56	54
−47				

7 Use the number lines.   p 63

a   4 2
    − 2 7

b   8 1
    − 5 6   p 63

8   p 65

a   6 7   b   8 8   c   9 5
   − 1 4   − 3 5   − 2 0

9 My frog jumped 58 cm.   p 66

Jill's frog jumped 37 cm.

What was the difference? _____

10 Write the next two fractions.   p 68

a $\frac{1}{5}, \frac{2}{5}, \frac{3}{5},$ ____, ____

b $\frac{3}{8}, \frac{4}{8}, \frac{5}{8},$ ____, ____

11 Order these fractions from smallest to largest.   p 70

a $\frac{2}{5}, \frac{5}{5}, \frac{1}{5}, \frac{4}{5}, \frac{3}{5}$

____ ____ ____ ____ ____

b $1, \frac{1}{2}, 2, 1\frac{1}{2}, 2\frac{1}{2}$

____ ____ ____ ____ ____

12 Place these mixed numbers on the number lines.   p 70

a $0, \frac{1}{2}, 1\frac{1}{2}, 2$

b $0, \frac{1}{3}, \frac{2}{3}, 1, 1\frac{1}{3}, 1\frac{2}{3}, 2$

Revision Term 2

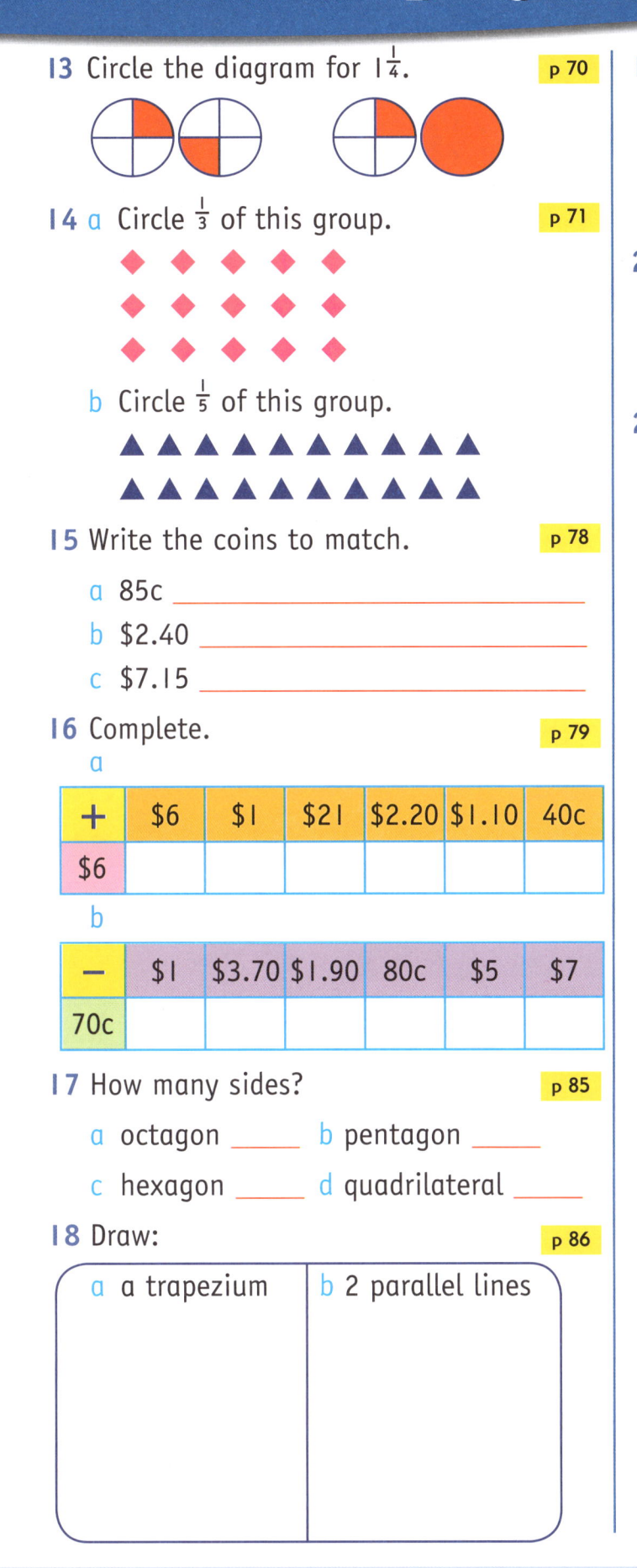

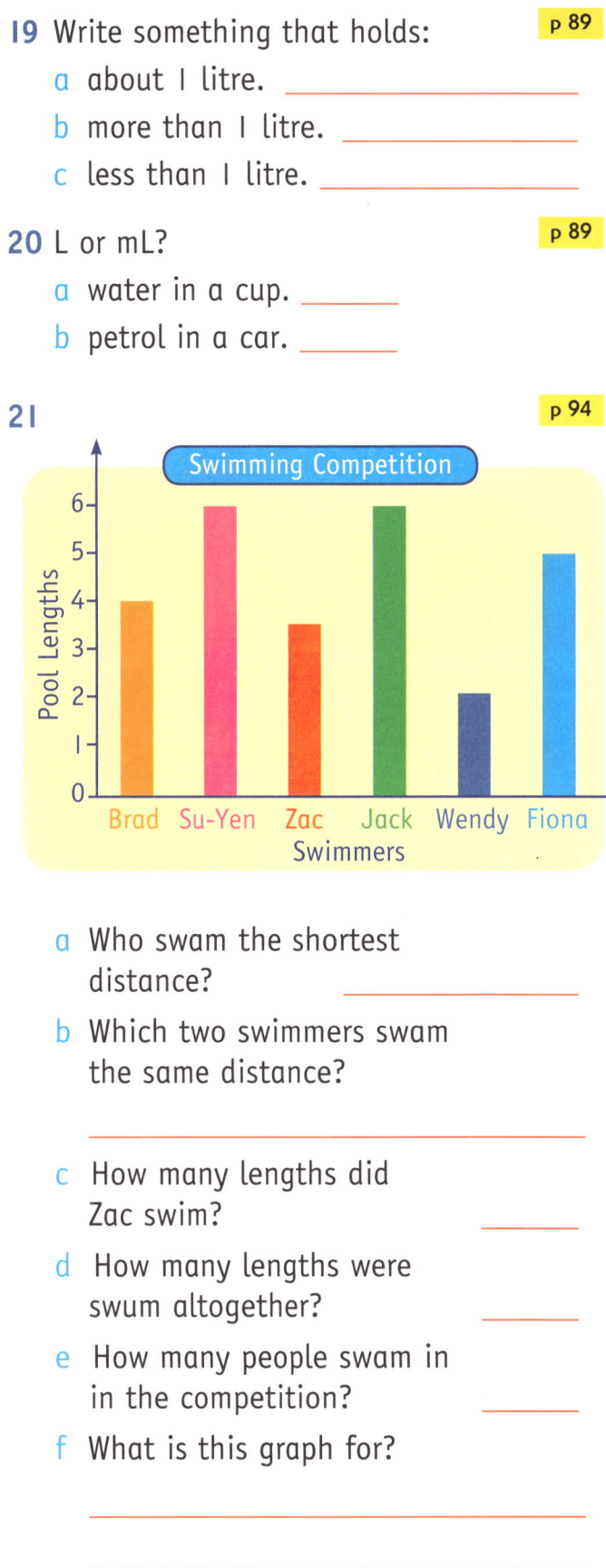

13 Circle the diagram for $1\frac{1}{4}$. 　　p 70

14 a Circle $\frac{1}{3}$ of this group. 　　p 71

   b Circle $\frac{1}{5}$ of this group.

15 Write the coins to match. 　　p 78

   a 85c _____
   b $2.40 _____
   c $7.15 _____

16 Complete. 　　p 79

   a

+	$6	$1	$21	$2.20	$1.10	40c
$6						

   b

−	$1	$3.70	$1.90	80c	$5	$7
70c						

17 How many sides? 　　p 85

   a octagon _____   b pentagon _____
   c hexagon _____   d quadrilateral _____

18 Draw: 　　p 86

   a a trapezium | b 2 parallel lines

19 Write something that holds: 　　p 89
   a about 1 litre. _____
   b more than 1 litre. _____
   c less than 1 litre. _____

20 L or mL? 　　p 89
   a water in a cup. _____
   b petrol in a car. _____

21 　　p 94

Swimming Competition

   a Who swam the shortest distance? _____
   b Which two swimmers swam the same distance? _____
   c How many lengths did Zac swim? _____
   d How many lengths were swum altogether? _____
   e How many people swam in in the competition? _____
   f What is this graph for?
   _____
   _____

97

Addition of money

Toys (with prices):
- Cario — $3.60
- Big Ears — $1.80
- Flame — $2.40
- Tum Tum — $2.50
- Toot — $1.60
- Blobby — $3.20
- Big Ice — $2.80
- Gurk — $1.70

Children:
- John has $5
- Ali has $3.50
- Ng has $4.50
- Mary has $7

1 Which two toys can each child buy?

   a Mary _____

   b John _____

   c Ali _____

   d Ng _____

2 How much change will they get?

   a Mary _____   b John _____

   c Ali _____   d Ng _____

3 How many different toys could Mary buy? _____

ACMNA059 Money and financial mathematics • Represent money values in multiple ways and count the change required for simple transactions to the nearest five cents.

Addition of 3-digit numbers

1 How many in each group? Find the total.

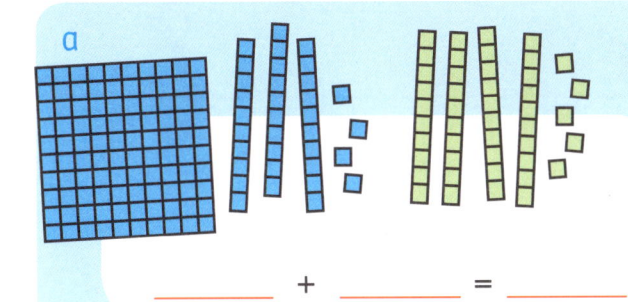

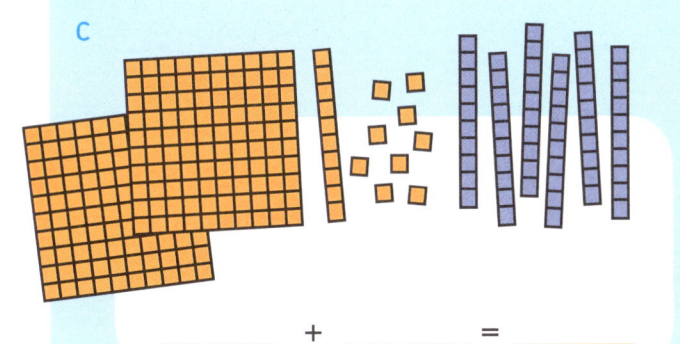

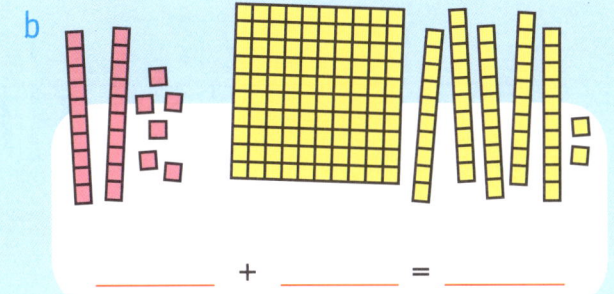

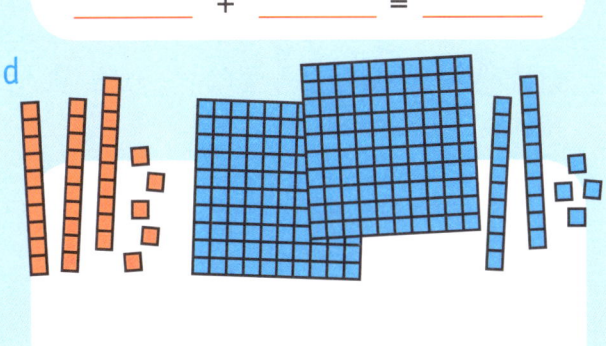

a _____ + _____ = _____

b _____ + _____ = _____

c _____ + _____ = _____

d _____ + _____ = _____

2
a 173
  + 16
  ─────

b 231
  + 45
  ─────

c 127
  +150
  ─────

d 284
  +115
  ─────

e 353
  +125
  ─────

f 126
  +472
  ─────

3
a   3 0
  + 2 ☐
  ─────
   ☐ 9

b   2 ☐
  + 6 3
  ─────
    ☐ 7

c   ☐ ☐
  + 2 4
  ─────
    9 9

d   1 2
  + ☐ 2
  ─────
    8 ☐

e   ☐ 5
  + 2 ☐
  ─────
    6 8

4 Match each to its answer.

a 172 + 27   278   199   289   b 283 + 13
c 35 + 243   d 333 + 46
e 41 + 146   296   379   187   f 49 + 240

Challenge! Can you buy all the toys on page 100 with $20? Use a calculator.

I love a challenge!

Addition of 3-digit numbers

1 Write a number sentence and the answer.

+	(123)	(212)	(143)
(24)	230 + 24 = 254		
(126)			
(236)			
(321)			

2

Tennis ball $1.50   Car $5.50   Boat $7.50
Monkey $7.50   Teddy $9   Donkey $4.50
Yo-yo $2   Mask $6.50   Softball $3.30

a Which two toys are the same price? _____ _____
b Which toy costs the most? _____
c Which toy is the cheapest? _____
d Which two toys together cost $8.50? _____ _____
e How much would it cost to buy the car and the yo-yo? _____
f Can I buy the donkey and the softball with $7.50? _____
g Which toys cost less than $5? _____
h If you had $10, what would you buy? _____
i If you had $20, what would you buy? _____

Mental addition

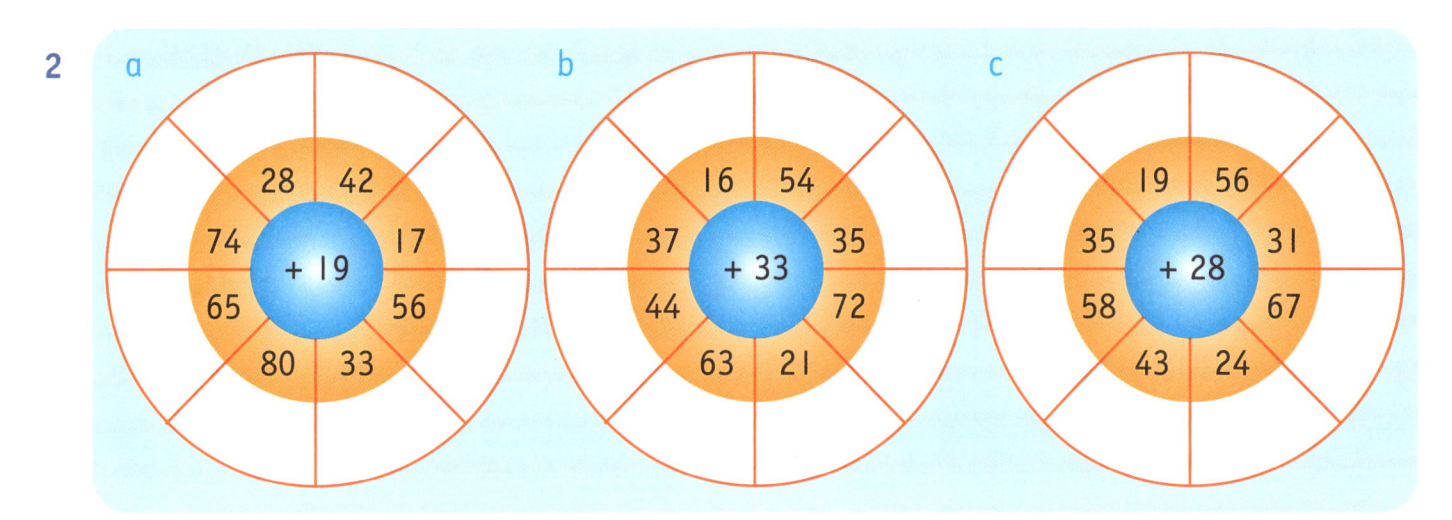

Compensation

1. a 65 + 29 = 65 + 30 − 1 = ____   b 38 + 43 = 38 + 40 + 3 = ____
   c 43 + 39 = ____ = ____   d 59 + 38 = ____ = ____
   e 38 + 61 = ____ = ____   f 47 + 22 = ____ = ____
   g 77 + 13 = ____ = ____   h 23 + 49 = ____ = ____
   i 14 + 28 = ____ = ____   j 26 + 31 = ____ = ____

2. a + 19 (28, 42, 17, 56, 33, 80, 65, 74)
   b + 33 (16, 54, 35, 72, 21, 63, 44, 37)
   c + 28 (19, 56, 31, 67, 24, 43, 58, 35)

3. Estimate first.

	Estimate	Answer
a 17 + 15		
b 39 + 24		
c 35 + 63		

	Estimate	Answer
d 28 + 13		
e 51 + 37		
f 46 + 29		

4. Jon paid 25c for an apple, 30c for an orange and 45c for a banana.

   a How much did he spend? ____

   b How much change from $2? ____

Work backwards

Look at question 2 on page 100. At the fair Mindy spent exactly $16 on 3 items. Which items did she buy? ____

ACMNA053 & ACMNA055 Number and place value • Apply place value to partition, rearrange and regroup numbers to at least 10 000 to assist calculations and solve problems. • Recall addition facts for single-digit numbers and related subtraction facts to develop increasingly efficient mental strategies for computation.

101

Multiplication

Lab 3 tables tennis

A B C
D E
F G H

1.

A	3 + 3 + 3 =	3 × 3 =
B	5 + 5 + 5 + 5 =	
C		
D		
E		
F		
G		
H		

2. Put A and G together and write an addition and a multiplication number sentence.

A and G

102

ACMNA056 & ACMNA057 Number and place value • Recall multiplication facts of two, three, five and ten and related facts. • Represent and solve problems involving multiplication using efficient mental and written strategies and appropriate digital technologies.

Multiplication

1 Use different colours to match.

a	2 + 2 + 2 + 2	6 bundles of 6	4 × 2	25
b	5 + 5 + 5 + 5 + 5	4 lots of 2	6 × 6	8
c	6 + 6 + 6 + 6 + 6 + 6	three nines	5 × 5	10
d	9 + 9 + 9	5 groups of 5	7 × 4	36
e	4 + 4 + 4 + 4 + 4 + 4 + 4	1 lot of 10	3 × 9	27
f	10	7 groups of 4	1 × 10	28

2 a 8 + 8 + 8 = ☐ ice creams   3 × 8 = ☐

b 9 + 9 + 9 + 9 + 9 + 9 + 9 = ☐ hearts   ☐ × 9 = ☐

c 5 + 5 + 5 + 5 = ☐ pencils   4 × ☐ = ☐

d 7 = ☐ cakes   ☐ × ☐ = ☐

e ☐ + ☐ + ☐ = ☐ apples   ☐ × ☐ = ☐

f ☐ + ☐ = ☐ balloons   ☐ × ☐ = ☐

4× table

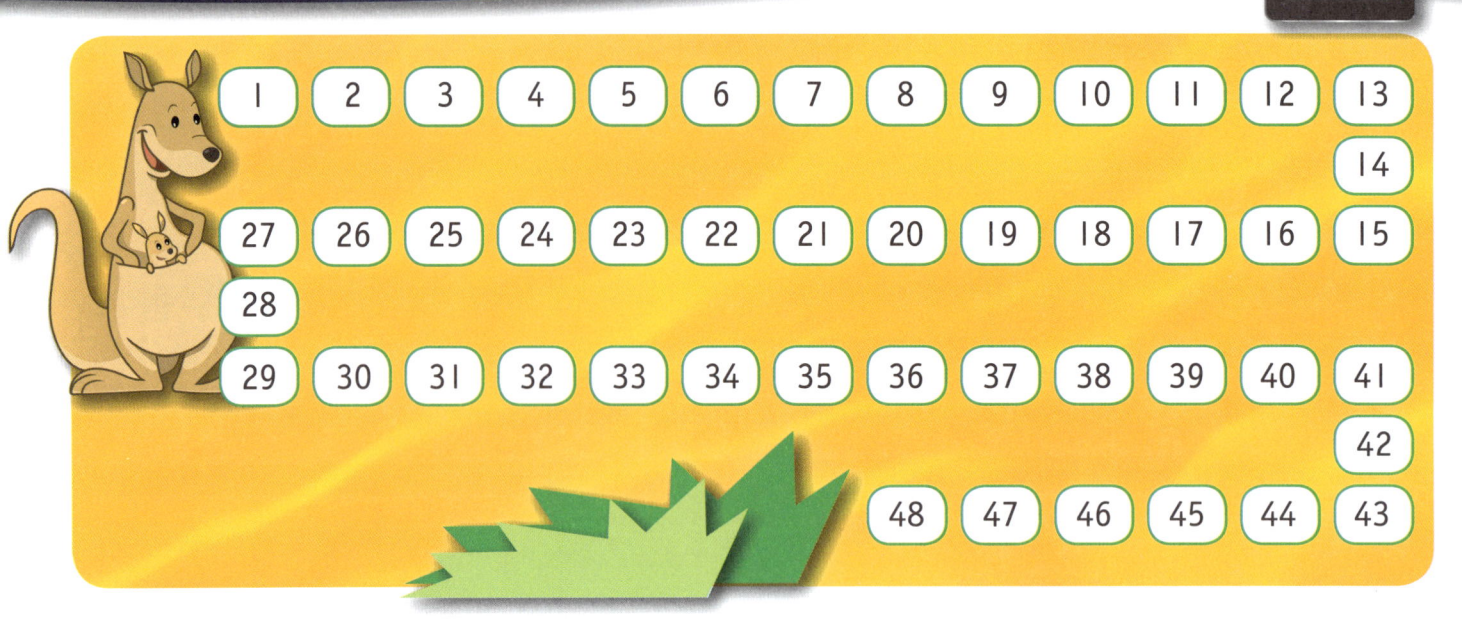

Lab 3 snowboard

3, 4 tables

1	2	3	4	5	6	7	8	9	10	11	12	13
												14
27	26	25	24	23	22	21	20	19	18	17	16	15
28
29	30	31	32	33	34	35	36	37	38	39	40	41
												42
						48	47	46	45	44	43

Kanga jumps along the path 4 spaces each time.

1. Colour the numbers she will land on.

2. How far did she go in:

   a 0 jumps? _____   b 1 jump? _____   c 2 jumps? _____   d 3 jumps? _____

   e 4 jumps? _____   f 5 jumps? _____   g 6 jumps? _____   h 7 jumps? _____

   i 8 jumps? _____   j 9 jumps? _____   k 10 jumps? _____

3. A dog has 4 paws. Add groups of 4 to find how many paws on:

   a 1 dog   4 × 1 = _____   b 2 dogs   4 × 2 = _____
   c 3 dogs   4 × 3 = _____   d 4 dogs   4 × 4 = _____
   e 5 dogs   4 × 5 = _____   f 6 dogs   4 × 6 = _____
   g 7 dogs   4 × 7 = _____   h 8 dogs   4 × 8 = _____
   i 9 dogs   4 × 9 = _____   j 10 dogs   4 × 10 = _____
   k How many paws would no dogs have? 4 × 0 = _____

4. a 4 × 10 = ____   b 10 × 4 = ____   c 4 × 6 = ____   d 1 × 4 = ____   e 4 × 0 = ____
   f 0 × 4 = ____   g 9 × 4 = ____   h 4 × 4 = ____   i 7 × 4 = ____   j 8 × 4 = ____

5. A butterfly has 4 spots on its wings. How many spots on 5 butterflies? ☐

6. Each car has 4 wheels. How many wheels on 7 cars? ☐

104

ACMNA056 & ACMNA057 Number and place value • Recall multiplication facts of two, three, five and ten and related division facts. • Represent and solve problems involving multiplication using efficient mental and written strategies and appropriate digital technologies.

Number facts practice

3, 4, 5, 10 tables

1 Write the a multiplication fact for each badge. Do some have more than one?

a. 90 — 10 x 9 =
b. 35
c. 24
d. 20
e. 18
f. 9
g. 50
h. 27
i. 45
j. 40
k. 28
l. 21

2

×	2	8	5	10	0	7	3	1	6	9	4
4											
10											
5											
3											

3

a. Mum drew a star with 3 points. How many points on 9 stars?

b. Aunt Jo drew a star with five points. How many points on 9 stars?

c. Uncle Bill drew a star with eight points. How many points on 9 stars?

d. How many more points are there on Uncle Bill's stars than on Aunt Jo's stars?

ACMNA056 & ACMNA057 Number and place value • Recall multiplication facts of two, three, five and ten and related division facts. • Represent and solve problems involving multiplication using efficient mental and written strategies and appropriate digital technologies.

105

Vertical multiplication

1 Write a number sentence for this picture.

☐ × ☐ = ☐

2 Write a number sentence and the answer.

  a 8 cars. 4 people in each car. How many people?   ☐ × ☐ = ☐
  b 5 tricycles. 3 wheels on each tricycle. How many wheels?   ☐ × ☐ = ☐
  c 6 cases each holding 8 pencils. How many pencils?   ☐ × ☐ = ☐
  d 5 rows with 10 boys in each row. How many boys?   ☐ × ☐ = ☐
  e 8 nests with 5 eggs in each nest. How many eggs?   ☐ × ☐ = ☐
  f 10 pies on each tray. There are 6 trays. How many pies?   ☐ × ☐ = ☐

3 Write the answers and match.

| 6 × 3 | 8 × 2 | 7 × 5 | 10 × 9 | 4 × 1 | 8 × 6 |

$7 \times 5 =$ ☐ $6 \times 3 =$ ☐ $8 \times 2 =$ ☐ $8 \times 6 =$ ☐ $10 \times 9 =$ ☐ $4 \times 1 =$ ☐

$5 \times 9 =$ ☐ $4 \times 0 =$ ☐ $10 \times 3 =$ ☐ $9 \times 5 =$ ☐ $6 \times 2 =$ ☐ $4 \times 4 =$ ☐

| 4 × 0 | 10 × 3 | 5 × 9 | 6 × 2 | 4 × 4 | 9 × 5 |

Draw a diagram

Draw pictures to show:

2 rows of 6

5 groups of 3 stars

4 lots of 7 apples

$2 \times 6 =$ ☐ $5 \times$ ☐ $=$ ☐   ☐ $\times$ ☐ $=$ ☐

106

Problem solving

Vegetable garden

Victor is planning gardens of lettuces, tomatoes and radishes. He wants to plant them in rows of equal numbers of plants. He has 30 lettuce, 32 tomato and 36 radish plants. How can he plant them in these garden beds?

Key: ● = lettuce   ▲ = tomato   ◆ = radish

Lab 3 — grandma crunch
Sharing

Sharing, Groups of

1. These dogs all need good homes. How many dogs are there? _____

2. How many dogs would each person get if they were fairly shared by:

   a 4 people? _____   b 3 people? _____

   c 2 people? _____   d 24 people? _____

   e 6 people? _____   f 8 people? _____

   g 1 person? _____   h 12 people? _____

3. Tom took half the dogs. How many did he take? _____

4. Jacky took one quarter of the dogs. How many did she take? _____

5. If five people wanted the dogs, would they each get a fair share? _____
   Why? _____

6. Are there other ways to share which are not fair? _____

108

ACMNA056 Number and place value • Recall multiplication and division facts of two, three, five and ten and related division facts.

Fair shares

Fair shares means an equal number in each share.

Sharing, Groups of

1 a Are these shares fair? _____

b Why? _____

_____

2 a Make 5 fair shares.　　b Make 4 fair shares.　　c Make 10 fair shares.

One share _____　　　One share _____　　　One share _____

3 Circle to make fair shares. How many in each share?

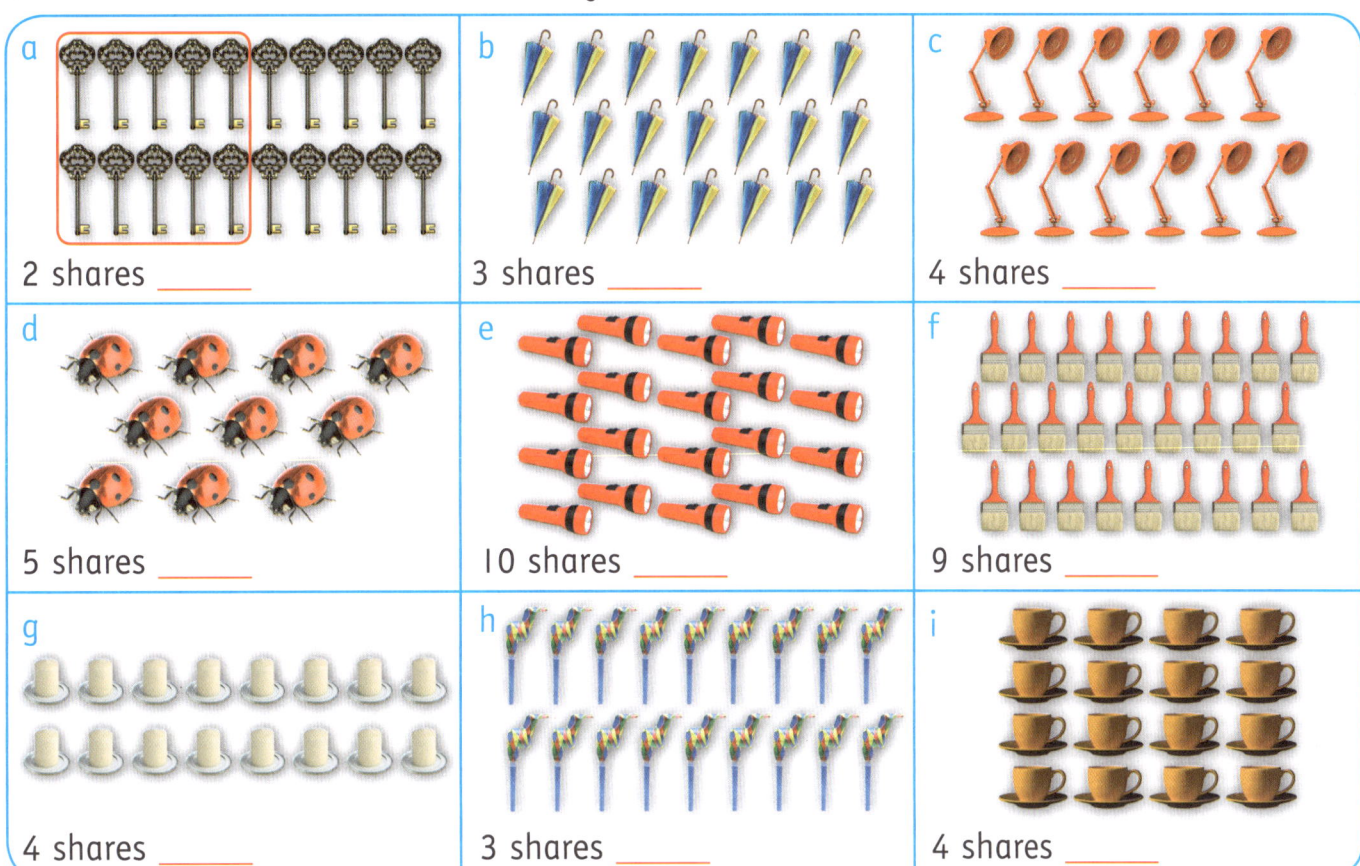

a 2 shares _____　　b 3 shares _____　　c 4 shares _____

d 5 shares _____　　e 10 shares _____　　f 9 shares _____

g 4 shares _____　　h 3 shares _____　　i 4 shares _____

4 a Share 20 lollies into 5 packets. How many lollies in each packet? _____

b Share 15 apples onto 5 plates. How many apples on each plate? _____

c Place 10 children into 2 equal groups. How many children in each group? _____

d Place 35 crayons equally into 7 boxes. How many crayons in each box? _____

e Share 27 coins among 3 girls. How many coins does each girl get? _____

ACMNA056 Number and place value • Recall multiplication and division facts of two, three, five and ten and related division facts.

Equal groups

1 a Circle groups of 5 pots.

How many pots? _____
How many groups? _____

b Circle groups of 5 hats.

How many hats? _____
How many groups? _____

c Circle groups of 3 eggs.

How many eggs? _____
How many groups? _____

2 a Circle groups of 3 hearts.

How many groups? _____
How many hearts? _____

b Circle groups of 4 hearts.

How many groups? _____
How many hearts? _____

c Circle groups of 2 hearts.

How many groups? _____
How many hearts? _____

3 There are 24 rockets.

a Circle 3 equal groups.

How many in each group? _____

b Circle 6 equal groups.

How many in each group? _____

c Circle 2 equal groups.

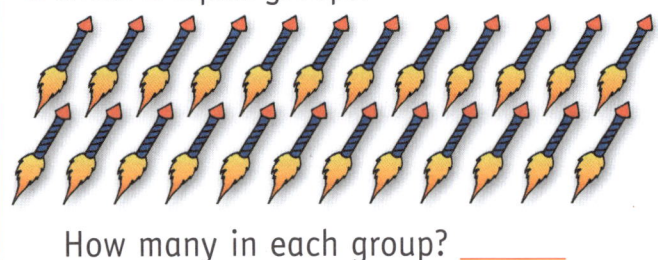

How many in each group? _____

d Circle 8 equal groups.

How many in each group? _____

110 ACMNA056 Number and place value • Recall multiplication and division facts of two, three, five and ten and related division facts.

Problem solving

Grandpa's treat

Grandpa has 36 fifty-cent coins. He says that he could share them evenly among his grandchildren even if he had 2, 3, 4, 5, 6, 7, 8 or 9 grandchildren. Is he right? Show your working.

Yes, he can share between 2. **36 ÷ 2 = 18   2 × 18 = 36**

Lab 3 — fraction 1
Equivalent fractions

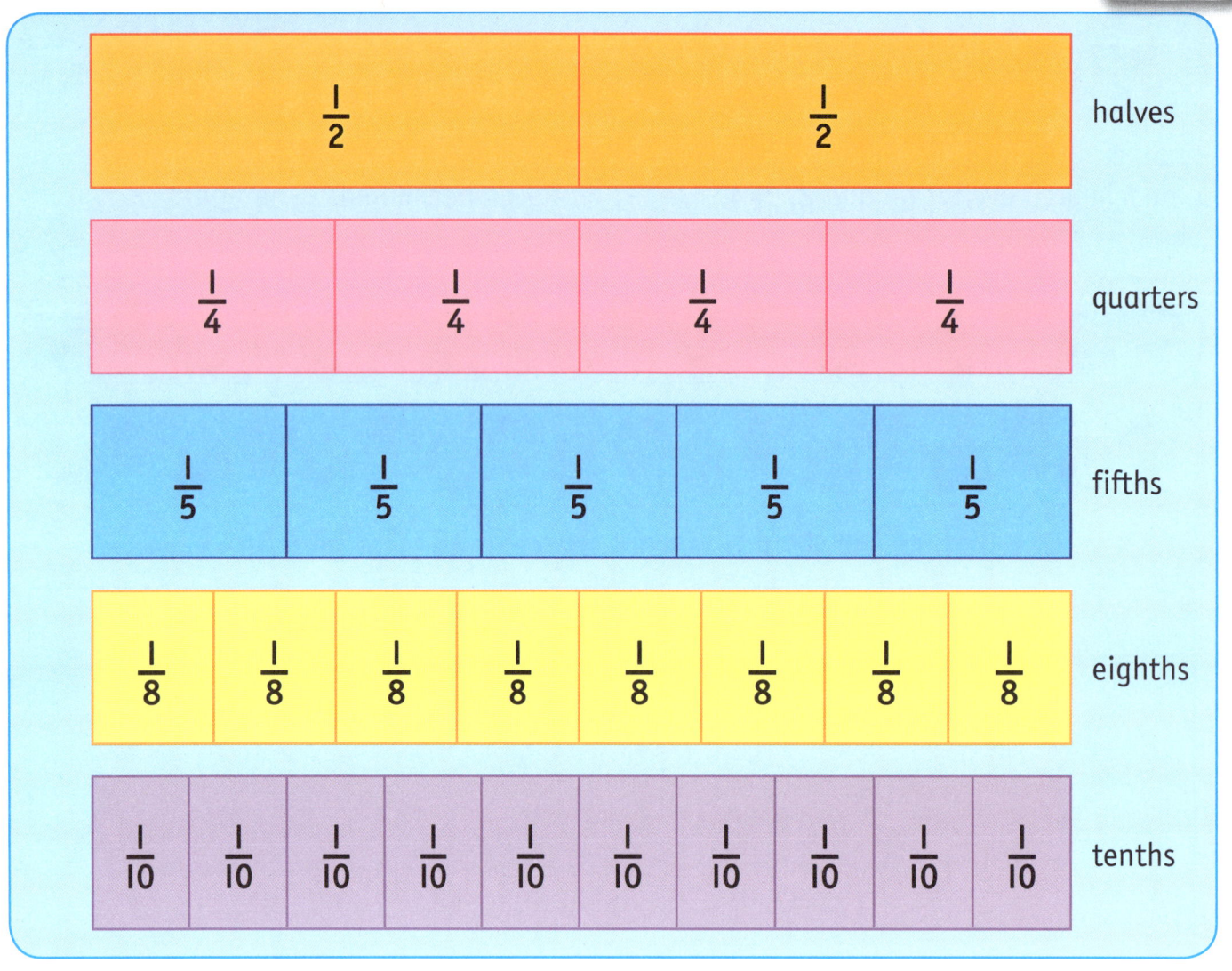

$\frac{1}{2}$ $\frac{1}{2}$	halves
$\frac{1}{4}$ $\frac{1}{4}$ $\frac{1}{4}$ $\frac{1}{4}$	quarters
$\frac{1}{5}$ $\frac{1}{5}$ $\frac{1}{5}$ $\frac{1}{5}$ $\frac{1}{5}$	fifths
$\frac{1}{8}$ $\frac{1}{8}$ $\frac{1}{8}$ $\frac{1}{8}$ $\frac{1}{8}$ $\frac{1}{8}$ $\frac{1}{8}$ $\frac{1}{8}$	eighths
$\frac{1}{10}$ $\frac{1}{10}$ $\frac{1}{10}$ $\frac{1}{10}$ $\frac{1}{10}$ $\frac{1}{10}$ $\frac{1}{10}$ $\frac{1}{10}$ $\frac{1}{10}$ $\frac{1}{10}$	tenths

1 How many in 1 whole?
   a halves _____   b fifths _____   c eighths _____   d tenths _____   e quarters _____

2 How many:
   a quarters make $\frac{1}{2}$? _____   b tenths make $\frac{1}{2}$? _____
   c eighths make $\frac{1}{2}$? _____   d eighths make $\frac{1}{4}$? _____

3 Circle the larger fraction.
   a $\frac{1}{5}$ $\frac{1}{10}$ b $\frac{1}{8}$ $\frac{1}{2}$ c $\frac{1}{4}$ $\frac{1}{5}$ d $\frac{1}{8}$ $\frac{2}{5}$ e $\frac{3}{5}$ $\frac{1}{2}$

4 True (T) or false (F). The larger the denominator the smaller the fraction. _____
   How do you know? _____

5 Write three fractions that are smaller than $\frac{1}{2}$. _____ _____ _____
   What do you notice about their denominators? _____

Fraction names

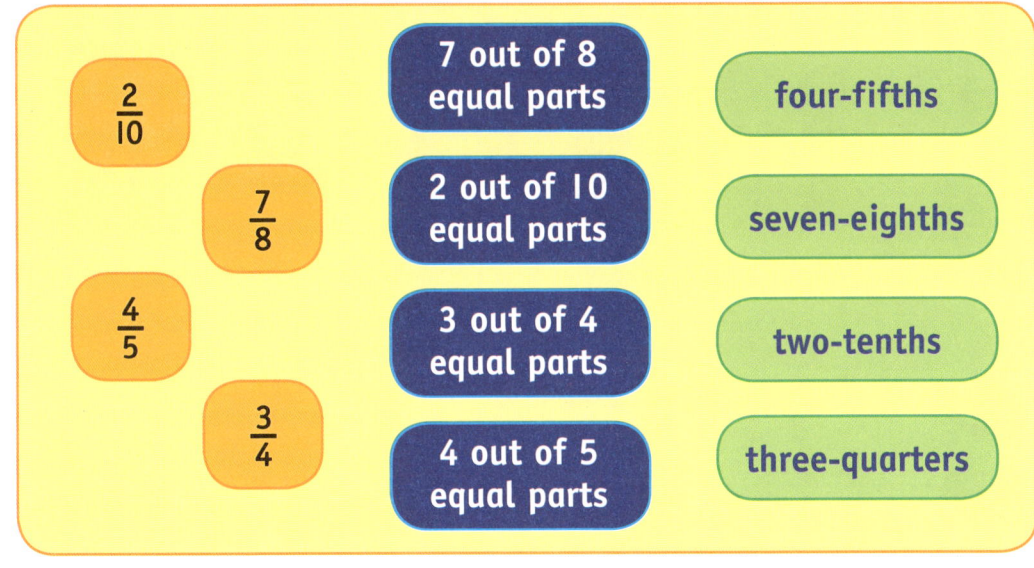

1 Match.

$\frac{2}{10}$	7 out of 8 equal parts	four-fifths
$\frac{7}{8}$	2 out of 10 equal parts	seven-eighths
$\frac{4}{5}$	3 out of 4 equal parts	two-tenths
$\frac{3}{4}$	4 out of 5 equal parts	three-quarters

$\frac{2}{5}$ = numerator / denominator

This means 2 equal parts out of 5.

2 Write the fraction coloured.

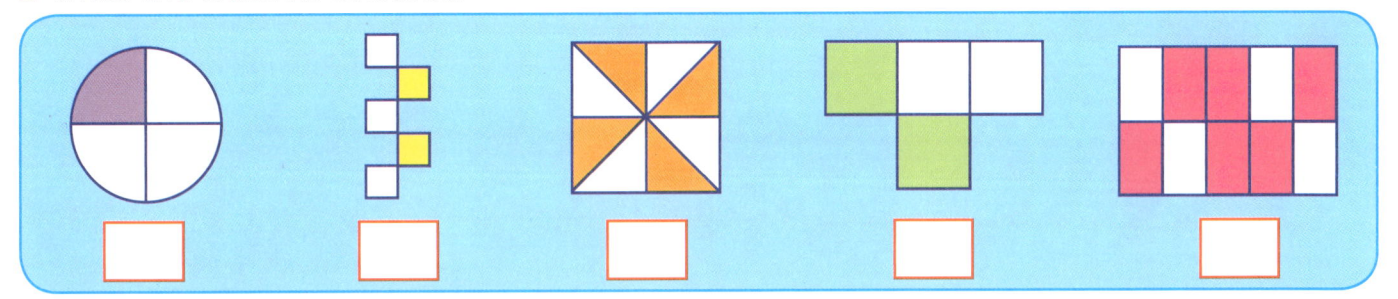

3 Colour to match the fraction.

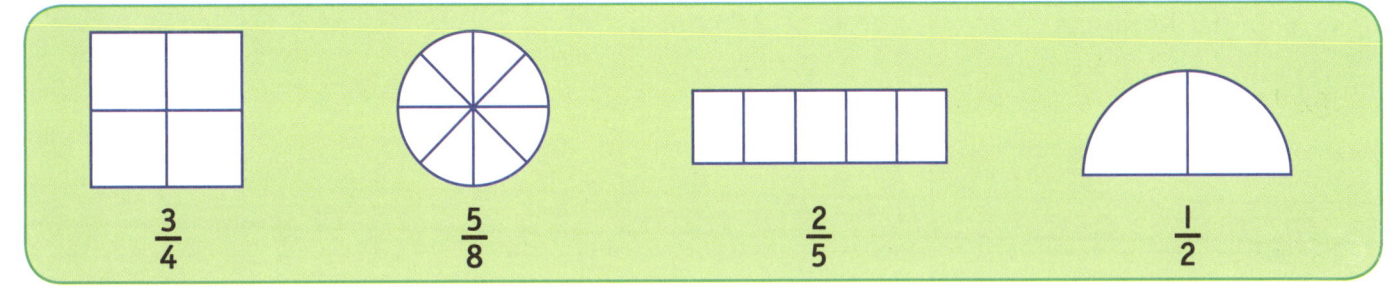

$\frac{3}{4}$ $\frac{5}{8}$ $\frac{2}{5}$ $\frac{1}{2}$

4 Look at page 112. Write another name for:

a one quarter _____

b one half _____

c one fifth _____

d five tenths _____

5 Draw a diagram to show:

$\frac{4}{5}$

$\frac{3}{8}$

ACMNA058 Fractions and decimals • Model and represent unit fractions including $\frac{1}{2}$, $\frac{1}{4}$, $\frac{1}{3}$, $\frac{1}{5}$ and their multiples to a complete whole.

113

Parts of a group

1 What is one-half of:

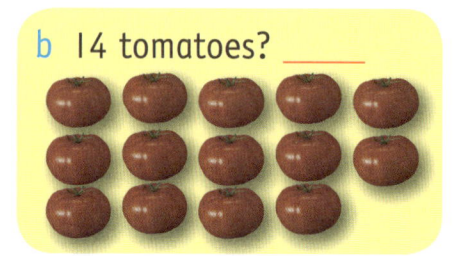

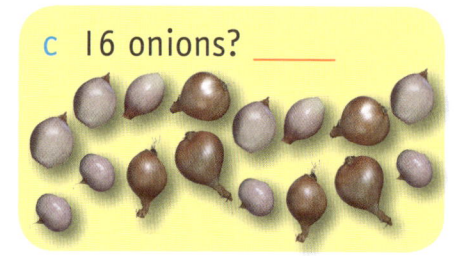

a 10 pears? _____

b 14 tomatoes? _____

c 16 onions? _____

2 What is one-quarter of:

a 8 mangoes? _____

b 12 peas? _____

c 16 mushrooms? _____

3 What is one-fifth of:

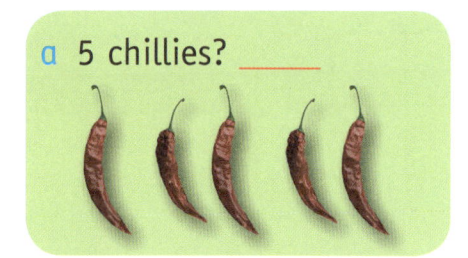

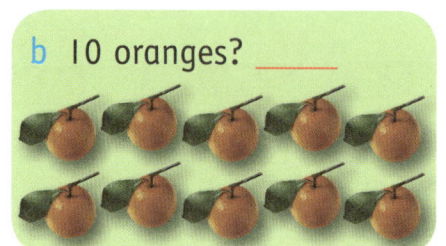

a 5 chillies? _____

b 10 oranges? _____

c 15 pumpkins? _____

4 Draw.

a $\frac{1}{5}$ of 10 bananas

b $\frac{1}{8}$ of 24 cherries

c $\frac{3}{4}$ of 8 apples

5 a $\frac{1}{2}$ of a bunch of grapes = 10. 1 whole bunch of grapes = _____

   b $\frac{1}{2}$ of a dozen eggs = 6. 1 whole dozen eggs = _____

   c $\frac{1}{4}$ of a bag of sweets = 3. 1 whole bag of sweets = _____

   d $\frac{1}{5}$ of a box of plums = 6. 1 whole box of plums = _____

   e $\frac{1}{10}$ of a packet of biscuits = 5. 1 whole packet of biscuits = _____

Challenge! At a basketball game the players eat $\frac{1}{4}$ of an orange each at every rest. There are 8 players and there are three rests. How many oranges are needed? ☐

Hint: A diagram might help!

Problem solving — Fractions at the party

1. There are 20 party hats to give out.
   $\frac{1}{2}$ of them are red. $\frac{1}{4}$ of them are blue.
   $\frac{1}{5}$ of them are green. The rest are pink.
   Colour the hats correctly. Circle and label the groups with their fractions.

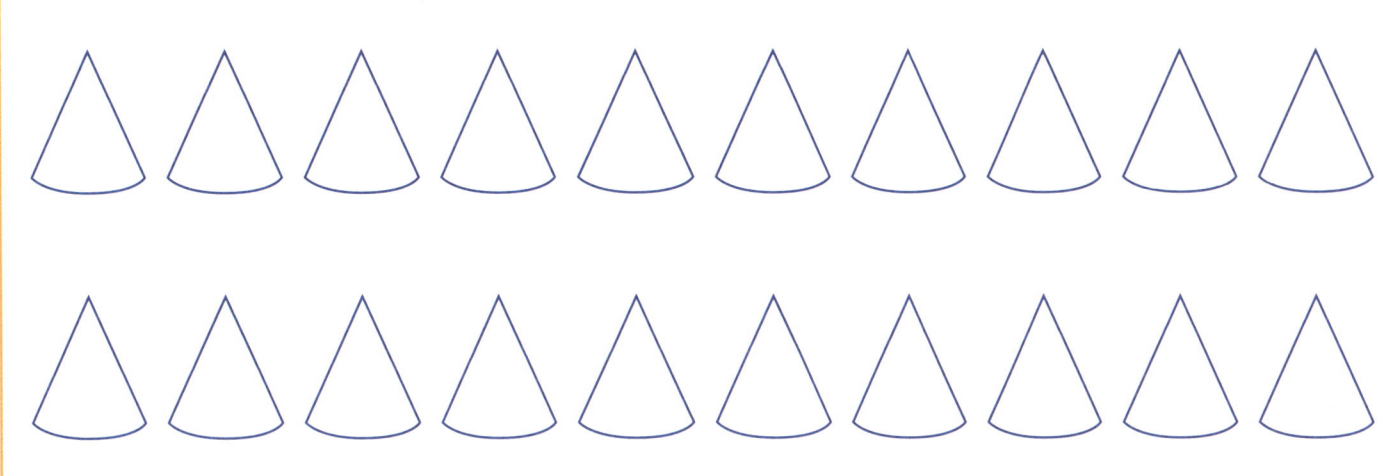

2. Answer true or false.
   a $\frac{1}{2}$ of 20 hats is more than $\frac{1}{5}$ of 20 hats. _____
   b $\frac{1}{5}$ of 20 hats is more than $\frac{1}{4}$ of 20 hats. _____
   c $\frac{1}{4}$ of 20 hats is half as much as $\frac{1}{2}$ of 20 hats. _____
   d $\frac{1}{2}$ is the same as $\frac{1}{5}$ of the hats and $\frac{1}{4}$ of the hats together. _____
       How do you know? _____
   e $\frac{1}{2}$ of the hats plus $\frac{1}{4}$ of the hats is all the hats. _____
       How do you know? _____

3. Write two of your own statements about the fractions of the hats.
   _____
   _____
   _____
   _____

ACMNA058 Fractions and decimals • Model and represent unit fractions including $\frac{1}{2}$, $\frac{1}{4}$, $\frac{1}{3}$, $\frac{1}{5}$ and their multiples to a complete whole.

Investigation 3

Holidays!

It's time for a holiday!
You need to plan everything.

Decide where you will go — camping, the snow, a city or the beach.

1 Survey your class to find the best place.

Tally

1 Camping _____
2 Snow _____
3 City _____
4 Beach _____

2 Display your results here.

3 Choose what holiday you want to go on.

_____

4 Choose the month you will be away. Fill in the calendar.
   Colour the 7 days you plan to be on holiday.

Month _____

Sun	Mon	Tues	Wed	Thurs	Fri	Sat

Leaving home: _____   Arriving back: _____

Holidays!

Investigation 3

5 What will you do on your holiday? Plan the days.

6 You can only take 3 shirts and 2 pairs of jeans or 2 skirts. Draw your clothes and the different outfits. How many different outfits can you wear? _____

To carry out these tasks I need to:
- ☐ ask survey questions.
- ☐ make a tally.
- ☐ make a horizontal column graph.
- ☐ read a calendar and record days on it.
- ☐ explain choice of time.
- ☐ calculate time and cost for activities.
- ☐ draw diagrams to show choices of clothing.

I enjoyed this task!
★★★★★

Revision

1.
   - koala $5.90
   - windmill $4.10
   - paints $2.40
   - wand $1.40
   - top $6.80

   Write your answer in the box.

   Su-Yin bought two toys and spent $7.30. Which two toys did she buy?

   ☐ and ☐

2. What is the total value of these notes and coins?

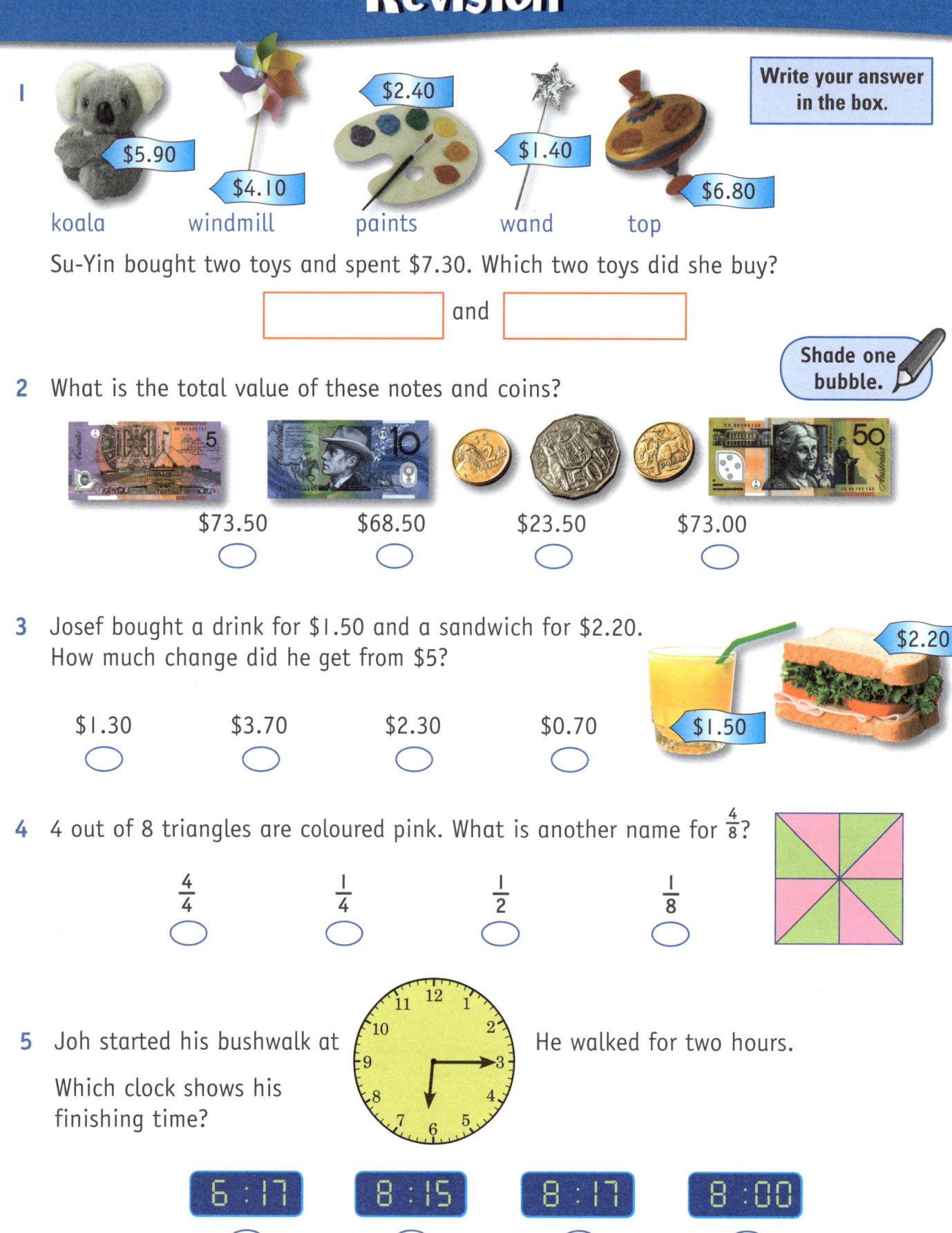

   Shade one bubble.

   $73.50 ○ $68.50 ○ $23.50 ○ $73.00 ○

3. Josef bought a drink for $1.50 and a sandwich for $2.20. How much change did he get from $5?

   $1.30 ○ $3.70 ○ $2.30 ○ $0.70 ○

   $2.20 $1.50

4. 4 out of 8 triangles are coloured pink. What is another name for $\frac{4}{8}$?

   $\frac{4}{4}$ ○ $\frac{1}{4}$ ○ $\frac{1}{2}$ ○ $\frac{1}{8}$ ○

5. Joh started his bushwalk at ⏰. He walked for two hours. Which clock shows his finishing time?

   6:17 ○   8:15 ○   8:17 ○   8:00 ○

118

Revision

6 Ahmed had to make 5 fair shares from these cupcakes.

How many in each share?

    3 ○   4 ○   5 ○   6 ○

Shade one bubble.

7 This graph shows how many glasses of water these children drank on Monday.

How many glasses did Murphy and Ari drink altogether?

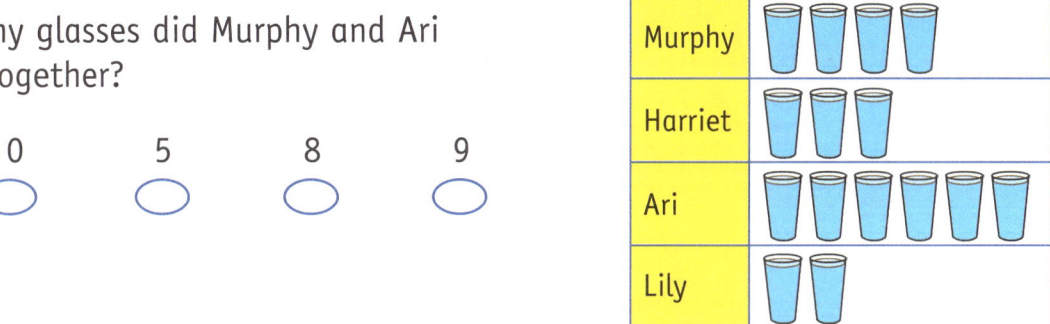

    10 ○   5 ○   8 ○   9 ○

8 Which child made correct estimations of the capacity of these containers?

	Tamsie ○	Jacque ○	Hiram ○	Lottie ○
Tea cup	Less than $\frac{1}{2}$ L	About 1 L	About $\frac{1}{2}$ L	About $\frac{1}{2}$ L
Juice carton	About 2 L	About 2 L	About 1 L	Less than $\frac{1}{2}$ L
Yoghurt carton	About $\frac{1}{2}$ L	About $\frac{1}{2}$ L	Less than $\frac{1}{2}$ L	About 1 L
Milk jug	About 1 L	Less than $\frac{1}{2}$ L	About 2 L	About 2 L

9 How many angles in this shape?

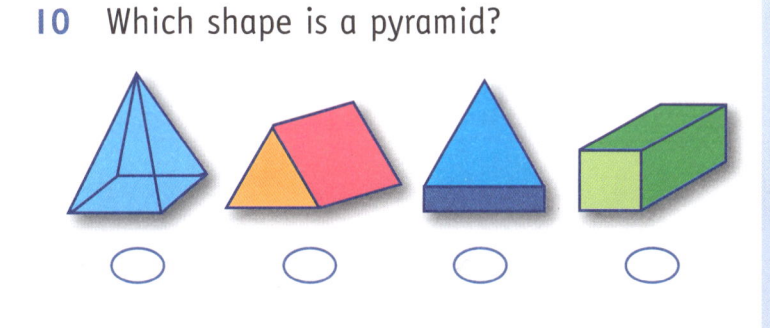

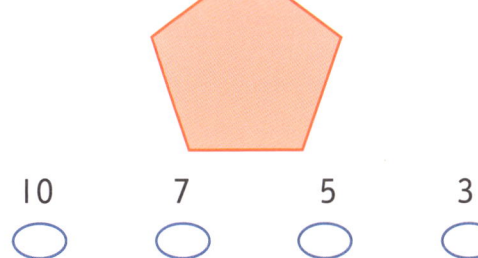

    10 ○   7 ○   5 ○   3 ○

10 Which shape is a pyramid?

○   ○   ○   ○

Lab 3 patterns 1

Missing terms

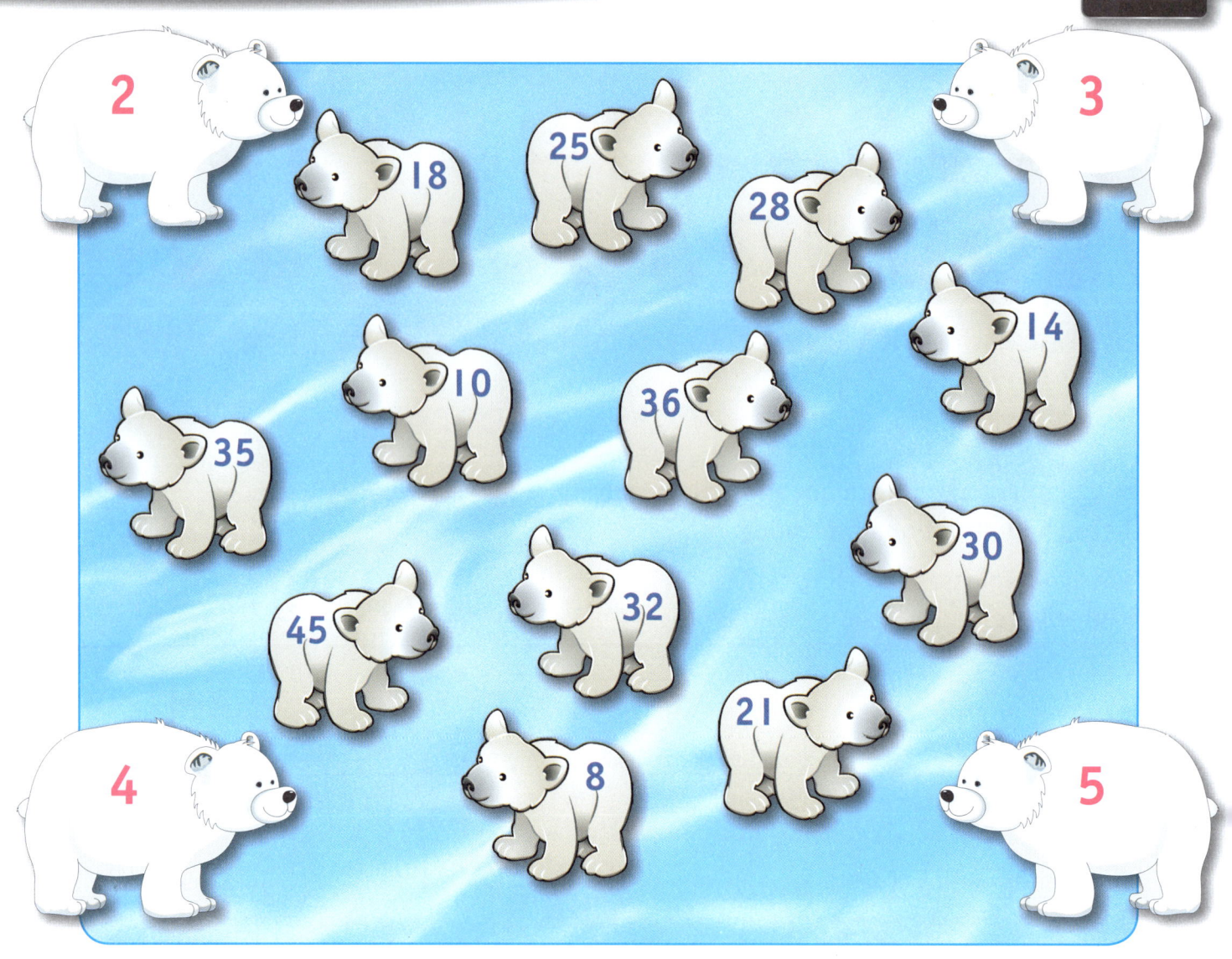

The young bears are lost. Match the mothers with their children. Give your reasons why.

2 _____ _____ _____
Reason _____

3 _____ _____ _____
Reason _____

4 _____ _____ _____
Reason _____

5 _____ _____ _____
Reason _____

HINT! Each mother can only have 3 children.

120

ACMNA060 Patterns and algebra • Describe, continue, and create number patterns resulting from performing addition or subtraction.

Describing patterns

1 Write the missing term, then write a reason for your answer.

a $\frac{1}{2}, \frac{1}{3}, \frac{1}{4},$ _____ , $\frac{1}{6}, \frac{1}{7}$

Reason _____

b $1.80, $1.70, _____ , $1.50, $1.40, $1.30

Reason _____

c 2, 7, 12, _____ , _____ , 27

Reason _____

d 25, 40, _____ , 70, _____ , _____

Reason _____

e 36, 45, 54, 63, _____ , 81

Reason _____

f 10, 120, 230, _____ , _____ , 560

Reason _____

2 Colour the terms that are equal.

- 9 × 6
- 3 × 4
- 8 + 7
- 36 − 4
- 9 + 3 + 4
- 100 − 55
- 5 × 3
- double 27
- 4 × 4
- 1 dozen
- 9 × 5
- 8 × 4

3 Use a calculator.

a Press AC   b Press 5   c Press +   +   d Press =

e What does your calculator show? _____   f Press = again.

g Keep pressing = and write the answers. _____ _____ _____ _____

h What is the pattern? _____

ACMNA060 Patterns and algebra • Describe, continue, and create number patterns resulting from performing addition or subtraction.

121

Number patterns

1 Complete these patterns.

a 2, 4, 6, ____, ____, ____, 14, 16, ____, ____, ____

b 15, 18, ____, ____, ____, 30, 33, ____, ____, ____

c 10, 20, ____, ____, ____, ____, 70, ____, ____, 100

d 62, 57, ____, ____, 42, ____, ____, ____, 22, ____

e 15, 20, ____, ____, ____, ____, 45, ____, ____, 60

2 Use the rule in each square to fill in the missing numbers.

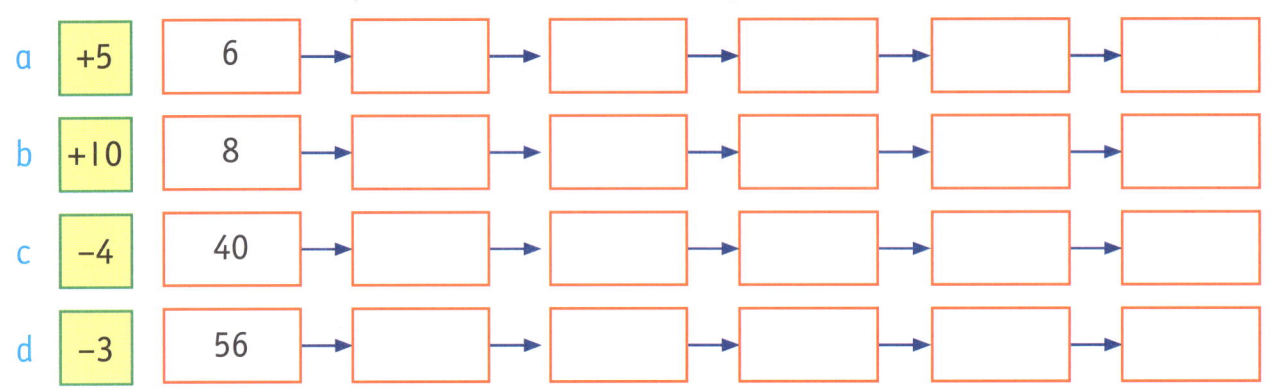

a +5 | 6 → ☐ → ☐ → ☐ → ☐ → ☐

b +10 | 8 → ☐ → ☐ → ☐ → ☐ → ☐

c −4 | 40 → ☐ → ☐ → ☐ → ☐ → ☐

d −3 | 56 → ☐ → ☐ → ☐ → ☐ → ☐

3 a Colour the 3s pattern red. Continue to 100.

b Colour the 4s pattern green. Continue to 100.

c Colour the 5s pattern yellow. Continue to 100.

d Which numbers are coloured on all three grids. _____

Challenge! Complete these patterns.

215, 224, 233, ☐, ☐, ☐, ☐, ☐

528, 519, 510, ☐, ☐, ☐, ☐, ☐

Table patterns

1 Write the pattern for adding 6 in this table.

Order of term	1	2	3							
Term	6	12								

2 Write the pattern for adding 7 in this table.

Order of term	1	2	3							
Term	7	14								

3 Complete these addition and subtraction patterns.

a 18 + 9 = _____
   _____ − 9 = 18

b 36 + 9 = _____
   _____ − 9 = 36

c 36 − 9 = _____
   _____ + 9 = 36

d _____ − 6 = 54
   54 + 6 = _____

e 72 − 8 = _____
   _____ + 8 = 72

f 81 − 7 = _____
   _____ + 7 = _____

4 a Write your own pattern using addition or subtraction.

_____ _____ _____ _____ _____ _____ _____ _____

b Write the rule. _____

c Make a table for adding 9.

Order of term	1	2	3							
Term	9	18								

5 Colour each path across the river.

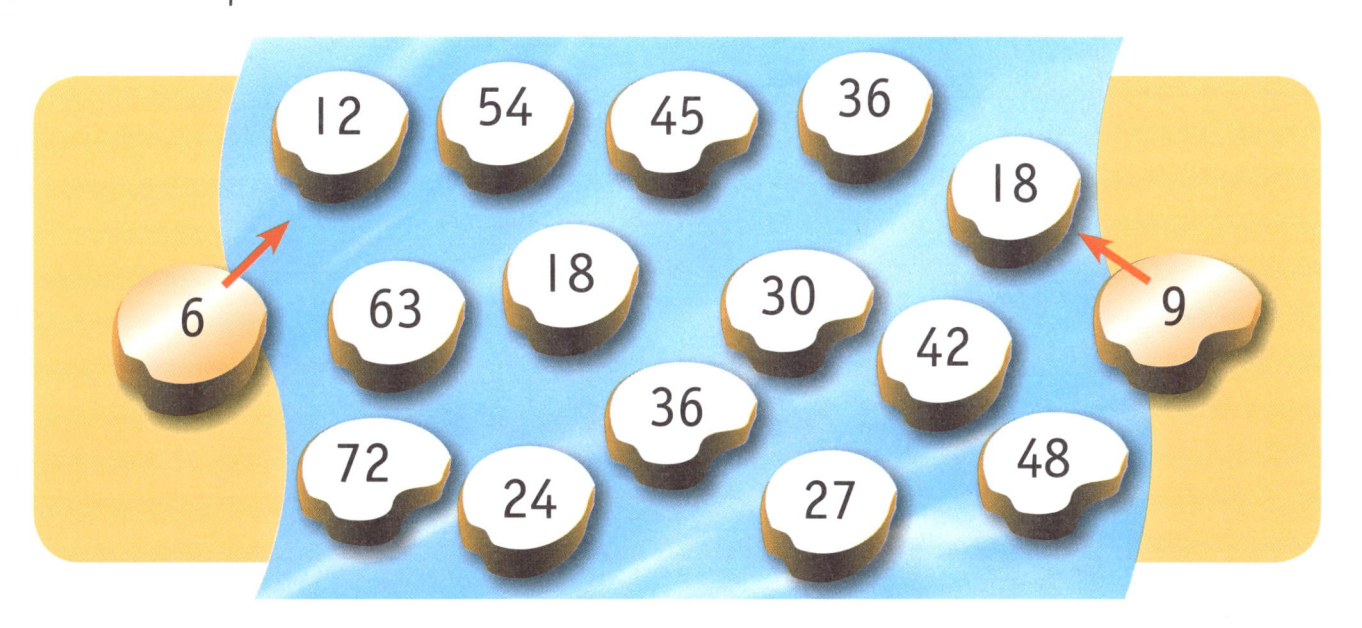

Stones: 12, 54, 45, 36, 18, 6, 63, 18, 30, 42, 9, 72, 36, 24, 27, 48

Lab 3 — position words

Position

1 Draw the cake they choose.

Mandy	Mitch	Milly	Min	Mark
top row, on the left	bottom row, 2nd from the right	middle row, on the right	bottom row, on the left	top row, in the middle

2 Write the position of:

a the cupcake with the cherry on top. _____

b the meringue snowman. _____

c the cream frog. _____

d the apricot cheesecake. _____

e the strawberry slice. _____

3 Write the names and positions of the three cakes you like best.

a _____

b _____

c _____

ACMMG065 Location and transformation • Create and interpret simple grid maps to show position and pathways.

Rows and columns

1 Which letter is:
  a third column, top row? _____
  b last column, first row? _____
  c fifth column, second row? _____
  d second last column, third row from the bottom? _____
  e third column from the right, fourth row from the top? _____
  f These letters spell a word. What is the word? _____

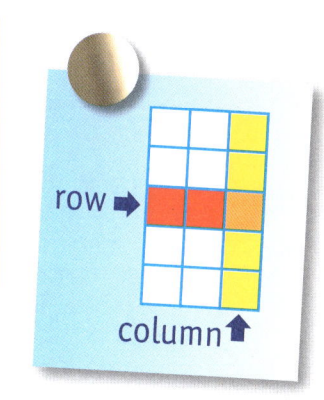

	1	2	3	4	5	6
5	U	P	G	A	D	C
4	D	S	K	V	E	B
3	F	B	Y	O	A	N
2	G	R	O	T	E	F
1	H	I	L	N	M	R

2 Here is the map of 3B's classroom.

Tim	Simon		Kirsty	Zoe		Samad			
Lionel	Bob		Adam			Chloe	Gill		Lenny
	Chris		Brian	Amy		Samir	Lilly		Gopal
Lucy	Sam		Jim	Judith		Joe	Ajit		Leah
						Miss Brown			

  a How many children are in Miss Brown's class? _____
  b Who is sitting next to Brian? _____
  c Who is sitting in front of the teacher? _____ _____
  d Who is sitting behind Lionel? _____
  e How many children are in Chloe's row? _____
  f Rodger wants to sit in the third row. Who will he sit next to? _____
  g Joe was talking. He was sent to sit behind Kirsty. Mark his new seat on the map.
  h Draw in red how Joe would get to his new seat.
  i Lucy wanted to borrow a pencil. She walked across the front of the room and down the aisle between Ajit and Leah. She asked the person in the third row on her left. Who did she ask? _____
  j Write directions for the path Adam would take to sit next to Samad.

ACMMG065 Location and transformation • Create and interpret simple grid maps to show position and pathways.

Street map

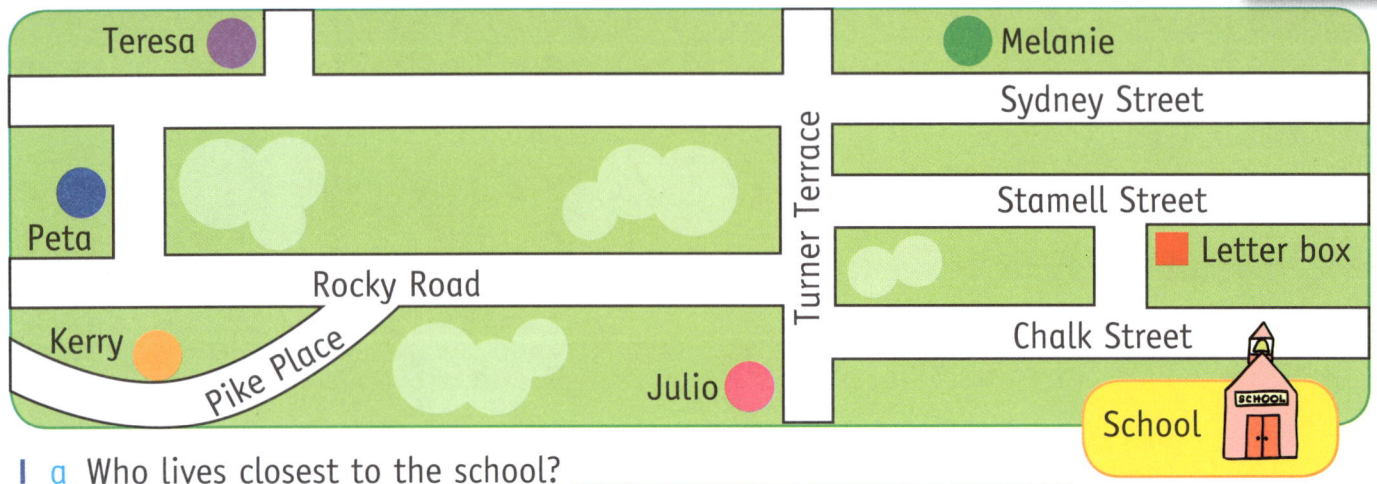

1. a Who lives closest to the school? _____
   b On which street does Melanie live? _____
   c Who lives at the corner of two streets? _____
   d Peta went to visit her friend. She walked out her front gate, turned left, then turned right. She walked past Turner Terrace, and entered a house on her left.
      Who did she visit? _____
   e Draw the path she followed in red.
   f Who lives furthest from Julio? _____

2. Teresa's mum asked her to post a letter on her way to school.
   In green draw her path to school.

3. Write directions to tell how Kerry walks home from school.

   _____

   _____

4. George has just moved into the area. He lives on the corner of Turner Terrace and Stamell Street closest to the school. Label the map to show where George lives.

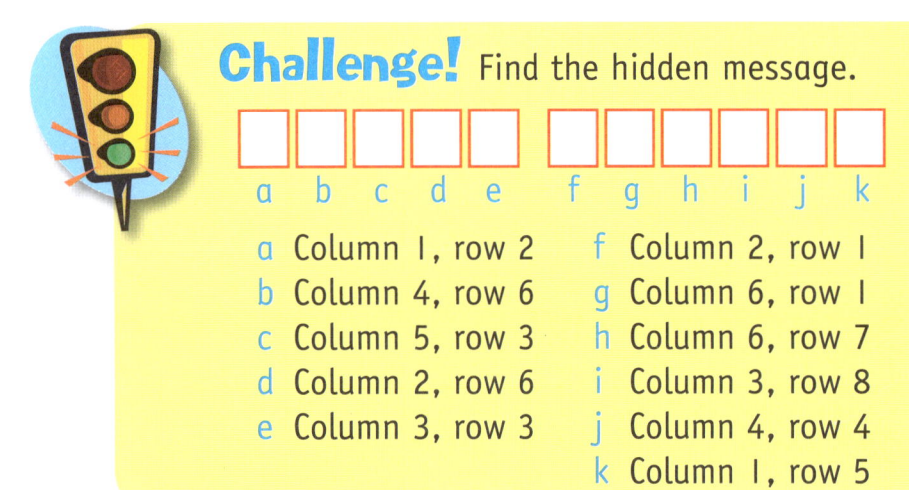

Challenge! Find the hidden message.

☐ ☐ ☐ ☐ ☐ ☐ ☐ ☐ ☐ ☐ ☐
a b c d e   f g h i j k

a Column 1, row 2
b Column 4, row 6
c Column 5, row 3
d Column 2, row 6
e Column 3, row 3
f Column 2, row 1
g Column 6, row 1
h Column 6, row 7
i Column 3, row 8
j Column 4, row 4
k Column 1, row 5

W	T	C	Y	U	I
A	R	E	P	O	A
S	N	D	O	F	G
S	D	F	J	X	H
C	V	B	E	N	K
A	N	G	M	I	L
G	E	R	D	B	Y
S	P	F	H	I	L

ACMMG065 Location and transformation • Create and interpret simple grid maps to show position and pathways.

Problem solving

Make a Picture Map

You and your friends are going on a mission to find lost gold.

	A	B	C	D	E	F	G
7							
6	N↑				🟫		
5							
4							
3							
2							
1		HOME					

1. Put these things on the map: mountains in the middle, a river to cross, swamps and a forest.
2. Write some directions for how you are going to get there. Use coordinates to describe your movements. Remember to put the letter first, eg B4.

_____
_____
_____
_____

Lab 3 basketball

Mass

Find three small boxes. Label them A, B and C. Fill each box with sand.

1 a Feel the weight of each box.

   b Write the boxes in order from lightest to heaviest.

   lightest _____ _____ _____ heaviest

2 Use balance scales to order the boxes.

   lightest _____ _____ _____ heaviest

3 a Empty the boxes and fill them with something different, eg marbles or blocks.

   b Order the boxes from lightest to heaviest.

   lightest _____ _____ _____ heaviest

4 Is the order the same each time? _____

5 How could you weigh this book using sand or marbles?

   _____

6 Do you know a better method to weigh this book?

   _____

ACMMG061 Using units of measurement • Measure, order and compare objects using familiar metric units of length, mass and capacity.

Introducing the kilogram

1 Hold a one kilogram weight. Feel how heavy it is.

Estimate whether these items are heavier or lighter than 1 kg. Use balance scales to check.

Objects are weighed in kilograms. kg is the short way to write kilograms.

Item	Estimate	Balance scales
a 2 maths books		
b a pencil case		
c a book box		
d a full lunch box		
e 1 brick		
f a bottle of water		
g a football		
h a backpack		
i a whiteboard marker		
j 20 pencils		

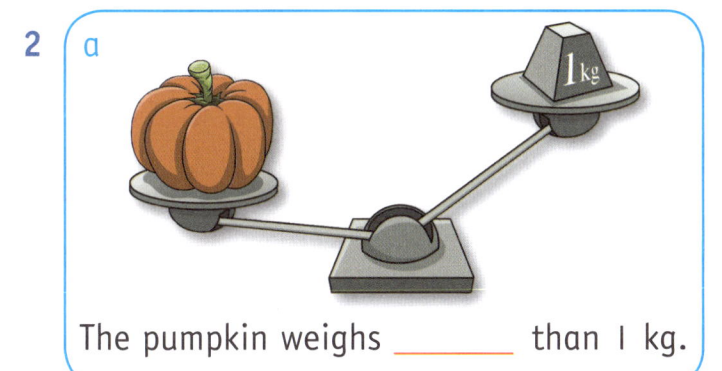

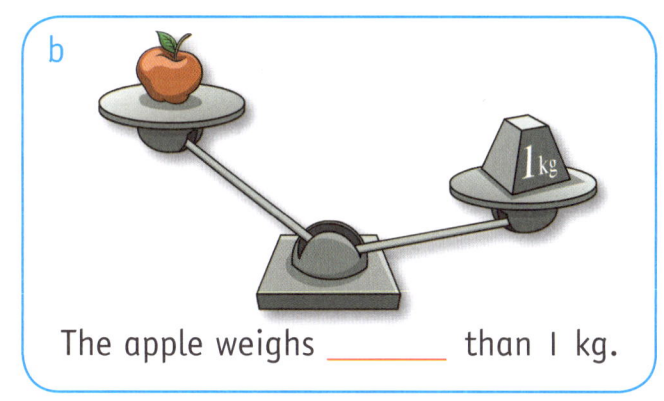

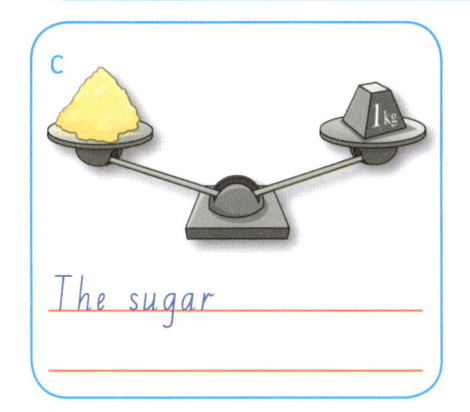

2

a The pumpkin weighs _____ than 1 kg.

b The apple weighs _____ than 1 kg.

c The sugar _____

d _____

e _____

3 Write five items that are weighed in kilograms, eg sugar.

_____ _____ _____ _____ _____

4 How many kilograms do you weigh? _____

Weighing in kilograms

1 What is the mass for each box?

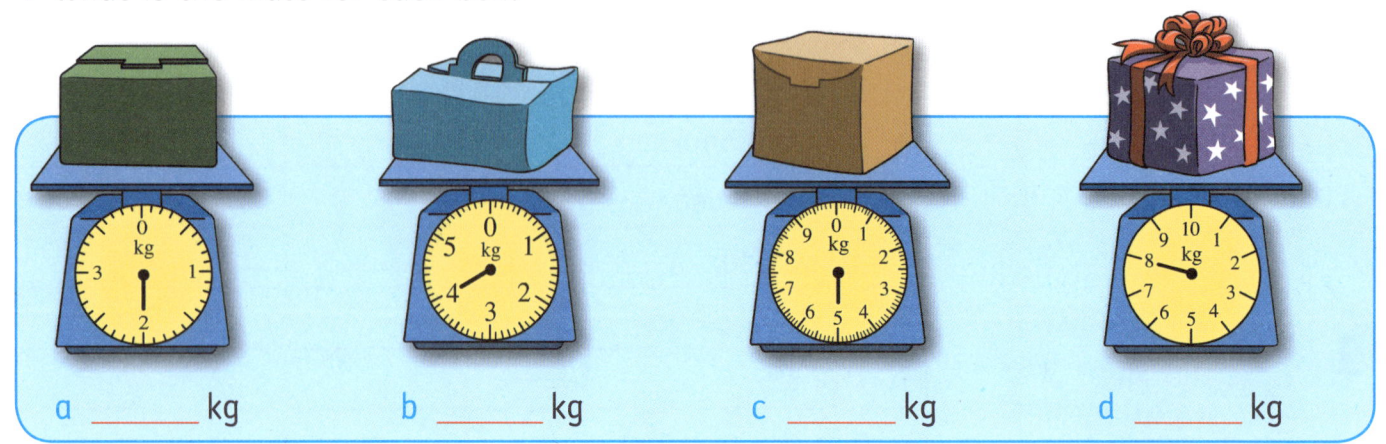

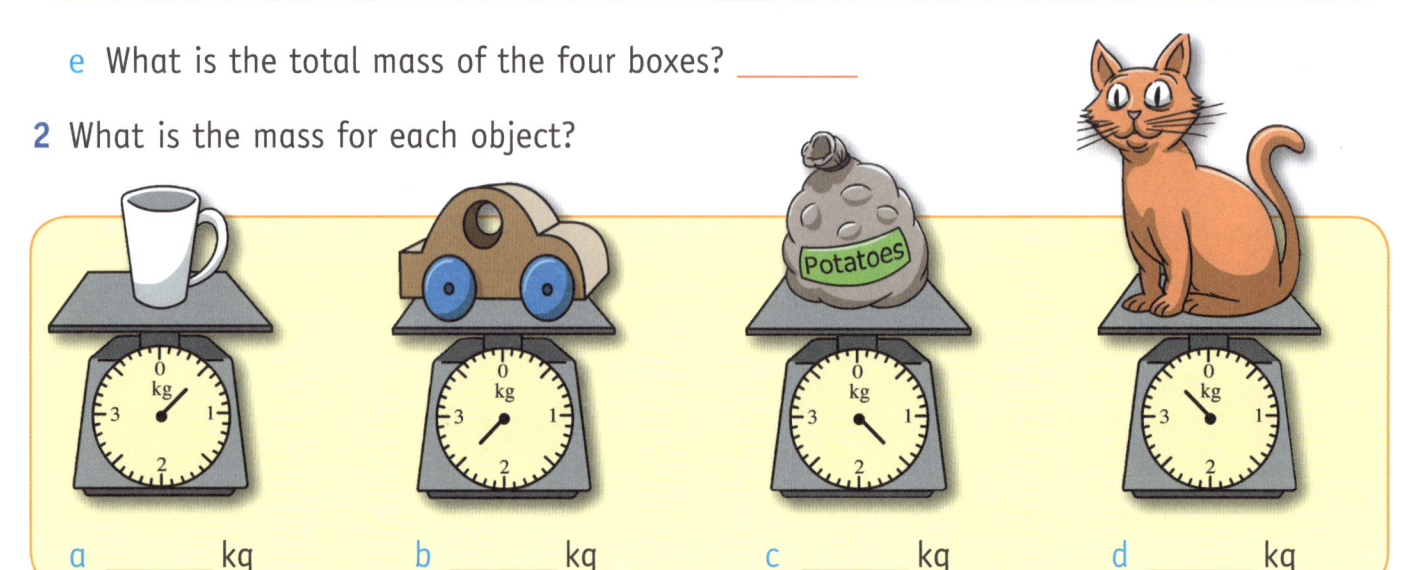

a _____ kg   b _____ kg   c _____ kg   d _____ kg

e What is the total mass of the four boxes? _____

2 What is the mass for each object?

a _____ kg   b _____ kg   c _____ kg   d _____ kg

e Order the objects from lightest to heaviest.

_____ _____ _____ _____

3 Use balance scales to find:

a two things that weigh about 1 kg. _____ _____

b two things that weigh about 2 kg. _____ _____

c two things that weigh about $\frac{1}{2}$ kg. _____ _____

d two things that are exactly the same weight. _____ _____

How heavy are they? _____

Challenge! Find something that has the same mass as you.

ACMMG061 Using units of measurement • Measure, order and compare objects using familiar metric units of length, mass and capacity.

Problem solving

Heavy duty

1. You can carry 7 kg and your little sister can carry 5 kg.

   How many ways can you carry all these bags between you?

   Solutions: _____
   _____
   _____
   _____

2. How can you find the heaviest of three similar objects with only a balance scale and no weights?

   Solution: _____
   _____
   _____
   _____

3. How can you weigh your dog when he won't stand still on the scales?

   Hint: Use these.

Symmetry

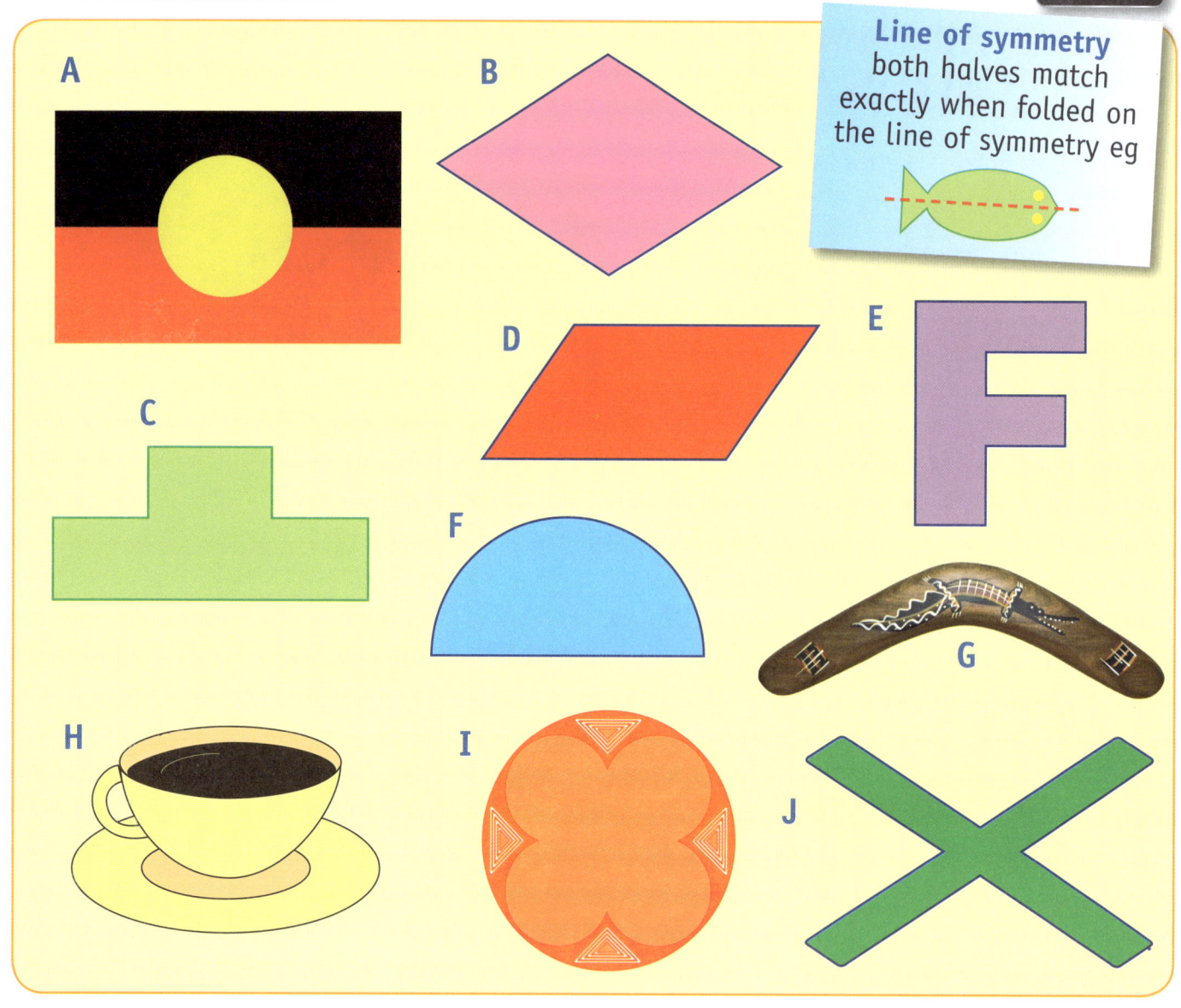

Line of symmetry both halves match exactly when folded on the line of symmetry eg

A

B

C

D

E

F

G

H

I

J

1 Inspect the shapes. If possible, draw in 1 line of symmetry.

2 Which shapes have more than 1 line of symmetry? _____

3 a Which shapes do not have a line of symmetry? _____

   b Why? _____

4 Draw two more letters and two more shapes that have a line of symmetry.

   a Letters

   b Shapes

Symmetrical shapes

1 Place a mirror on each dotted line. Write the name of the object. Draw the missing part.

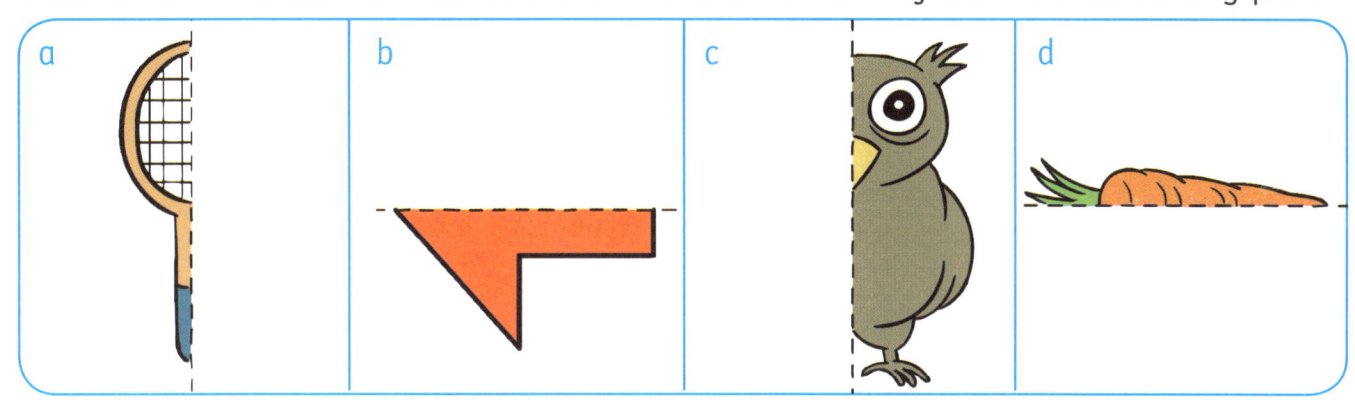

| a | b | c | d |

_____   _____   _____   _____

2 a Look at these shapes. Colour those that are symmetrical.

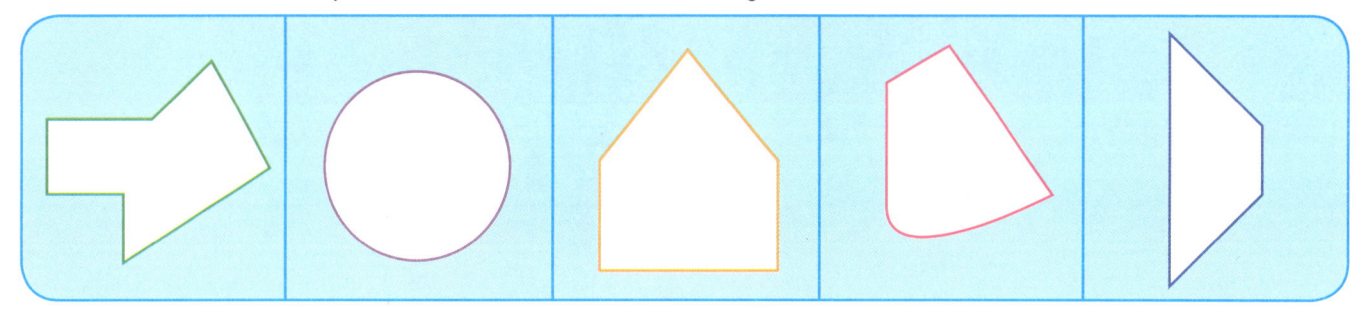

b Draw a line of symmetry on those you coloured.

3 Complete each of these drawings to make a symmetrical design.

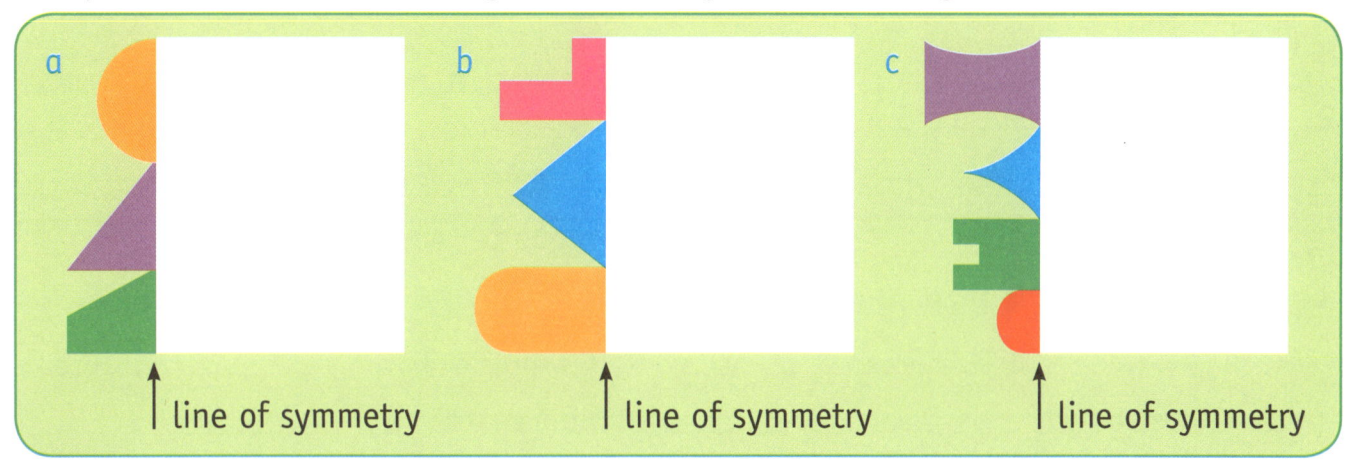

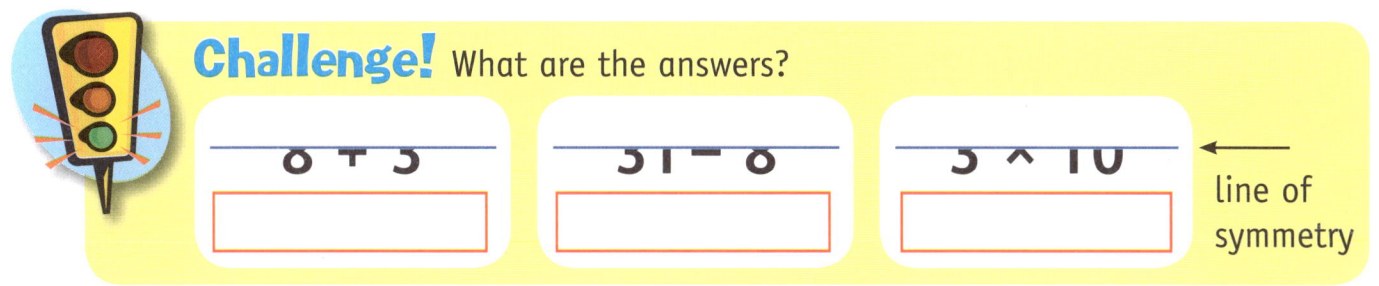

| a | b | c |

↑ line of symmetry   ↑ line of symmetry   ↑ line of symmetry

Challenge! What are the answers?

8 + 5   31 − 8   3 × 10 ← line of symmetry

Passing time

1 Study the analogue clock and count the minutes between the letters, counting clockwise.

   a A and B _____   b X and Y _____   c T and Z _____

2 Write the analogue time 5 minutes after:

   a 10 past 5 _____   b 20 past 4 _____

   c 5 past 3 _____   d a quarter past 7 _____

3 Write the analogue time 10 minutes before:

   a 20 past 2 _____   b a quarter past 6 _____

   c 10 past 8 _____   d half past 9 _____

4 Write the analogue time 15 minutes after:

   a 25 past 4 _____   b twenty to 11 _____

   c half past 7 _____   d ten to 5 _____

5 Write the analogue time 5 minutes before:

   a twenty to 3 _____   b ten to 12 _____

Time and action

1 How many hours have passed:

   a between 1 pm and 4 pm? _____   b between 11 am and 1 pm? _____

   c between 6 pm and 12 midnight? _____   d between 10 am and 9 pm? _____

2 Write a reasonable activity that takes about this much time.

   a 15 minutes _____   b 25 minutes _____

   c 2 hours _____   d 1 hour 5 minutes _____

3 How many minutes have passed? What might you do in this time?

   a between 3:45 pm and 4:15 pm?   b between 5:10 am and 5:24 am?

   _____   _____

   _____   _____

   _____   _____

   c between 12 noon and 12:32 pm?   d between 11:26 am and 11:38 am?

   _____   _____

   _____   _____

   _____   _____

4 Show the two times on the clocks and answer the question.

   a Cam started to clean the car at 9:10 am. He finished at 9:45 am.

   b Joan's appointment was at 3:20 pm but she arrived at 3:50.

   How long did it take him to clean the car?

   _____

   How late was she?

   _____

Challenge! Mum says, "Meet me here at four o'clock." As time passes, you look at your watch 4 times. How long do you have each time?

2:45 [ ]   3:05 [ ]   3:25 [ ]   3:50 [ ]

Lab 3 — Reading a table

jetpack jenny

Tallies and graphs

SSL Table — Central Districts

	Games	Won	Lost	Drawn	Points
Giants	8	6	1	1	26
Bradies	8	6	2	0	24
Dragons	8	5	3	0	20
Furies	8	4	3	1	18
Brongoes	7	4	3	0	16
Tigers	8	4	4	0	16
Meteors	7	2	5	0	8
Wallabies	8	2	6	0	8

Here is the Schools Soccer League results table for this year.

1. What are the points for the:
   a. Wallabies? _____   b. Giants? _____
   c. Dragons? _____   d. Meteors? _____

2. a. How many points do the teams score for a win? _____
   b. How many points do they get for a draw? _____

3. How many rounds have been played by most teams? _____

4. Who has yet to play their eighth game? _____

5. Which two teams had a draw? _____

6. If the Brongoes win their 8th round match, what will the top 4 teams be?
   _____

7. Could the Furies become the league leaders after playing two more games? _____
   How? _____

8. If the Tigers win the next 4 games, will they be leaders? _____
   Why? _____

Challenge! Update the table using these results:
Round 8   Brongoes 4   Meteors 2
Round 9   Giants 3   Wallabies 1   Bradies 2   Dragons 1
          Meteors 4   Furies 3   Brongoes 2   Tigers 2

Who is top of the table now? _____

Graphs

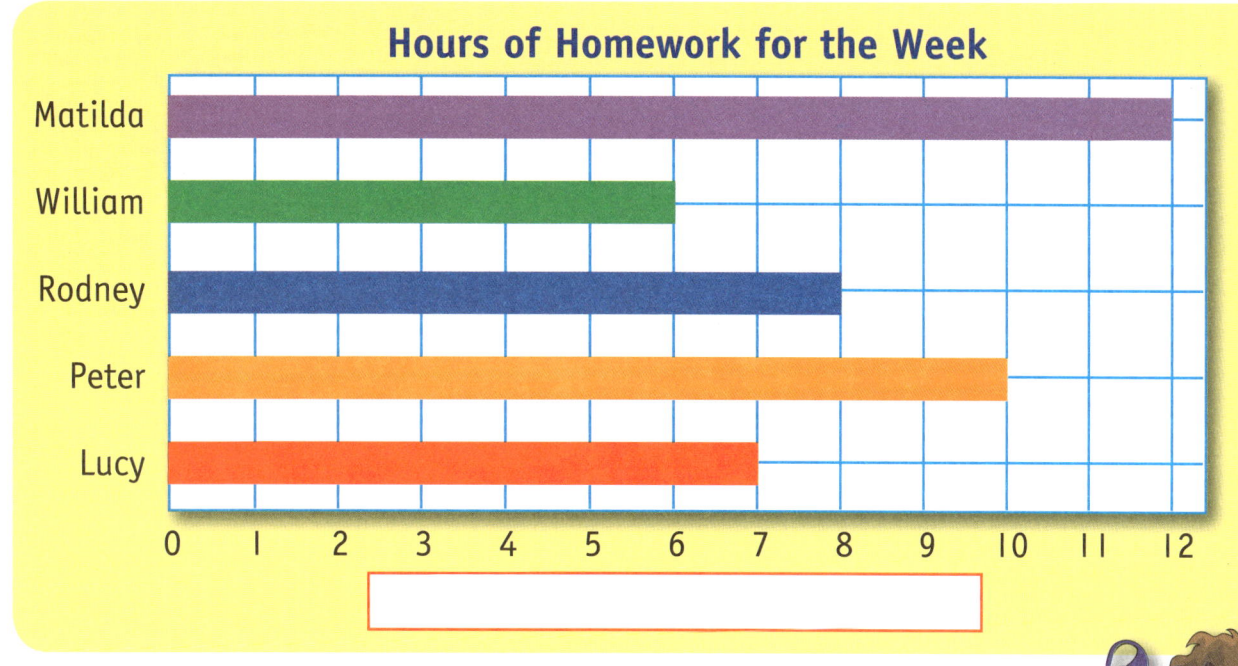

Hours of Homework for the Week

Matilda	12
William	6
Rodney	8
Peter	10
Lucy	7

0 1 2 3 4 5 6 7 8 9 10 11 12

1 a How many students compared homework? _____
   b Write the label for the bottom numbers.
   c Who did the most homework? _____
   d Who did the least homework? _____
   e Who did 8 hours of homework? _____
   f Name two students who did more homework than Lucy?
      _____ _____

2 Draw a picture graph to show the same information. Use one clock to show one hour. Label your graph clearly.

ACMSP070 Data representation and interpretation • Interpret and compare data displays.

137

Tally marks are in groups of 5
~~||||~~ || = 7

Collecting data

Tallies and graphs

Which do they like most?

1 Ask each child in your class to choose one.

   a Use this tick sheet.

   b Now use tally marks.

2 Make a column graph to show these choices. Remember all the labels.

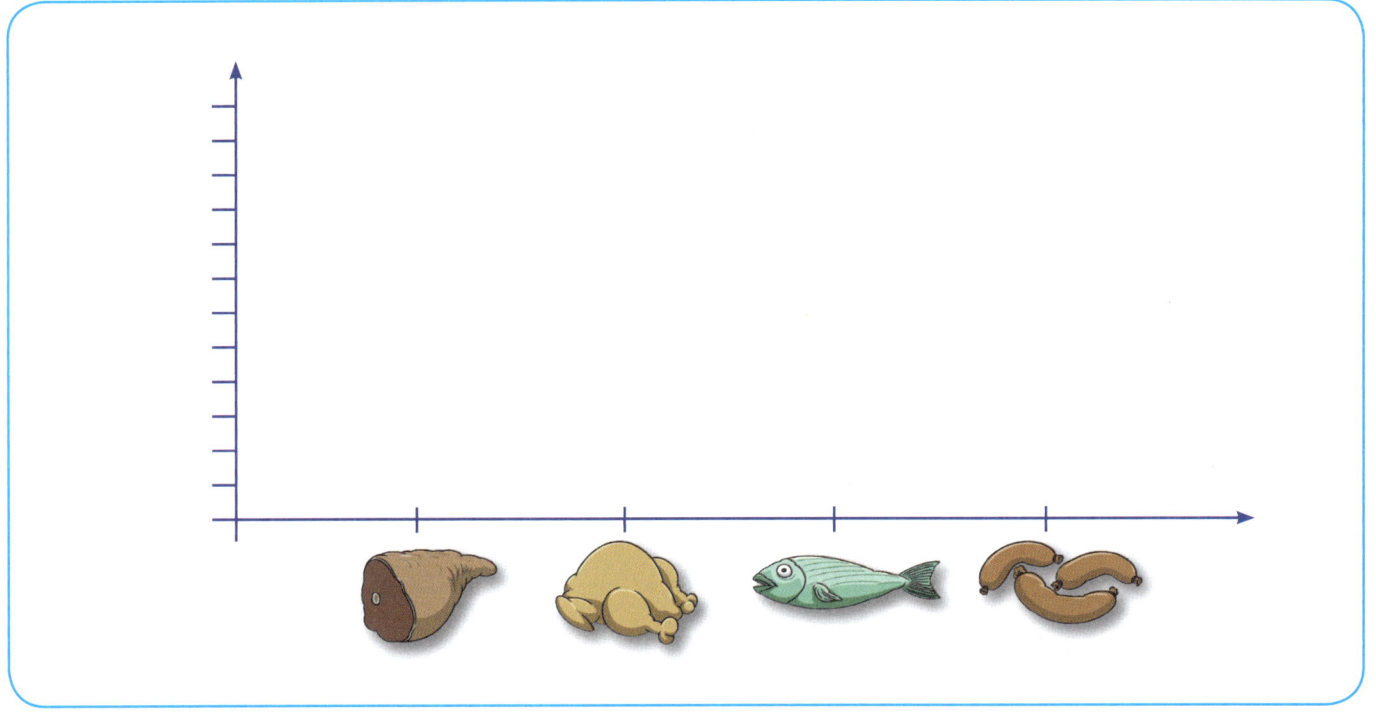

Chance

1 What is the likelihood of each happening? Use one of these words.

> certain   likely   unlikely   impossible

a You will eat a boiled egg for breakfast tomorrow.
_____

b Your teacher will have purple hair next week.
_____

c It will rain next Wednesday.
_____

d My mother is older than me.
_____

e You will eat food tomorrow.
_____

f Next month is September.
_____

g Our cat will have puppies next year.
_____

h February will have 28 days.
_____

i My family will win the lottery.
_____

j It will be cloudy sometime this year.
_____

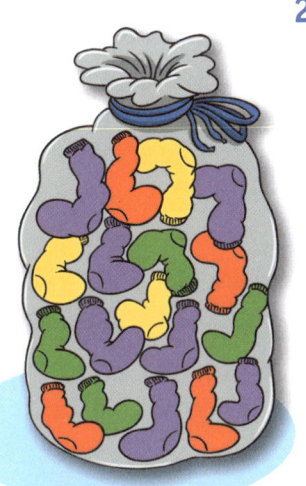

2 From this bag which colour:

a is most likely to be drawn out? _____
   Why? _____

b is least likely to be drawn out? _____
   Why? _____

c will never be drawn out? _____
   Why? _____

d Which colours have the same chance? _____
   Why? _____

Challenge! Write down 3 things you think are FAIR and 3 things you think are UNFAIR.

FAIR	UNFAIR

Revision Term 3

1 Sam had $5. He bought one chocolate for $3.20 and one lollipop for 60c. *p 98*

   a How much did he spend? _____

   b How much change did he get? _____

2 a   1 7 4   b   3 8 3   c   4 6 0   *p 99*
      +   1 3   +   1 5   +   3 7

3 Fill in the boxes. *p 99*

   a   2 ☐   b   ☐ 2   c   6 4
      + 5 4   + 3 4   + ☐☐
      ☐ 9   7 ☐   7 8

4 a 9 × 5 = _____   b 9 × 0 = _____   *p 102*

   c 3 × 9 = _____   d 9 × 4 = _____

5 Use colours to match. *p 103*

9 + 9 + 9	six fours
7 × 5	27
6 groups of 4	6 × 3
10 × 0	7 + 7 + 7 + 7 + 7
3 + 3 + 3 + 3 + 3 + 3	0

6 Each chapter in a book has 8 pages. How many pages has Liam read if he's read 4 chapters? _____ *p 104*

7 *p 105*

   a How many kites? _____

   b How many bows on each kite? _____

   c How many bows altogether? _____

   d _____ × _____ = _____

8 a   4   b   5   c   4   d   10   *p 106*
     × 1   × 3   × 9   × 6

9 Make fair shares. *p 108*

   7 shares. 1 share = _____

10 a Draw 24 balls. *p 110*

   b How many groups of 4? _____

   c How many groups of 3? _____

   d How many groups of 12? _____

11 Circle the larger fraction. $\frac{1}{2}$, $\frac{1}{5}$ *p 112*

12 True or false. *p 112*

   a $\frac{1}{2}$ is the same as $\frac{2}{4}$ _____

   b $\frac{1}{2}$ is more than $\frac{2}{5}$ _____

13 Colour the fraction to match. *p 113*

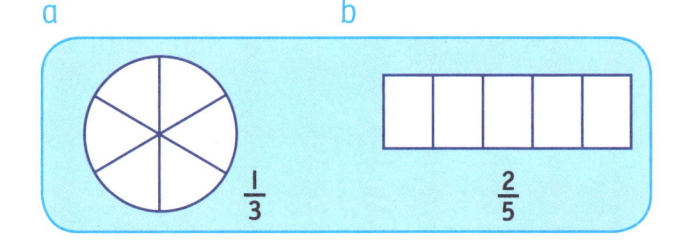

   a   b

   $\frac{1}{3}$ $\frac{2}{5}$

14 What is: *p 114*

   a $\frac{1}{4}$ of 12 oranges? _____

   b $\frac{1}{3}$ of 15 beans? _____

Revision Term 3

15 Write the missing terms.   p 121

    a $1.80, $1.60, _____, $1.20, _____

    b   25, 33, 41, _____, _____, 65

16 Write the pattern for adding 6 in this table.   p 122

Order of the term	1	2	3			
Term	6					

17   p 124

What is:

a on the top row in the middle?

_____

b in the middle row on the left?

_____

Write the position of:

c the jacket. _____

d the sunglasses. _____

18 Name something that is: p 128

    a   heavier than 1 kg.

_____

    b   lighter than 1 kg. _____

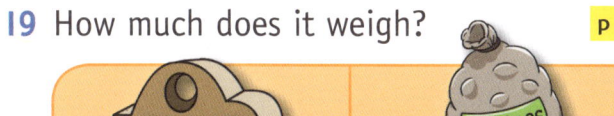

19 How much does it weigh?   p 130

20 Draw in all lines of symmetry.   p 132

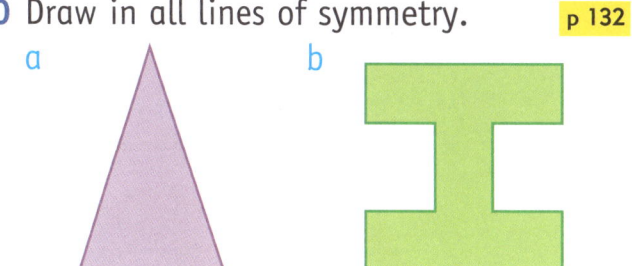

    a   b

21 Complete this drawing.   p 133

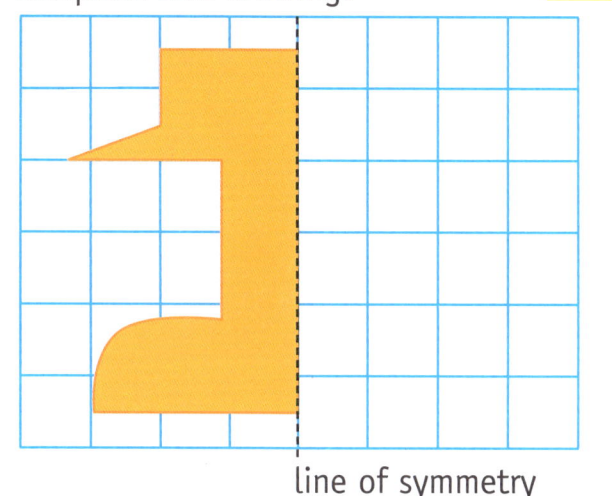

line of symmetry

22 Draw both times on the clocks.   p 135

The writing lesson started at 11:40 am and went for 35 minutes. Write the time it finished in words.

_____

23 What is the likelihood of: p 139

    a   the school holidays being 3 months long? _____

    b   it raining next week? _____

Lab 4 — Writing four-digit numbers

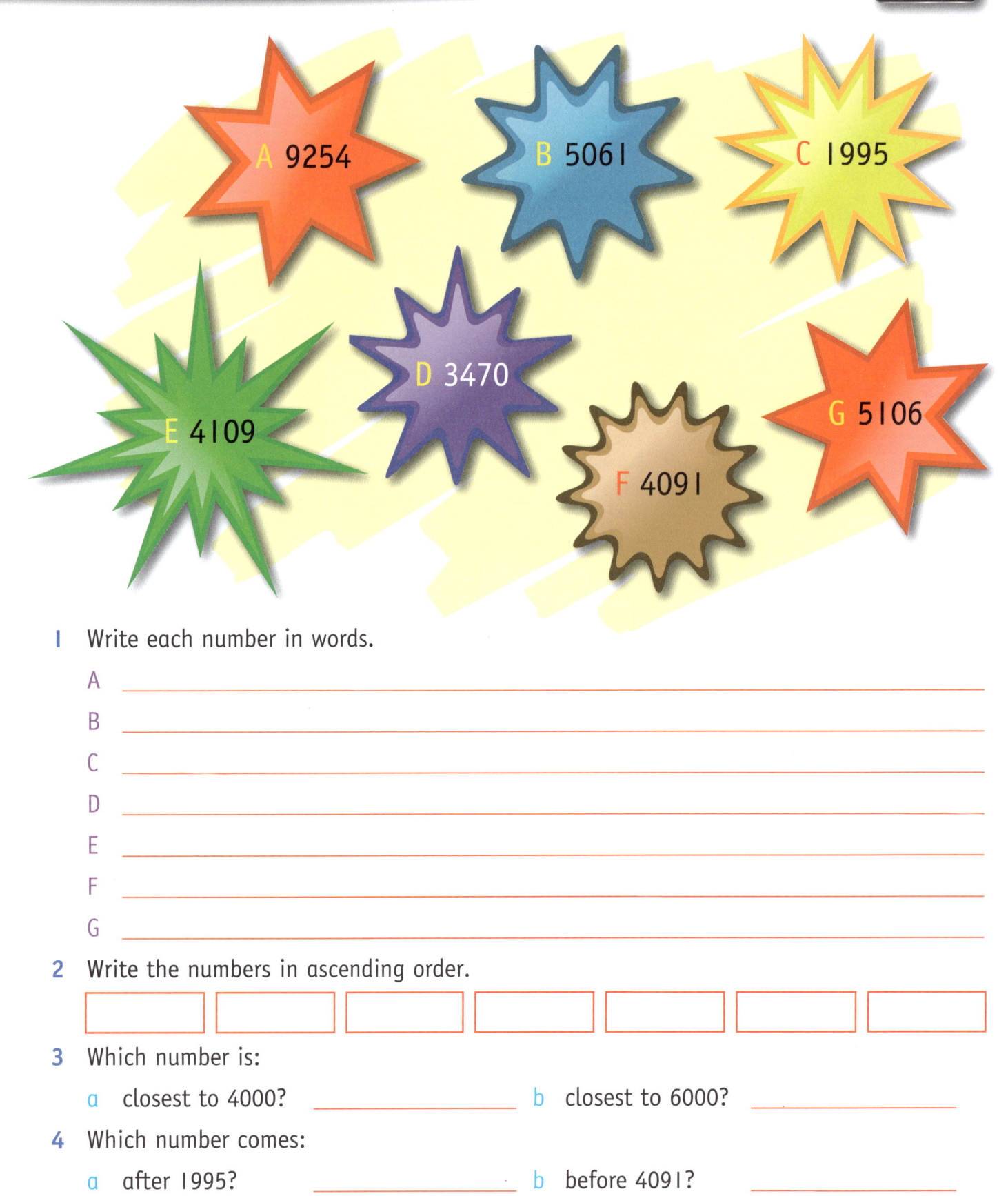

expander dog

Number words

A 9254
B 5061
C 1995
D 3470
E 4109
F 4091
G 5106

1. Write each number in words.

   A _____
   B _____
   C _____
   D _____
   E _____
   F _____
   G _____

2. Write the numbers in ascending order.

   ☐ ☐ ☐ ☐ ☐ ☐ ☐

3. Which number is:

   a closest to 4000? _____   b closest to 6000? _____

4. Which number comes:

   a after 1995? _____   b before 4091? _____
   c before 5061? _____   d after 4109? _____

142

ACMNA052 Number and place • Recognise, model represent and order numbers to at least 10 000.

Rounding thousands

1 Round these numbers to the nearest thousand.

a 7430 _____   b 8199 _____
c 2506 _____   d 6794 _____
e 1245 _____   f 4009 _____
g 8952 _____   h 3673 _____
i 9367 _____   j 5801 _____

> To round to the nearest thousand look at the hundreds place.
> 1<u>7</u>04 → 2000
> 1<u>4</u>07 → 1000
> **Remember**
> 1, 2, 3, 4 go down.
> 5, 6, 7, 8, 9 go up.

2 Write the number 10 more than:

a	3654	
b	2871	
c	9108	
d	8235	
e	5096	

3 Write the number 10 less than:

a	8463	
b	2028	
c	9612	
d	5579	
e	3105	

4 Write the number 100 more than:

a	7398	
b	1427	
c	5006	
d	2192	
e	945	

5 Write the number 100 less than:

a	5650	
b	1901	
c	9436	
d	3198	
e	8072	

6 6105   5160   5016   5601   6510

Write the number:
a with thousands digit 5 and ones digit 1. ____
b with hundreds digit 1 and ones digit 5. ____
c with hundreds digit 5 and ones digit 0. ____
d with thousands digit 5 and ones digit 6. ____

Work backwards

What number am I?
My thousands digit is 2 more than my tens digit.
My tens digit is 3 less than my hundreds digit.
My hundreds digit is 4 more than my ones digit which is 2. ____

Less than and more than

> **<** means less than
> **>** means more than

1 Use the signs < and >.

　　a 764 _____ 674　　b 991 _____ 919　　c 538 _____ 583

　　d 1465 _____ 1456　　e 2091 _____ 2109　　f 8691 _____ 8961

2 Choose numbers from page 142 to fill in the blanks.

　　a _____ < _____　　b _____ < _____　　c _____ < _____

　　d _____ > _____　　e _____ > _____　　f _____ > _____

3 Write the value of the 9 in:

　　a 9254 _____　　b 1995 _____ and _____

　　c 4109 _____　　d 4091 _____

4 Write the value of the 4 in:

　　a 9254 _____　　b 3470 _____　　c 4109 _____　　d 4091 _____

5 a 9254 = 9000 + 200 + _____ + _____　　b 1995 = _____ + _____ + _____ + _____

　　c 3470 = _____ + _____ + _____　　d 5106 = _____ + _____ + _____

　　e 5061 = _____ + _____ + _____　　f 4091 = _____ + _____ + _____

6 True or false?

　　a There were about 9000 people at the cinema. _____

　　b There are about 5000 children in our school. _____

　　c In our class there are less than 2000 toes. _____

　　d There are 1000 cents in $10. _____

　　e A large bottle can hold 2000 mL. _____

　　f There are 6914 birds sitting on the window sill. _____

　　g Grandma read 3011 books last week. _____

　　h There are more than 2000 words in this book. _____

Challenge! If you turn a calculator upside down some numbers look like letters, eg 1 = i, 7 = L, 4 = h etc. 7714 = hill
What numbers make these words?

　　sell　　lose　　shoe　　goes　　legs

Using numeral expanders

1 Write these numbers.

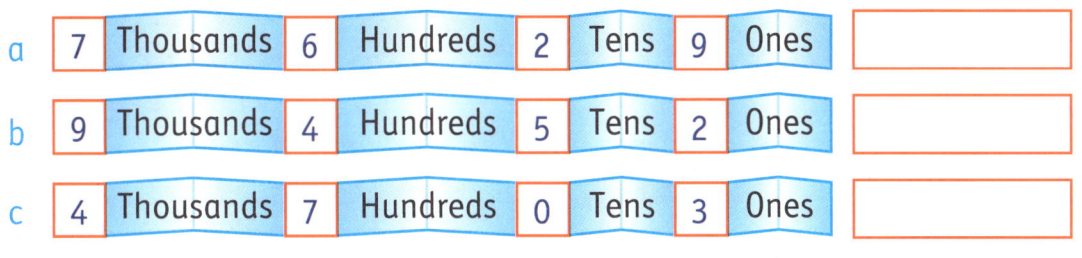

a | 7 Thousands | 6 Hundreds | 2 Tens | 9 Ones |

b | 9 Thousands | 4 Hundreds | 5 Tens | 2 Ones |

c | 4 Thousands | 7 Hundreds | 0 Tens | 3 Ones |

d | 1 Thousands | 0 Hundreds | 8 Tens | 6 Ones |

e | 6 Thousands | 3 Hundreds | 5 Tens | 0 Ones |

These are expanded numbers.

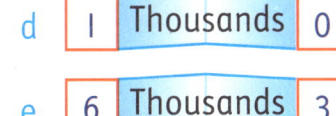

2 Complete these numeral expanders.

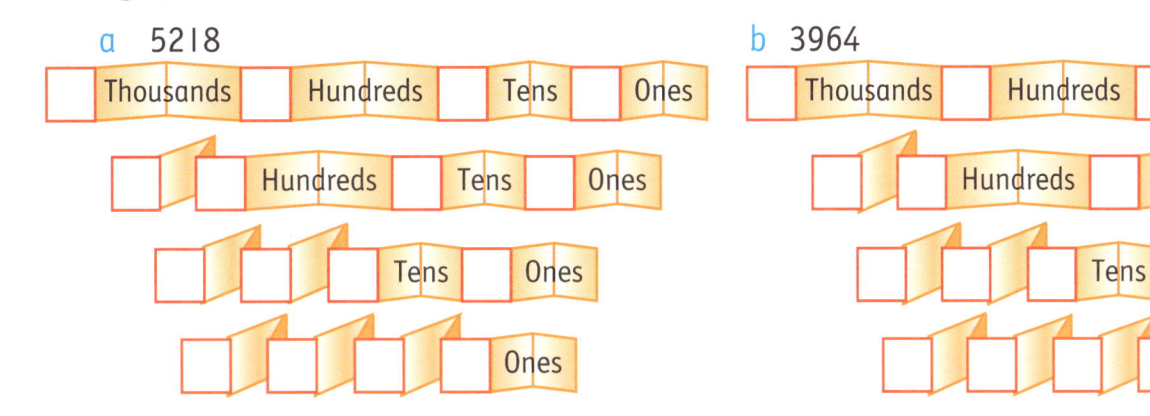

a 5218

☐ Thousands ☐ Hundreds ☐ Tens ☐ Ones

☐ ☐ Hundreds ☐ Tens ☐ Ones

☐ ☐ ☐ Tens ☐ Ones

☐ ☐ ☐ ☐ Ones

b 3964

☐ Thousands ☐ Hundreds ☐ Tens ☐ Ones

☐ ☐ Hundreds ☐ Tens ☐ Ones

☐ ☐ ☐ Tens ☐ Ones

☐ ☐ ☐ ☐ Ones

3 Use the numeral expanders above to express:

a 5218 as _____ thousands, _____ tens, _____ ones

b 5218 as _____ hundreds, _____ tens, _____ ones

c 5218 as _____ tens, _____ ones

d 3964 as _____ thousands, _____ tens, _____ ones

e 3964 as _____ hundreds, _____ tens, _____ ones

f 3964 as _____ tens, _____ ones

4 How many hundreds in:

a 7450? _____   b 6307? _____   c 2094? _____   d 8813? _____

5 How many tens in:

a 1638? _____   b 5920? _____   c 4107? _____   d 9022? _____

6 How many ones in:

a 7004? _____   b 2500? _____   c 1234? _____   d 9990? _____

ACMNA052 Number and place value • Recognise, model represent and order numbers to at least 10 000.

Lab 3
tables tennis

3x table

Here are 10 groups of 3 children.

1. How many children in:
   - a 3 groups? _____
   - b 6 groups? _____
   - c 4 groups? _____
   - d 2 groups? _____
   - e 10 groups? _____
   - f 8 groups? _____
   - g 5 groups? _____
   - h 7 groups? _____
   - i 9 groups? _____
   - j 0 groups? _____
   - k 11 groups? _____
   - l 12 groups? _____

2. Complete.

   0   3   6   __   __   __   __   __   __   __   __

3.
×	6	10	2	8	4	0	7	3	9	1	5
3											

4. It takes 3 minutes to walk around the oval. How long will it take to walk around the oval 8 times? _____

5. 1 toy costs $3. How much will 5 toys cost? _____

6. There are 3 flowers on each plant. How many flowers are there on 7 plants?

7. Make up your own '3' story. _____

ACMNA057 Number and place value • Represent and solve problems involving multiplication using efficient mental and written strategies and appropriate digital technologies.

4x table

1 How many paws on:

a 1 cat? _____   b 6 cats? _____   c 4 cats? _____   d 9 cats? _____

e 2 cats? _____   f 10 cats? _____   g 3 cats? _____   h 8 cats? _____

i 7 cats? _____   j 5 cats? _____   k 0 cats? _____   l 11 cats? _____

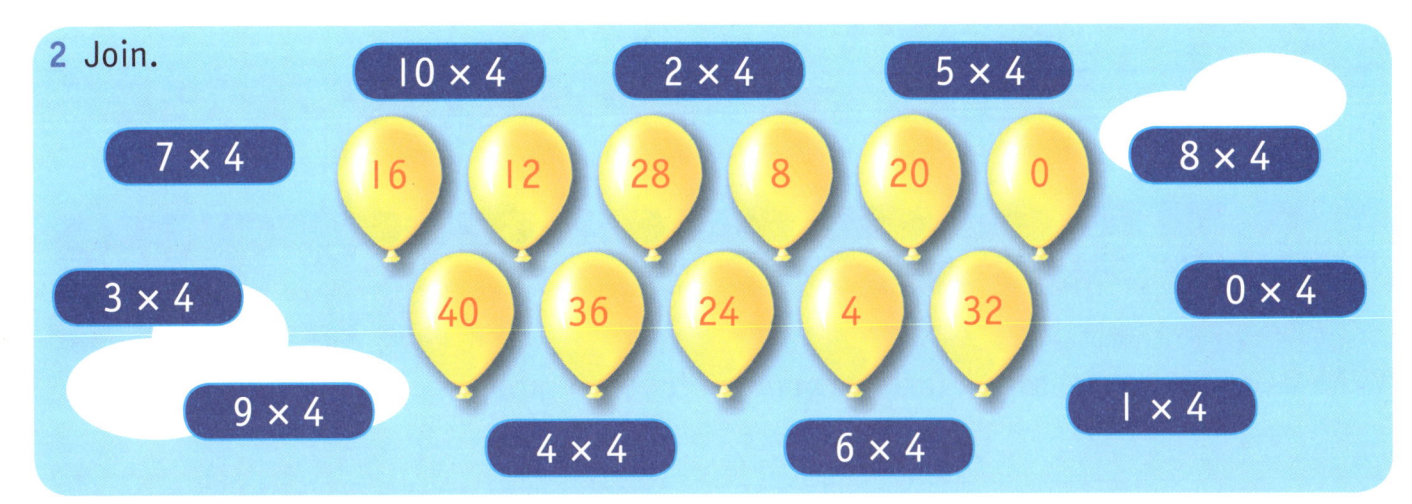

2 Join.

10 × 4 — 40
2 × 4 — 8
5 × 4 — 20
7 × 4 — 28
8 × 4 — 32
3 × 4 — 12
0 × 4 — 0
9 × 4 — 36
1 × 4 — 4
4 × 4 — 16
6 × 4 — 24

3 Complete these as quickly as you can.

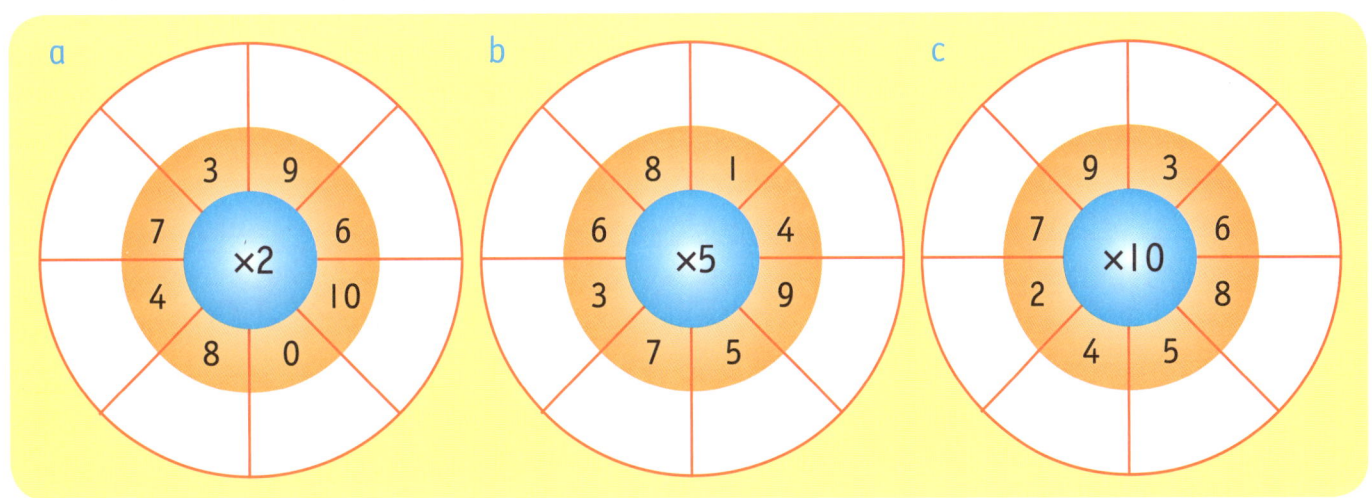

a) ×2 with 3, 9, 6, 10, 0, 8, 4, 7

b) ×5 with 8, 1, 4, 9, 5, 7, 3, 6

c) ×10 with 9, 3, 6, 8, 5, 4, 2, 7

ACMNA057 Number and place value • Represent and solve problems involving multiplication using efficient mental and written strategies and appropriate digital technologies.

147

Multiplication facts

Lab 3 snowboard

A B  C  D 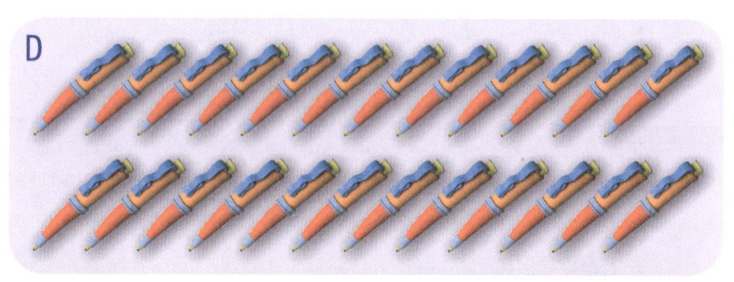 E  F

Write as many multiplication facts as you can for each group.

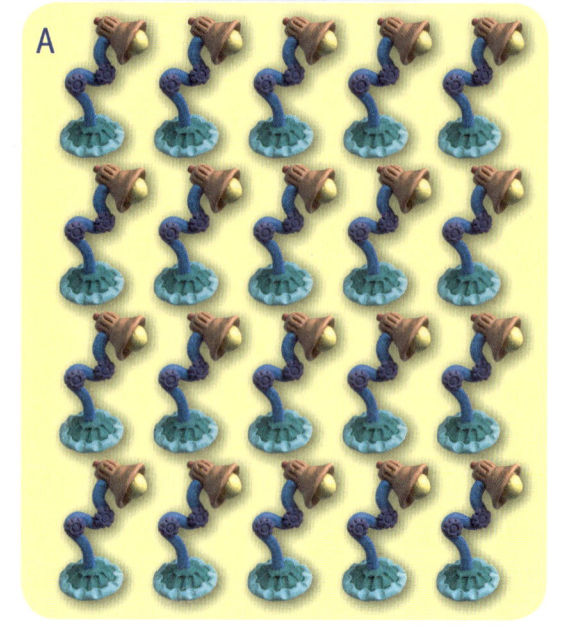

A

B

C

D

E

F

148

ACMNA057 Number and place value • Represent and solve problems involving multiplication using efficient mental and written strategies and appropriate digital technologies.

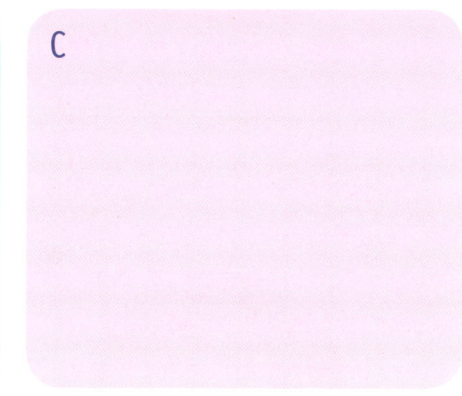

Products

Product is the answer when numbers are multiplied.

Multiplication

Match the number sentence to its answer.
Then write the letter in the secret message.

1. 6 × 7 =
2. 9 × 8 =
3. 4 × 4 =
4. 8 × 6 =
5. 3 × 7 =
6. 5 × 4 =
7. 9 × 6 =
8. 7 × 7 =

R 20   A 16   S 42   O 21
H 48   E 72   F 54   I 49

☐☐☐ ☐☐☐☐☐ ☐☐☐☐☐☐
1 2 3   4 5 6 1 2 1   3 6 2 7 8 1 4

9 a 8   b 9   c 6   d 7   e 5   f 4
   × 5   × 3   × 0   × 10   × 7   × 8
   ___   ___   ___   ___   ___   ___

10 Write the product of:

a 6 and 4 ____   b 3 and 6 ____   c 10 and 2 ____   d 2 and 5 ____

e 4 and 3 ____   f 7 and 4 ____   g 6 and 6 ____   h 8 and 3 ____

11 Fill in the missing facts.

eg	(dots)	4 groups of 6	6 × 4	6 × 4	24
a		3 groups of 5			
b			5 × 5		
c					16

ACMNA057 Number and place value • Represent and solve problems involving multiplication using efficient mental and written strategies and appropriate digital technologies.

Multiples

3, 4, 5, 10 tables

1	2	3	4	5	6	7	8	9	10
11	12	13	14	15	16	17	18	19	20
21	22	23	24	25	26	27	28	29	30
31	32	33	34	35	36	37	38	39	40
41	42	43	44	45	46	47	48	49	50
51	52	53	54	55	56	57	58	59	60
61	62	63	64	65	66	67	68	69	70
71	72	73	74	75	76	77	78	79	80
81	82	83	84	85	86	87	88	89	90
91	92	93	94	95	96	97	98	99	100

1 a Colour the multiples of 7 yellow.

   b Colour the multiples of 8 red.

   c Colour the multiples of 9 green.

   d Which numbers have been coloured more than once? _____

   e Why? _____

2 Colour the multiples of the middle number.

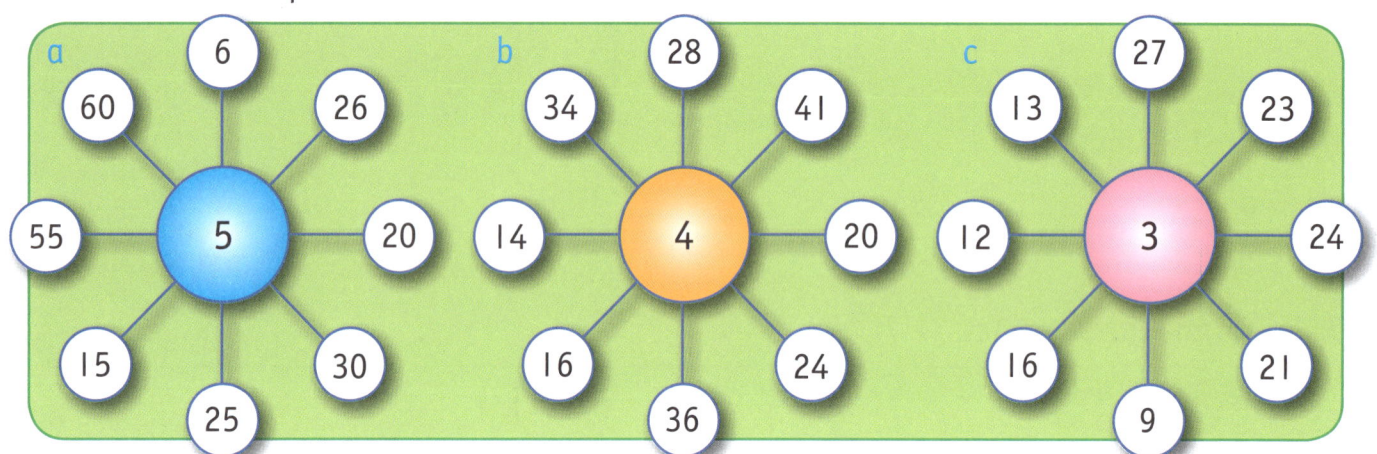

   a 5 — 6, 60, 26, 55, 20, 15, 30, 25

   b 4 — 28, 34, 41, 14, 20, 16, 24, 36

   c 3 — 27, 13, 23, 12, 24, 16, 21, 9

3 What is the value of each pile?

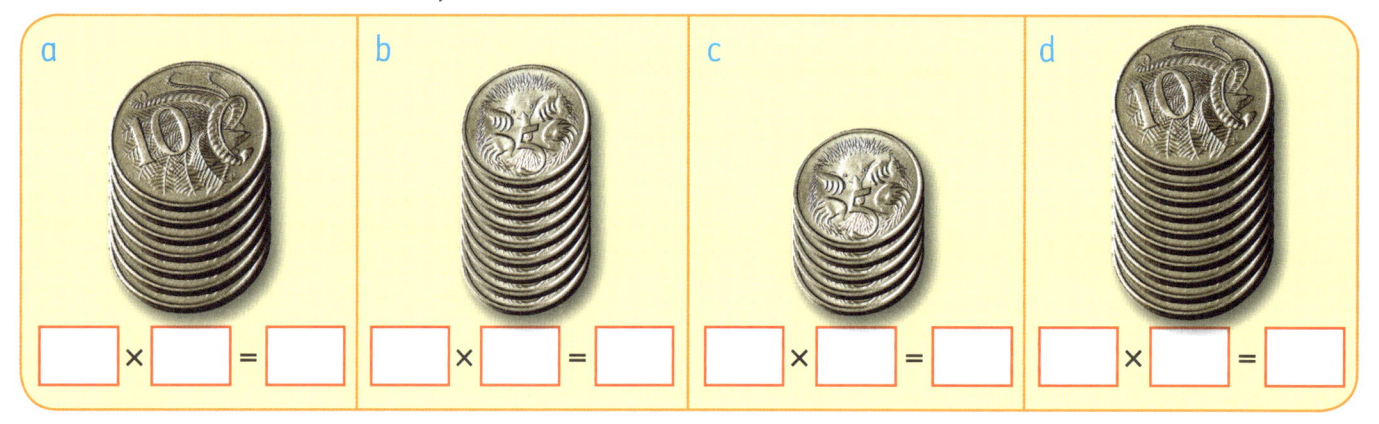

   a ☐ × ☐ = ☐
   b ☐ × ☐ = ☐
   c ☐ × ☐ = ☐
   d ☐ × ☐ = ☐

150

ACMNA057 Number and place value • Represent and solve problems involving multiplication using efficient mental and written strategies and appropriate digital technologies.

Problem solving   Operations

1. John has 8 pairs of socks. How many socks altogether?

    8 × 2 = ☐

    Answer ☐ socks

2. Sammy bought 7 apples for 10 cents each. How much did he spend?

    ☐ × ☐ = ☐

    Answer ☐

3. Mrs Tiredout has 9 children. Each child has 4 T-shirts. How many T-shirts altogether?

    ☐ × ☐ = ☐

    Answer ☐ T-shirts

4. Jack gathers 4 eggs every day. How many eggs in 1 week?

    ☐ × ☐ = ☐

    Answer ☐ eggs

You write the questions.

5. _____

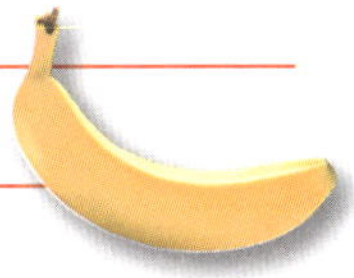

    ☐ × ☐ = ☐   Answer 30 bananas

6. _____

    ☐ × ☐ = ☐   Answer 48 monsters

7. Use a calculator.

    Farmer Joe had 14 paddocks. There were 25 cows in each of 6 paddocks and 34 sheep in each of 8 paddocks.

    a. How many cows?   ☐ × ☐ = ☐

    b. How many sheep? ☐ × ☐ = ☐

    c. How many animals altogether?

    _____

Division

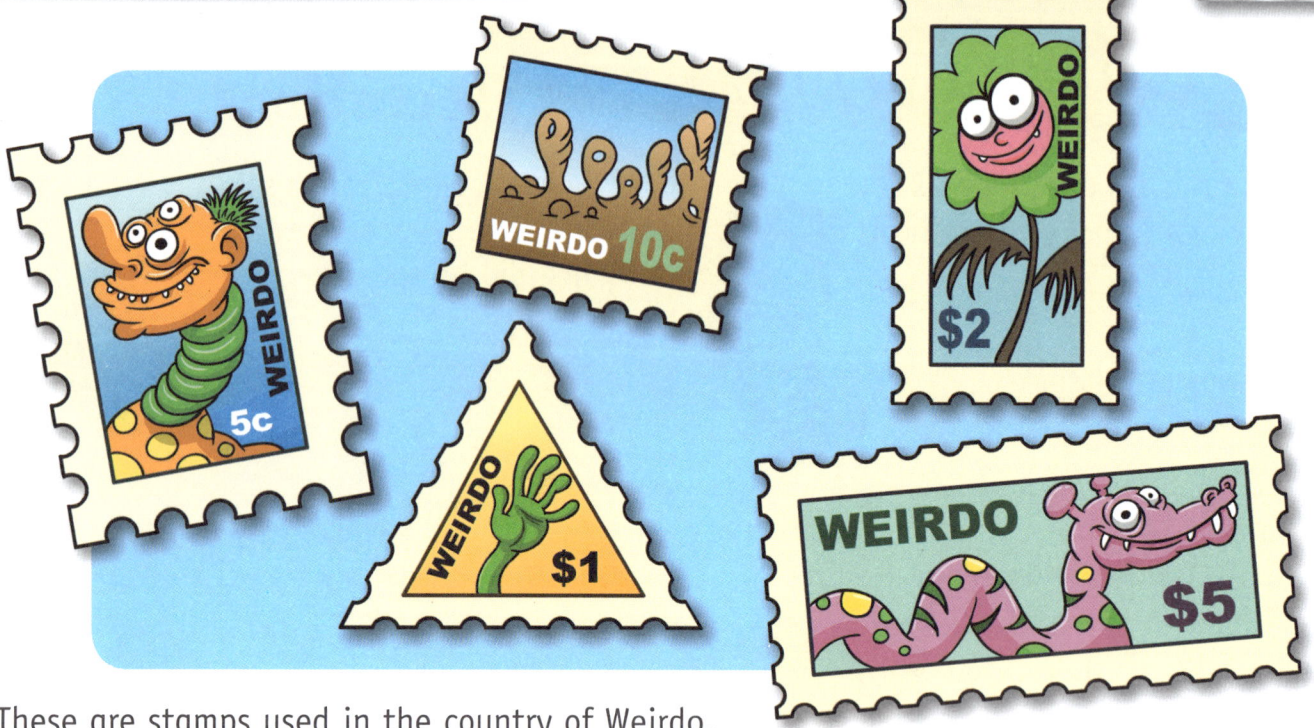

These are stamps used in the country of Weirdo.

1. Wrod only ever bought 5c stamps. How many could he buy for:

   a 40c? _____   b 30c? _____   c 15c? _____   d 5c? _____   e 50c? _____

2. Wred only bought 10c stamps. How many could she buy for:

   a 60c? _____   b 90c? _____   c 20c? _____   d 50c? _____   e 70c? _____

3. Weid only bought $2 stamps. How many could he buy for?

   a $14? _____   b $8? _____   c $18? _____   d $6? _____   e $12? _____

4. Wido had $13. Could she buy eight $2 stamps? _____

   Why? _____

5. How much for: a seven 5c stamps? _____   b five $5 stamps? _____

6. Wodi has 85c. How many 10c stamps can she buy? _____

7. a How much to buy 1 of each stamp? _____

   b How much change from $10? _____

Challenge! Make a list

Werd has a package to send. List the ways she can make $3.10 using 5 or less stamps.

The division sign

÷ means to divide.

1 Divide 20 cars into 4 equal groups.

20 ÷ 4 = _____

There are _____ cars in each group.

2 Divide 16 leaves into 8 equal groups.

16 ÷ 8 = _____

There are _____ leaves in each group.

3 Divide 24 stars into 6 equal groups.

24 ÷ 6 = _____

There are _____ stars in each group.

4 Divide 18 cats into 3 equal groups.

18 ÷ 3 = _____

There are _____ cats in each group.

5 Divide 32 dice into 8 groups.

32 ÷ 8 = _____

There are _____ dice in each group.

6 Divide 24 foxes into groups of 8.

24 ÷ 8 = _____

There are _____ groups of foxes.

7 Divide 15 girls into groups of 3.

15 ÷ 3 = _____

There are _____ groups of girls.

8 Divide 20 bugs into groups of 5.

20 ÷ 5 = _____

There are _____ groups of shells.

9 Divide 22 fish into groups of 2.

22 ÷ 2 = _____

There are _____ groups of fish.

ACMNA057 Number and place value • Represent and solve problems involving multiplication using efficient mental and written strategies and appropriate digital technologies.

12 ÷ 3 = 4
12 ÷ 4 = 3
3 × 4 = 12
4 × 3 = 12

Using the division sign

÷ 5, ÷ 10

1 Use this group of 24 ice-creams to help you to divide.

a 24 ÷ 8 = _____   b 24 ÷ 6 = _____
c 24 ÷ 3 = _____   d 24 ÷ 24 = _____
e 24 ÷ 4 = _____   f 24 ÷ 1 = _____

2 Use this group of 30 bears to help you to divide.

a 30 ÷ 10 = _____
b 30 ÷ 6 = _____
c 30 ÷ 3 = _____
d 30 ÷ 5 = _____
e 30 ÷ 30 = _____
f 30 ÷ 1 = _____

3 Complete these number sentences.

a 5 × 6 = _____   b 3 × 6 = _____   c 4 × 8 = _____   d 10 × 9 = _____
   30 ÷ 5 = _____   18 ÷ 3 = _____   32 ÷ 4 = _____   90 ÷ 10 = _____
   30 ÷ 6 = _____   18 ÷ 6 = _____   32 ÷ 8 = _____   90 ÷ 9 = _____

4 a 42 ÷ 7 = _____   b 10 ÷ 5 = _____   c 20 ÷ 10 = _____   d 40 ÷ 10 = _____
     e 27 ÷ 9 = _____   f 48 ÷ 8 = _____   g 49 ÷ 7 = _____   h 36 ÷ 6 = _____
     i 54 ÷ 9 = _____   j 35 ÷ 5 = _____   k 9 ÷ 9 = _____   l 100 ÷ 10 = _____

5 a 30 balls are packed into boxes of 6.
     How many boxes are needed? ☐ ÷ ☐ = ☐

   b Mrs Lim is making 50 cupcakes.
     She puts 10 cupcakes on each tray.
     How many trays are needed? ☐ ÷ ☐ = ☐

   c 5 children share 25 biscuits equally.
     How many biscuits each? ☐ ÷ ☐ = ☐

   d Mr Baker has 60 apples.
     He puts 6 apples in each bag.
     How many bags? ☐ ÷ ☐ = ☐

ACMNA057 Number and place value • Represent and solve problems involving multiplication using efficient mental and written strategies and appropriate digital technologies.

Problem solving

Bags to pack

Jerry, Sam and Tye bought 48 grocery items. They wanted to find how many ways they could pack them equally into bags. Jerry found the most ways. Sam thought of 3 ways, 1 less than Tye. Tye thought of 4 less than Jerry. How many ways did Jerry find?

_____

_____

_____

What might be the ways that Jerry thought of, apart from this way?

24 + 24 = 48

2 × 24 = 48

48 ÷ 2 = 24

equivalent – having the same value, equal to

Denominators

Equivalent fractions

$$\frac{1}{1} = 1$$

The denominator 1 divides one whole into 1 part.

| $\frac{1}{2}$ | $\frac{1}{2}$ |

The denominator 2 divides one whole into two equal parts.

| $\frac{1}{4}$ | $\frac{1}{4}$ | $\frac{1}{4}$ | $\frac{1}{4}$ |

The denominator 4 divides one whole into 4 equal parts.

| $\frac{1}{8}$ | $\frac{1}{8}$ | $\frac{1}{8}$ | $\frac{1}{8}$ | $\frac{1}{8}$ | $\frac{1}{8}$ | $\frac{1}{8}$ | $\frac{1}{8}$ |

The denominator 8 divides one whole into 8 equal parts.

1 $\frac{1}{4}$ is one of four parts. a $\frac{2}{4}$ is _____ of four parts.

b $\frac{3}{4}$ is _____ of four parts. c $\frac{4}{4}$ is _____ of four parts.

d Are all four parts the same size? _____ Why? _____

e Which fraction is the largest? _____

What is another name for this? _____

2 a Colour the fractions.

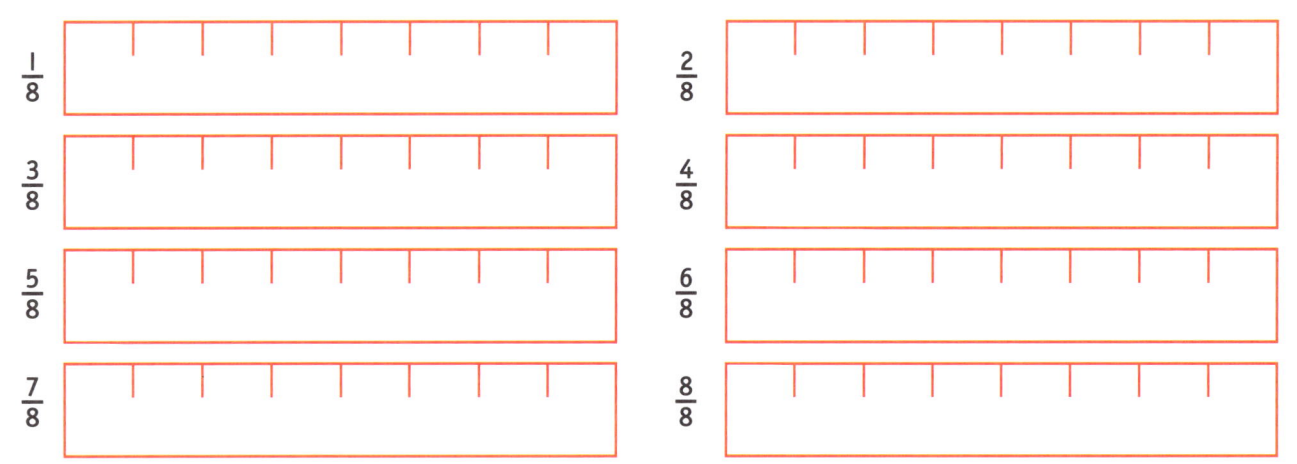

$\frac{1}{8}$ $\frac{2}{8}$

$\frac{3}{8}$ $\frac{4}{8}$

$\frac{5}{8}$ $\frac{6}{8}$

$\frac{7}{8}$ $\frac{8}{8}$

b Find the fraction which is equivalent to $\frac{1}{4}$. _____ = $\frac{1}{4}$.

c Find the fraction which is equivalent to $\frac{3}{4}$. _____ = $\frac{3}{4}$.

ACMNA058 Fractions and decimals • Model and represent unit fractions including $\frac{1}{2}, \frac{1}{4}, \frac{1}{3}, \frac{1}{5}$ and their multiples to a complete whole.

Fractions

1 Colour and complete.

   a Colour one half.
     1 out of 2 = $\frac{1}{2}$

   b Colour one third.
     1 out of _____ = $\frac{1}{3}$

   c Colour one quarter.
     1 out of _____ = $\frac{1}{4}$

   d Colour one fifth.
     _____ out of 5 = $\frac{1}{5}$

2 Colour the fractions. Then order the fractions from smallest to largest.

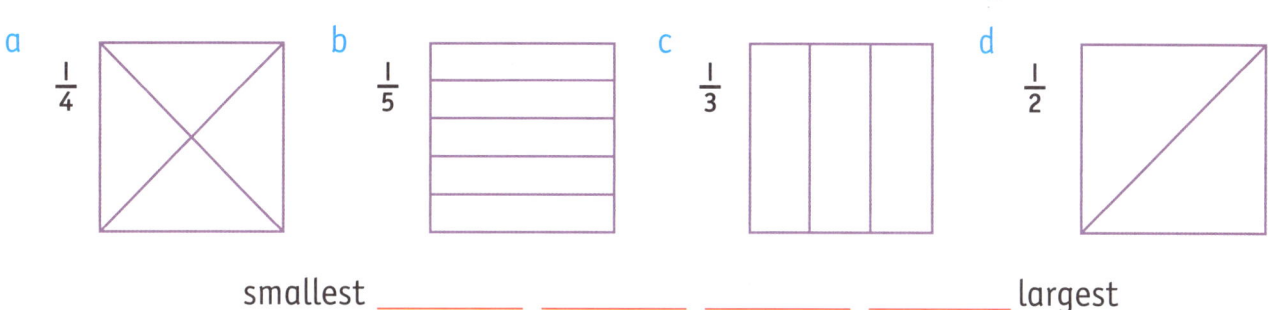

   a $\frac{1}{4}$ b $\frac{1}{5}$ c $\frac{1}{3}$ d $\frac{1}{2}$

   smallest _____ _____ _____ _____ largest

3 Circle the larger fraction in each pair.

   a $\frac{1}{2}$ $\frac{1}{3}$ b $\frac{1}{5}$ $\frac{1}{4}$ c $\frac{1}{4}$ $\frac{1}{3}$ d $\frac{1}{5}$ $\frac{1}{4}$

4 a Colour the correct fractions.

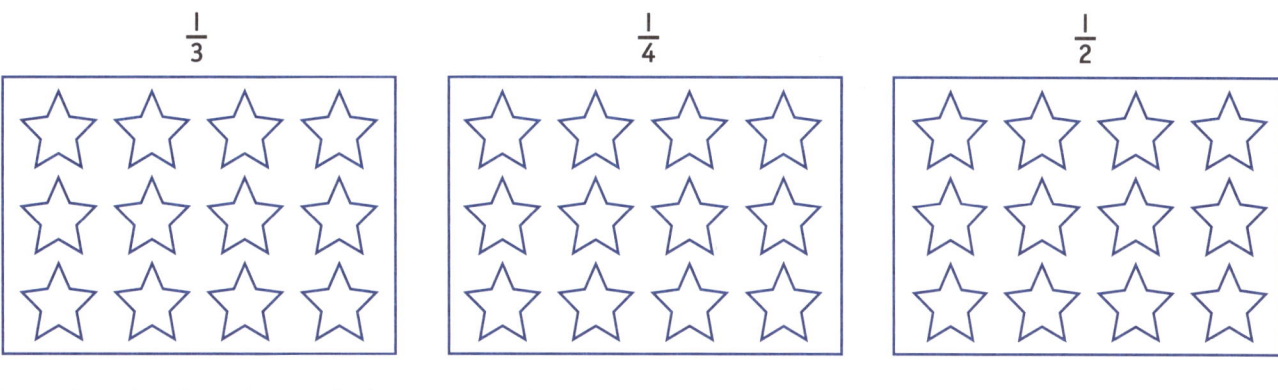

   $\frac{1}{3}$ $\frac{1}{4}$ $\frac{1}{2}$

   b Order the fractions of the group of 12 stars from smallest to largest. _____ _____ _____

5 a The denominator of the fraction tells how many _____.

   b As the denominator gets bigger, the fraction gets _____.

More denominators

1. a $\frac{1}{3}$ means one of _____ parts.

   b Write all the thirds in order. _____ _____ _____

   c If you cut one into three equal parts, what is each piece called? _____

   d Cut each shape into thirds.

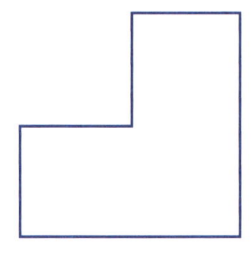

2. a $\frac{1}{5}$ means one of _____ parts.

   b Write all the fifths in order. _____ _____ _____ _____ _____

   c Write $\frac{3}{5}$ in other ways. Use words _____

   Use numbers _____

   d Make each number sentence equal 1 whole.

   _____ + $\frac{1}{5}$ = 1 whole   _____ + $\frac{2}{5}$ = 1 whole

   _____ + $\frac{3}{5}$ = 1 whole   _____ + $\frac{4}{5}$ = 1 whole

   _____ _____ _____ _____ _____ _____ _____ _____ _____ _____

3. Fifths and tenths.

   a Colour one fifth ($\frac{1}{5}$) and two tenths ($\frac{2}{10}$) to show they are equivalent.

   b Answer true or false.

   $\frac{4}{10} = \frac{1}{5}$ _____ $\frac{3}{10} < \frac{1}{5}$ _____ $\frac{7}{10} > \frac{3}{5}$ _____

   c Place these on the number line.

   $\frac{1}{2}, \frac{3}{5}, \frac{7}{10}, \frac{2}{5}, \frac{2}{10}$

ACMNA058 Fractions and decimals • Model and represent unit fractions including $\frac{1}{2}, \frac{1}{4}, \frac{1}{3}, \frac{1}{5}$ and their multiples to a complete whole.

Problem solving

Zoo fractions

At Jimmy's zoo, he has an empty area for some new animals. Look at the animals below and decide which area they will need. Then put fences on the map and draw in the animals.

one crocodile	four rock wallabies	three emus	three koalas	one dingo

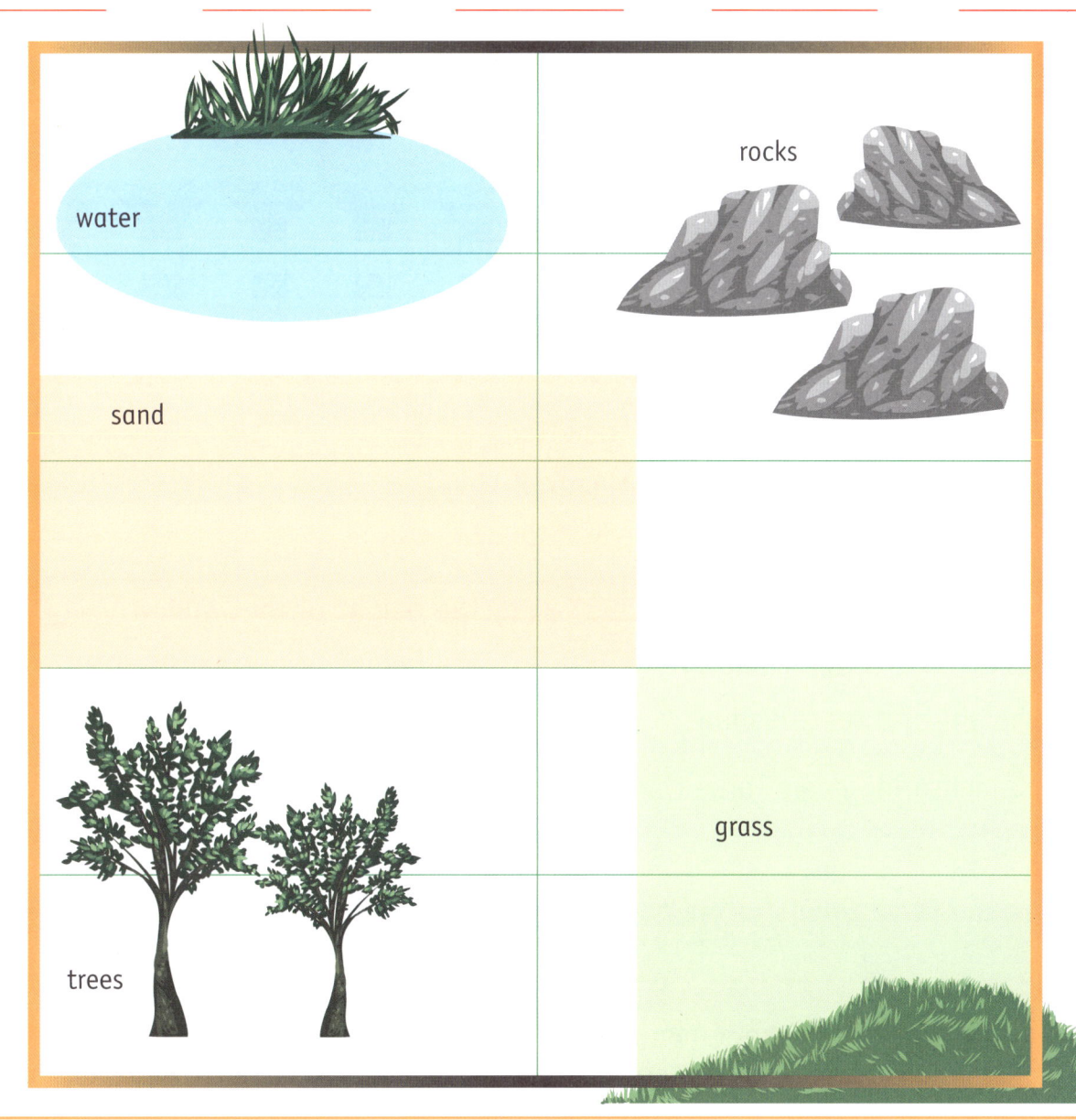

ACMNA058 Fractions and decimals • Model and represent unit fractions including $\frac{1}{2}$, $\frac{1}{4}$, $\frac{1}{3}$, $\frac{1}{5}$ and their multiples to a complete whole.

Lab 3 — Centimetres and millimetres

1. a Is a millimetre smaller than a centimetre? _____
   b How many millimetres in one centimetre? _____

2. Measure in centimetres:
   a the width of the house. _____
   b the height of the window. _____
   c the short side of the chimney. _____
   d the height of the house wall. _____
   e the height of a fence paling. _____
   f the width of a tree branch. _____

3. Without measuring name three things that are about 2 cm.
   a _____ b _____ c _____

4. Measure the three things to see how close you are.
   a _____ b _____ c _____

5. Draw a line that is: a 4 cm 6 mm long.
   b 3 cm 2 mm long.

160

ACMMG061 Using units of measurement • Measure, order and compare objects using familiar metric units of length, mass and capacity.

m is metre
cm is centimetre
mm is millimetre
10 mm = 1 cm
100 cm = 1 m

Millimetres

Length

1 How many centimetres in:
   a 2 m? ____   b 5 m? ____   c 3 m? ____   d 4½ m? ____   e 1½ m? ____

2 How many millimetres in:
   a 3 cm? ____   b 7 cm? ____   c 10 cm? ____   d 1 cm? ____   e 9 cm? ____

3 Change these to metres.
   a 100 cm ____   b 700 cm ____   c 900 cm ____   d 350 cm ____   e 550 cm ____

4 Change these to centimetres.
   a 50 mm ____   b 10 mm ____   c 40 mm ____   d 20 mm ____   e 70 mm ____

5 Name three things you might measure in millimetres.
   a _____   b _____   c _____

6 Draw these straight lines and label them.
   A 10 mm   B 40 mm   C 55 mm   D 25 mm   E 38 mm   F 73 mm

7 Give each alien a name then measure its height.

   Name _____   Name _____   Name _____   Name _____
   Height _____   Height _____   Height _____   Height _____

Challenge! Measure your height in: centimetres. ☐
                                         millimetres. ☐

ACMMG061 Using units of measurement • Measure, order and compare objects using familiar metric units of length, mass and capacity.

161

Area is the size of the surface. It is measured in squares.

Area

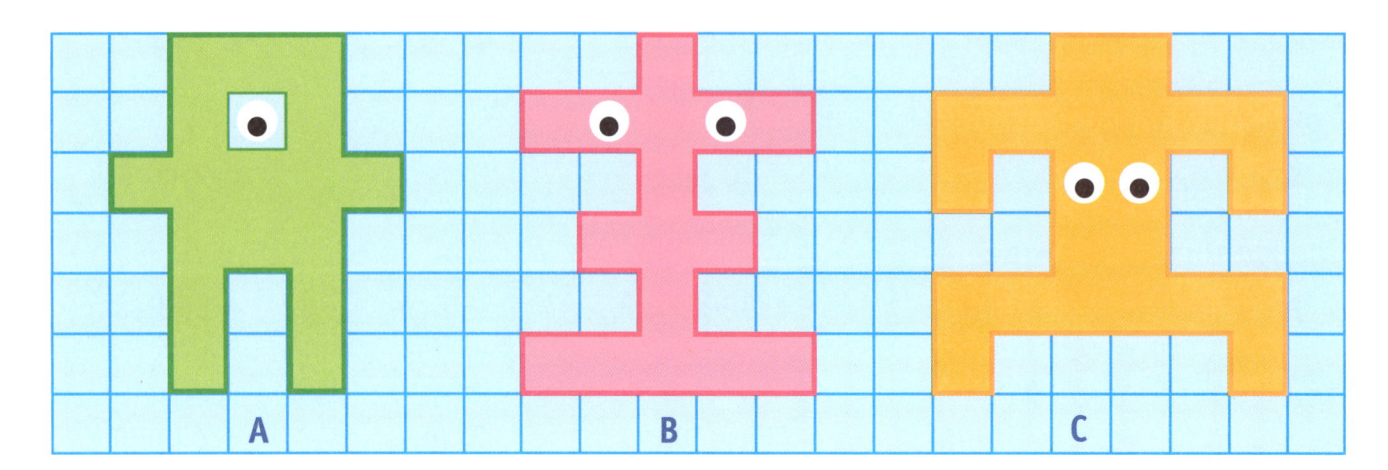

A   B   C

1 a Estimate the area of these robots in squares.

   A = _____ squares   B = _____ squares   C = _____ squares

  b Now count the squares.

   A = _____ squares   B = _____ squares   C = _____ squares

2 Which robot has: a the largest area? _____   b the smallest area? _____

3 Draw a robot with an area of 30 squares.

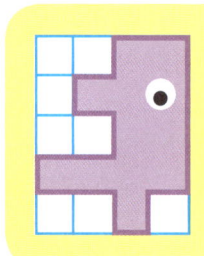

4 This is half a robot. What will be the area of the whole robot?

5 a Are the squares in Questions 1, 3 and 4 the same size? _____

  b Will the area of robot A be the same if it is drawn on smaller squares? _____

  c Will the area of robot B be the same if it is drawn on bigger squares? _____

6 a Cover your desk with counters. What is its area? _____ counters

  b Cover your desk with books. What is its area? _____ books

  c Are the answers the same? _____ Why not? _____

7 What would you use to find the area of the board? _____

162 ACMMG061 Using units of measurement • Measure, order and compare objects using familiar metric units of length, mass and capacity.

Square centimetres

To measure area we can use square centimetres.
We write 1 square centimetre as 1 cm².

Area

1 This is a square centimetre grid.
   What is the area of these shapes? Estimate first.

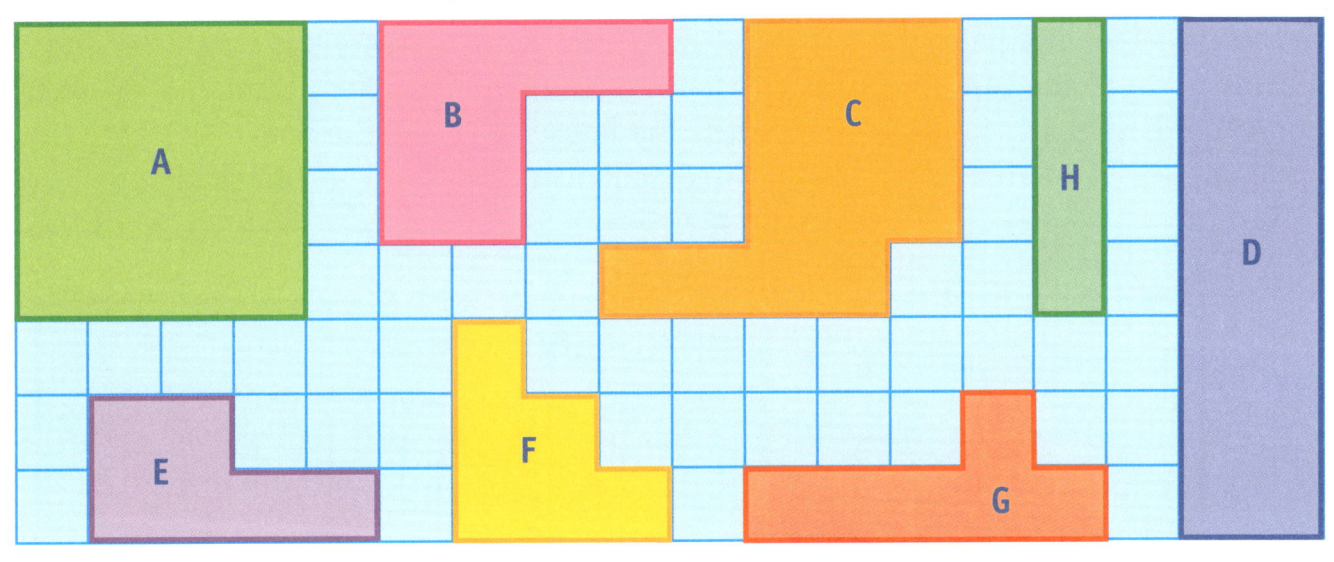

Area **A** = _____ cm²   Area **B** = _____ cm²   Area **C** = _____ cm²
Area **D** = _____ cm²   Area **E** = _____ cm²   Area **F** = _____ cm²
Area **G** = _____ cm²   Area **H** = _____ cm²

a Which shape has the largest area?   _____
b Which shape has the smallest area? _____
c Which shapes have the same area?   _____ _____

2 On this grid draw and colour 5 different shapes that each have an area of 5 cm².

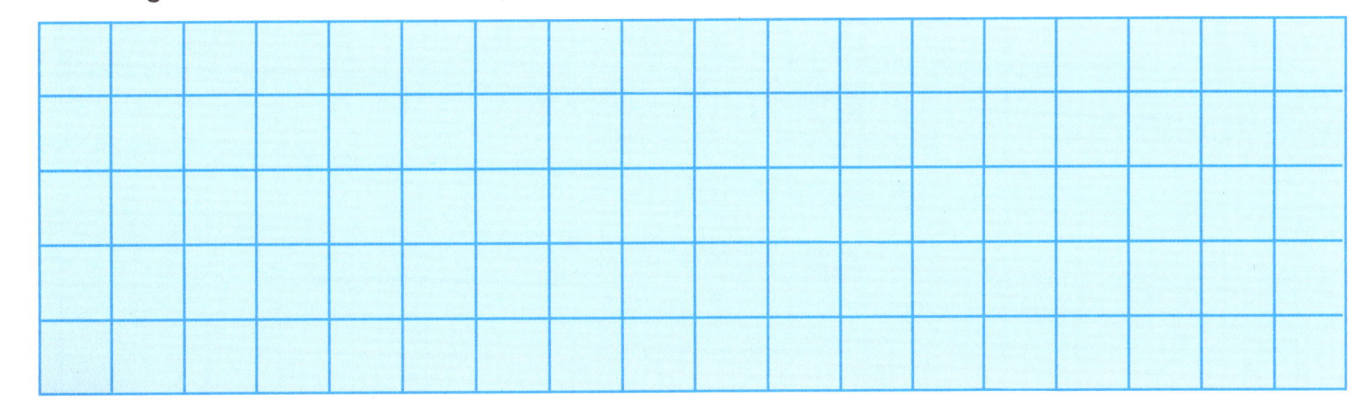

Challenge! Use a 1 cm² sheet to work out the area in square centimetres of:
• this book cover.
• your desk.

ACMMG061 Using units of measurement • Measure, order and compare objects using familiar metric units of length, mass and capacity.

Investigation 4

Farmer Zoop's Farm!

Farmer Zoop has forgotten where his animals live.
Read the clues and label each area.

The cows live in a paddock of 20 squares. The pigs live in a sty of 15 squares. The horse lives north of the cows. The pigs are south of the hens. The hens' yard is 5 squares. The orchard covers 36 squares in two areas. The house yard and the horse yard both have perimeters of 14. The sheep live in three paddocks which add to 100 squares.

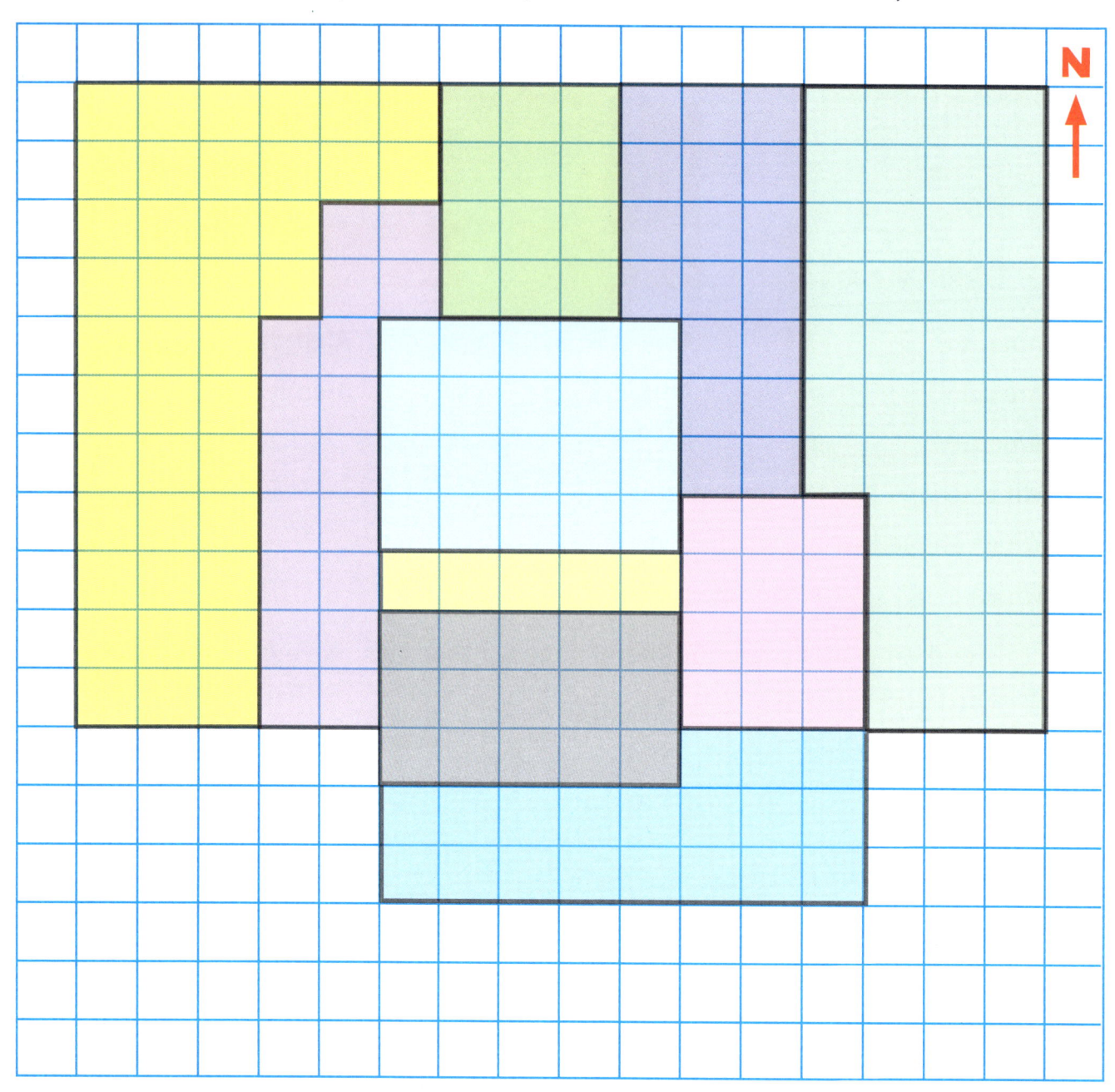

Farmer Zoop has 120 animals altogether. How many of each might he have?

Cows _____   Pigs _____   Horses _____   Hens _____   Sheep _____

Your Own Farm!

Investigation 4

You have 120 animals. What will you keep on your farm?

_____

_____

_____

Design your own farm. Fill this space. Make paddocks and yards for each of the animals. Remember, larger animals need larger paddocks. Bigger numbers of animals need bigger paddocks too. Label your plan.

To carry out these tasks I need to:
- ☐ count squares for area.
- ☐ use trial and error to solve problems.
- ☐ use draw a diagram to solve problems.
- ☐ understand that same areas can have different shapes and perimeters.

I enjoyed this task!
★★★★

Revision

Shade one bubble.

1. Which operation shows these shells divided into 6 equal groups?

   18 ÷ 3 ○   18 − 6 ○   18 − 4 ○   18 ÷ 6 ○

2. $\frac{1}{4}$ $\frac{1}{2}$

   Which sign can go between these fractions?

   < ○   > ○   = ○   * ○

3. Mum cut some oranges into quarters.

   How many whole oranges did she cut?

   16 ○   4 ○   8 ○   6 ○

4. This fruit was placed in a bag.
   Jay closed his eyes to pick one piece.
   What is the chance he picked a banana?

   certain ○   impossible ○   likely ○   unlikely ○

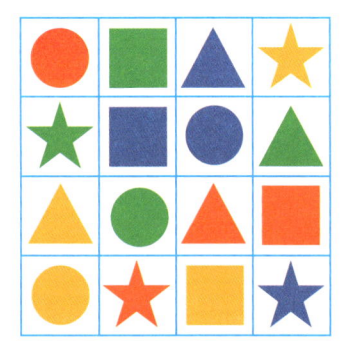

5. What shape is second from the left in the top row?

   ▲ ○   ● ○   ★ ○   ■ ○

166

Revision

Shade one bubble.

6   Which number is 356 written to the closest ten?

   360   350   400   355
    ○   ○   ○   ○

7   Which shape does not have an axis of symmetry?

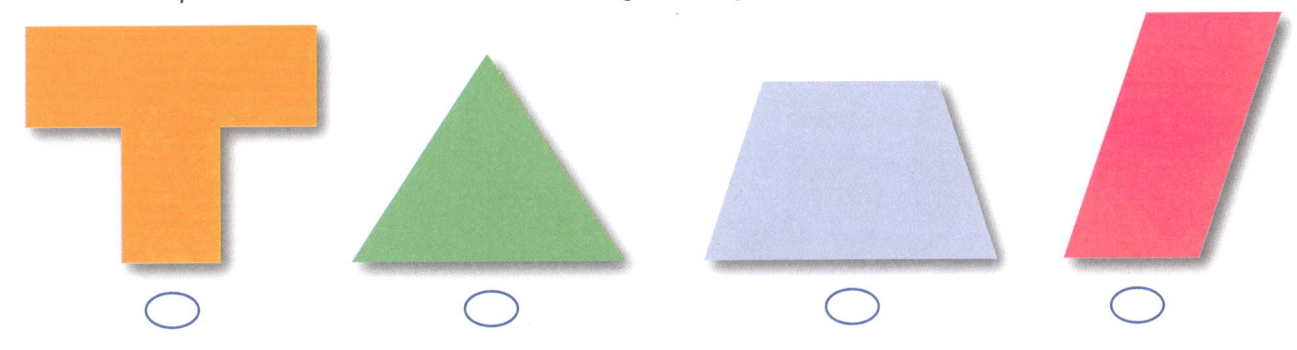

    ○   ○   ○   ○

8   What is the height of this alien?

     4 cm   4 mm   4 m   40 cm
      ○   ○   ○   ○

9   Fifi thought of a number. She then doubled it and added 3. The answer was 19. What number did she first think of?

     5   6   7   8
     ○   ○   ○   ○

10 Which star shows a number that is not a multiple of 4?

    36   24   34   28
    ○   ○   ○   ○

167

Changing numbers

Lab 3 stomper

Sequences

In this amazing machine, numbers are changed into a pattern of four more numbers.

1 What comes out if these numbers are put into D?
 a 7 ___ ___ ___ ___   b 9 ___ ___ ___ ___
 c 4 ___ ___ ___ ___   d 11 ___ ___ ___ ___

2 What comes out if these numbers are put into B?
 a 24 ___ ___ ___ ___   b 19 ___ ___ ___ ___
 c 16 ___ ___ ___ ___   d 27 ___ ___ ___ ___

3 What comes out if these numbers are put into E?
 a 3 ___ ___ ___ ___   b 15 ___ ___ ___ ___
 c 30 ___ ___ ___ ___   d 41 ___ ___ ___ ___

4 3, 15 and 41 are odd numbers.
 When an odd number is added to an odd number the answer is _____.

5 When an even number is added to an odd number the answer is _____.

Don't put me in the machine.

ACMNA060 Patterns and algebra • Describe, continue, and create number patterns resulting from performing addition and subtraction.

Matching answers

1 True (T) or false (F)?

 a 6 + 4 = 4 + 6 ____   b 8 + 5 = 5 + 8 ____   c 1 + 7 = 7 + 1 ____   d 3 + 9 = 9 + 3 ____

 e 5 + 8 = 8 + 5 ____   f 7 + 6 = 6 + 7 ____   g 3 + 7 = 7 + 3 ____   h 4 + 5 = 5 + 4 ____

 i What rule can you make? _____

2 True (T) or false (F)?

 a 2 × 9 = 9 × 2 ____   b 7 × 4 = 4 × 7 ____   c 8 × 5 = 5 × 8 ____   d 5 × 9 = 9 × 5 ____

 e 3 × 5 = 5 × 3 ____   f 6 × 2 = 2 × 6 ____   g 9 × 4 = 4 × 9 ____   h 10 × 8 = 8 × 10 ____

 i What rule can you make? _____

3 Are the rules the same? _____

4 True (T) or false (F)?

 a 6 − 2 = 2 − 6 ____   b 9 − 5 = 5 − 9 ____   c 8 − 3 = 3 − 8 ____   d 7 − 4 = 4 − 7 ____

 e Can you make a rule? _____

5 True (T) or false (F)?

 a 18 ÷ 3 = 3 ÷ 18 ____   b 25 ÷ 5 = 5 ÷ 25 ____

 c 40 ÷ 4 = 4 ÷ 40 ____   d 9 ÷ 3 = 3 ÷ 9 ____

 e Can you make a rule? _____

8 + 2 = 2 + 8 This makes maths easier!

6 True (T) or false (F)?

 a 9 + 7 = 7 + 9 ____   b 21 ÷ 3 = 3 ÷ 21 ____

 c 14 − 6 = 6 − 14 ____   d 9 × 9 = 9 + 9 ____

 e 8 + 11 = 11 + 8 ____   f 6 + 8 = 8 − 6 ____

 g 90 ÷ 10 = 10 ÷ 90 ____   h 26 + 42 = 42 + 26 ____

 i 68 × 97 = 97 × 68 ____   j 42 − 36 = 42 + 36 ____

7 What happens to all numbers if they are multiplied by 1? _____

Challenge! a Add these numbers together in four different ways. Are the answers always the same? ____

b Use a calculator to multiply the numbers together in four different ways. Are the answers always the same? ____

3 7 4

Lab 3 — patterns 1

Making patterns

Mary used matches to make some shapes. Draw the next shape in the box, then complete the table. Look for patterns.

1 a

b

Number of shapes	1	2	3	4	5	6	7	8
Number of matches	4	7	10					

2 a

b

Number of shapes	1	2	3	4	5	6	7	8
Number of matches								

3 a

b

Number of shapes	1	2	3	4	5	6	7	8
Number of matches								

4 a

b

Number of shapes	1	2	3	4	5	6	7	8
Number of matches								

Draw a diagram

Make your own pattern using match sticks. Draw it. Write a table.

ACMNA060 Patterns and algebra • Describe, continue, and create number patterns resulting from performing addition and subtraction.

When two straight lines meet they make an angle.
eg

Angle search

Lines and angles

1 a What shape is the aquarium? _____

   b What type of angles are at the corners? _____

2 How many angles can you see inside:
   a the red fish? _____   b the purple fish? _____
   c the green fish? _____   d the yellow fish? _____

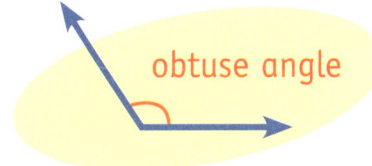

3 How many right angles can you see inside:
   a the red fish? _____   b the purple fish? _____
   c the green fish? _____   d the yellow fish? _____

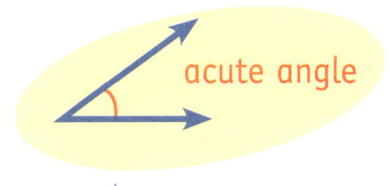

4 How many obtuse angles can you see inside:
   a the red fish? _____   b the yellow fish? _____

5 How many acute angles can you see inside:
   a the green fish? _____   b the purple fish? _____

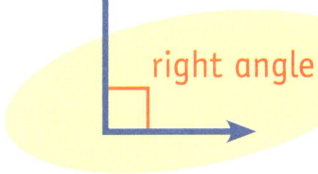

6 Draw another angle fish.

obtuse angle

acute angle

right angle

ACMMG064 Geometric reasoning • Identify angles as measures of turn and compare angle sizes in everyday situations.

Angle size

1
A	B	C	D
Here are 4 angles.	Copy the angle.	Draw a larger angle.	Draw a smaller angle.
a	b	c	d
e	f	g	h
i	j	k	l
m	n	o	p

2 Which angle is the largest in:

a column A? _____   b column B? _____   c column C? _____   d column D? _____

3 Which angle is the smallest in:

a column A? _____   b column B? _____   c column C? _____   d column D? _____

4 Look around the classroom and write 3 places where you can see right angles.

_____   _____   _____

Draw a diagram Draw a house. Colour the right angles blue, colour the acute angles pink, colour the obtuse angles orange.

172

ACMMG064 Geometric reasoning • Identify angles as measures of turn and compare angle sizes in everyday situations.

Comparing angles

The corners of this page are square corners.
A square corner is called a right angle.

Acute angles are smaller than right angles. 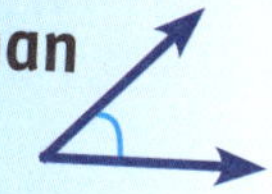
Obtuse angles are larger than right angles.

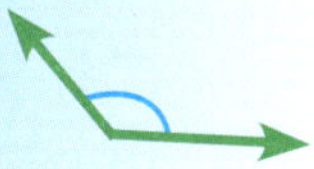

1 Colour the right angles red; the angles bigger than a right angle green; the angles smaller than a right angle yellow.

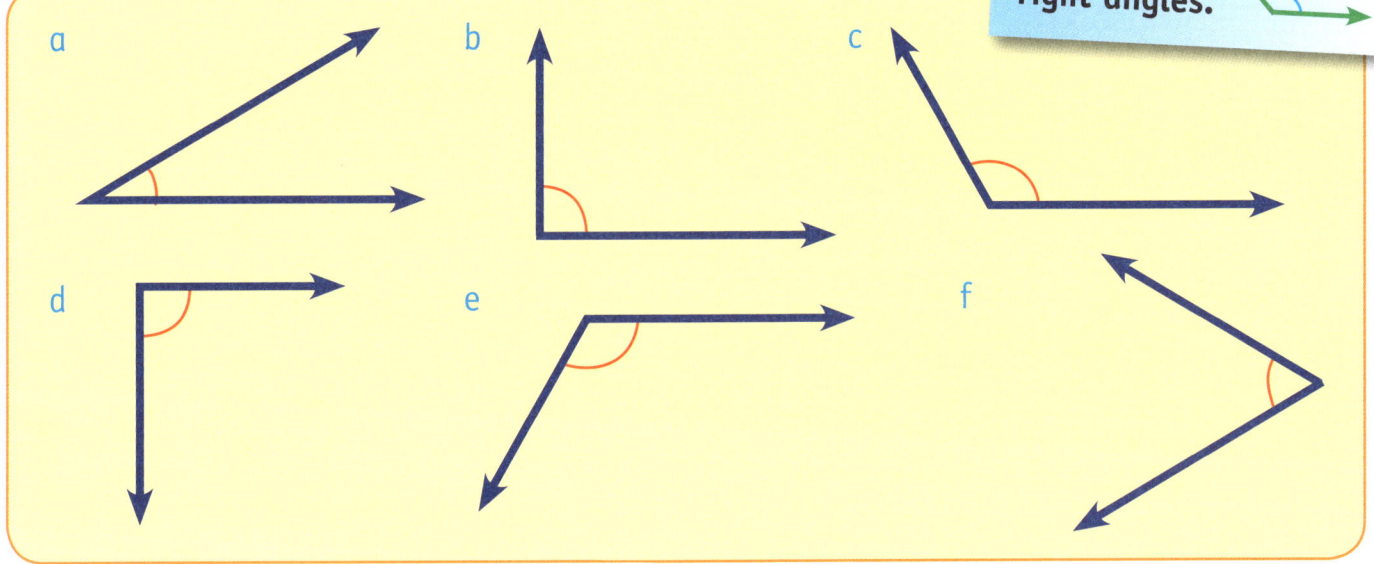

a   b   c
d   e   f

2 a Draw a right angle.   b Draw an acute angle.   c Draw an obtuse angle.

3 Make a movable angle with 2 strips of cardboard and a fastener.

Use your movable angle to find and circle angles the same as A.

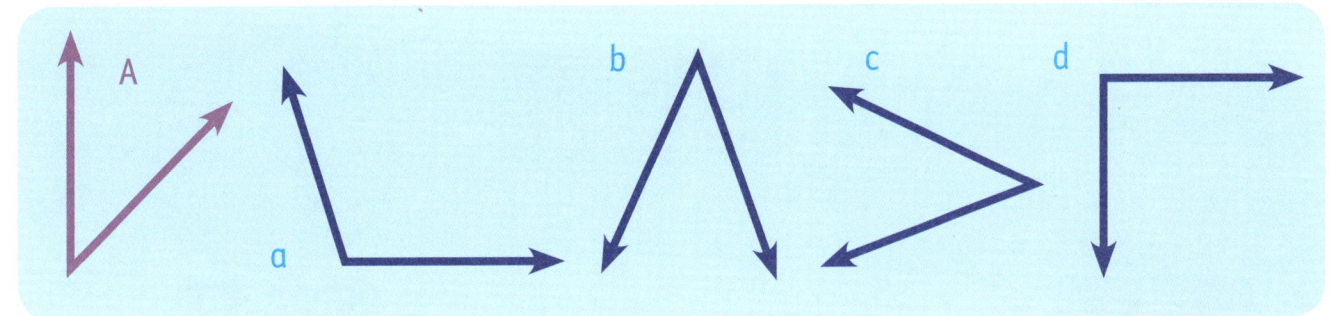

A   a   b   c   d

ACMMG064 Geometric reasoning • Identify angles as measures of turn and compare angle sizes in everyday situations.

173

Reading a timetable

This is Tim's school day.

A		B	
7:15	Wake up	12:30	Lunch break
7:20	Shower and clean teeth	1:10	Back to class
7:30	Get dressed	3:10	School finishes
7:45	Have breakfast		Arrive home and have a snack
8:00	Feed dog, cat and rabbit	4:00	Begin homework
8:20	Walk to school	5:00	Finish homework
8:45	Arrive at school	5:05	Play
9:00	Start school	6:15	Dinner
10:55	Morning recess	7:00	Watch TV
11:10	Back to class	8:30	Bed

1. Which column shows pm time? _____

2. When does Tim begin his shower? _____

3. How long does it take for him to get dressed? _____ minutes

4. Does Tim have any pets? _____ How do you know? _____

5. a How long does it take for Tim to walk to school? _____ minutes

   b It takes him the same time to walk home from school.
     Complete the timetable by writing the time Tim arrives home.

6. How long is school lunchtime? _____ minutes

7. How many minutes does Tim spend on his homework? _____ minutes

8. How long in hours and minutes does Tim spend watching TV? _____ hours _____ minutes

9. Tim watches the same amount of TV each night from Monday to Friday.
   How much TV is this for the 5 days? _____ hours _____ minutes

10. What is Tim doing at each of these times?

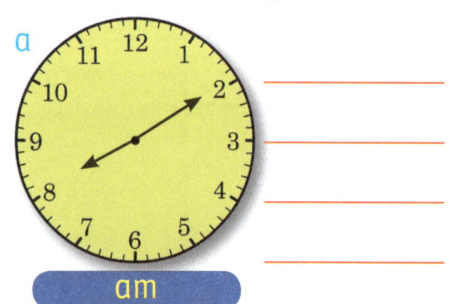

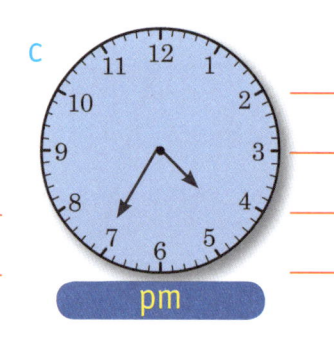

    a (clock) am

    b 3:30 pm

    c (clock) pm

Position

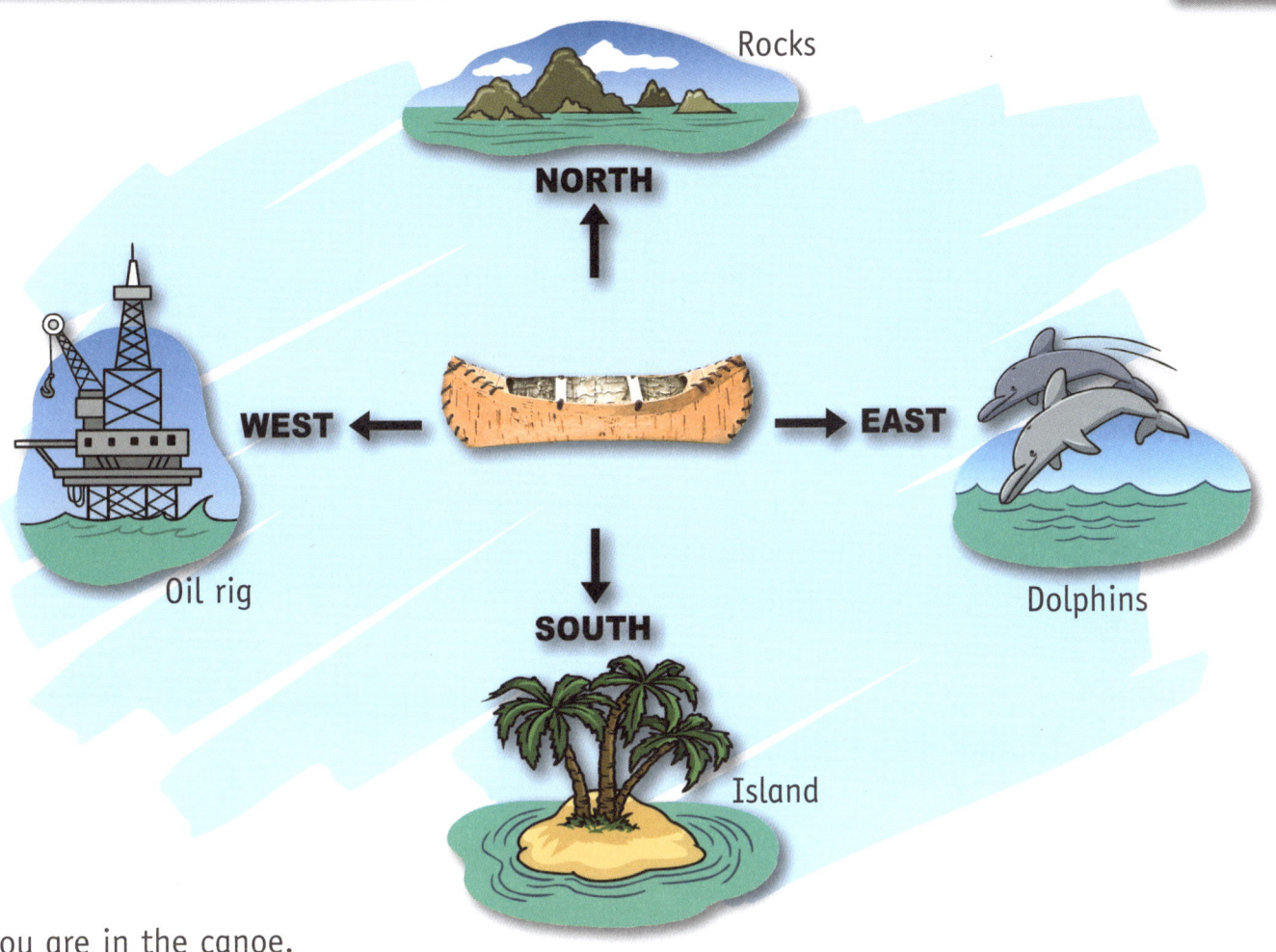

Lab 3 position words

You are in the canoe.

1 You are facing West. What direction is:

   a on your right? _____   b on your left? _____   c behind you? _____

2 What do you see if you look:

   a North? _____   b South? _____

   c East? _____   c West? _____

3 Face East. What do you see:

   a on your right? _____   b on your left? _____

   c behind you? _____   d in front of you? _____

4 Face South. What do you see:

   a on your right? _____   b on your left? _____

   c behind you? _____   d in front of you? _____

5 If you are facing West, what will you see if:

   a you make a half turn? _____   b a full turn? _____

ACMMG065 Location and transformation • Create and interpret simple grid maps to show position and pathways.

175

Following directions

1 Write the moves made on the grid. Start at ✱.

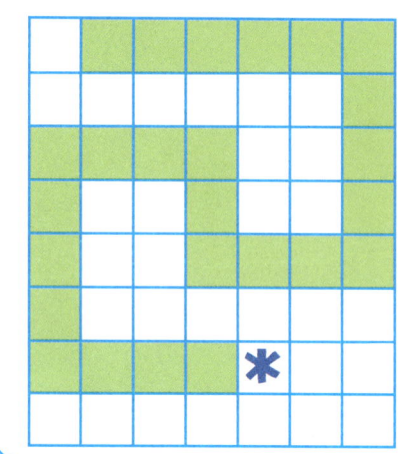

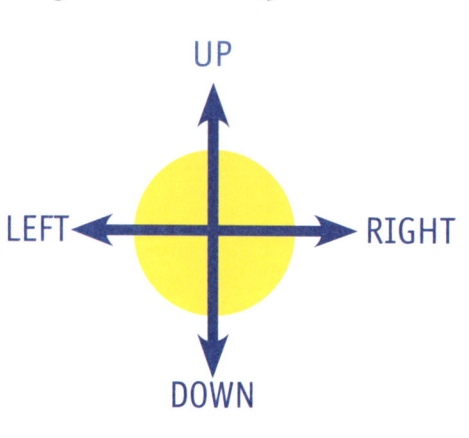

| 4 left |
| 4 |
| |
| |
| |
| |
| |

2 Start at ✱ and follow the directions. The first two moves have been done.

a 1 right   b 2 down   c 1 right
d 1 down   e 2 right   f 1 up
g 1 right   h 2 up   i 1 left
j 1 up   k 3 left   l 2 up
m 1 right   n 1 up   o 3 right
p 1 down

q What number have you drawn? _____

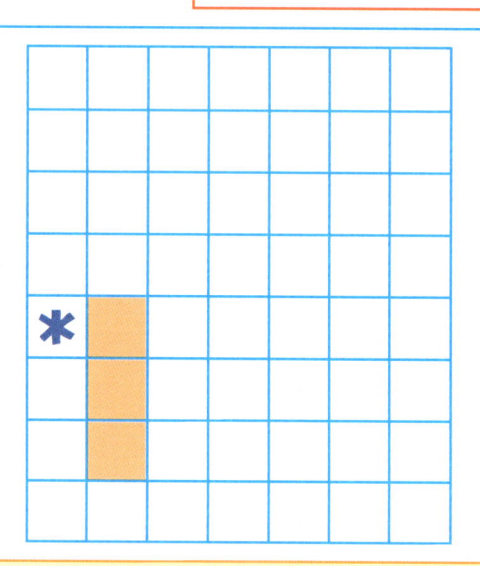

3 a Write the compass points.

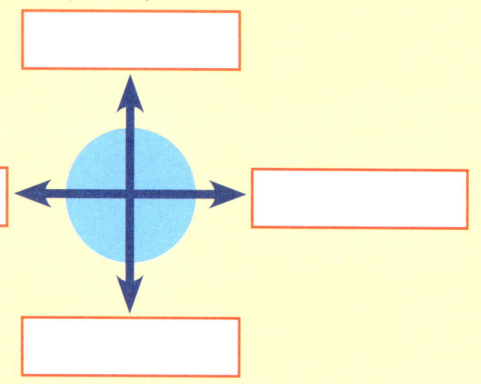

Ed wants to know where his friends are. Write the directions from Ed.

b Gerry Gorilla _____   c Horace Hippo _____
d Leo Lion _____   e Cate Camel _____

Where is Ed from: f Horace? _____   g Cate? _____   h Leo? _____   i Gerry? _____

176

ACMMG065 Location and transformation • Create and interpret simple grid maps to show position and pathways.

Island maps

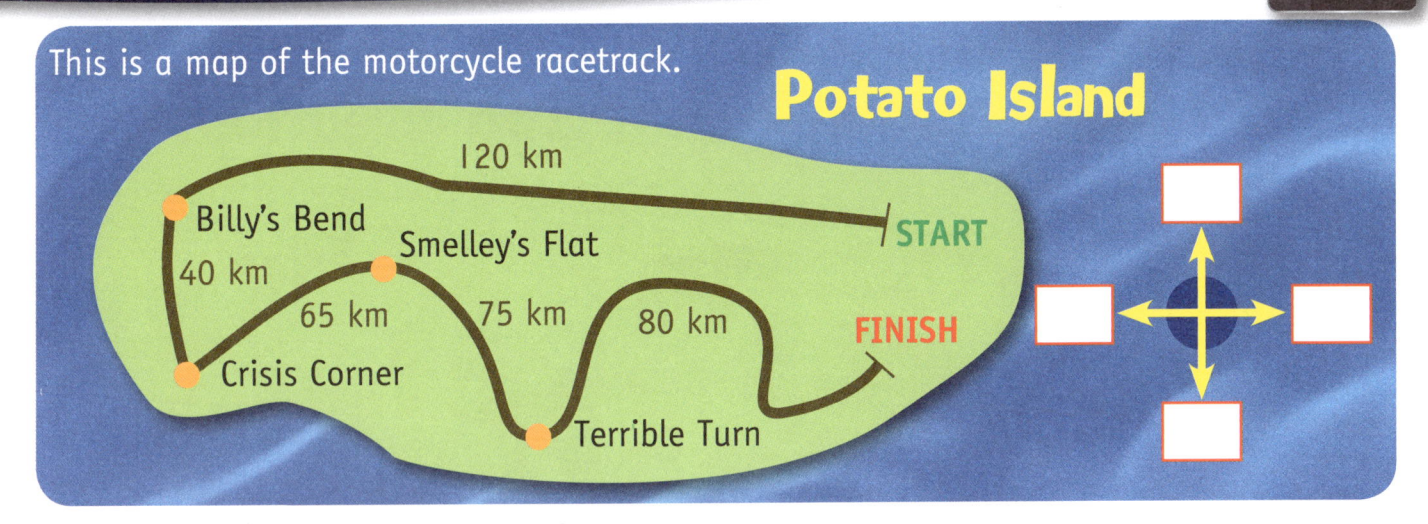

Position

This is a map of the motorcycle racetrack.

Potato Island

- 120 km
- Billy's Bend
- 40 km
- Smelley's Flat
- 65 km
- 75 km
- 80 km
- Crisis Corner
- Terrible Turn
- START
- FINISH

1
 a Write in the compass points.
 b What is the name of the island? _____
 c Where is the sharpest turn? _____
 d Where does the track make a turn that is nearly a right angle? _____
 e How far is it from the Start to Crisis Corner? _____
 f How far is it from Smelley's Flat to the Finish? _____
 g Use a calculator to find the length of the racetrack. _____

2 This is Kid Stuff Island. What is at:
 a A2? _____
 b D1? _____
 c C3? _____
 d B4? _____

Write the position of:
 e the parachute. _____
 f the helicopter. _____
 g the basketball hoop. _____

 h Draw what is at: D3   B3   C2

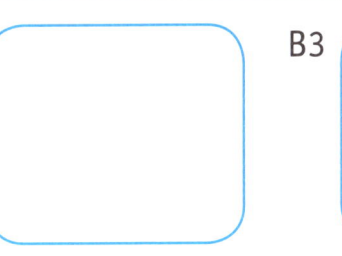

ACMMG065 Location and transformation • Create and interpret simple grid maps to show position and pathways.

Problem solving

Zoo directions

1. Place the following animals on the map and write their location.

   Monkeys _____ Giraffes _____ Platypus _____ Red panda _____ Kangaroo _____

2. Give instructions on how to find two of the animals, starting at the entrance. Use direction words: North, South, East, West, right, left and ahead.

   A _____

   B _____

Possible paths

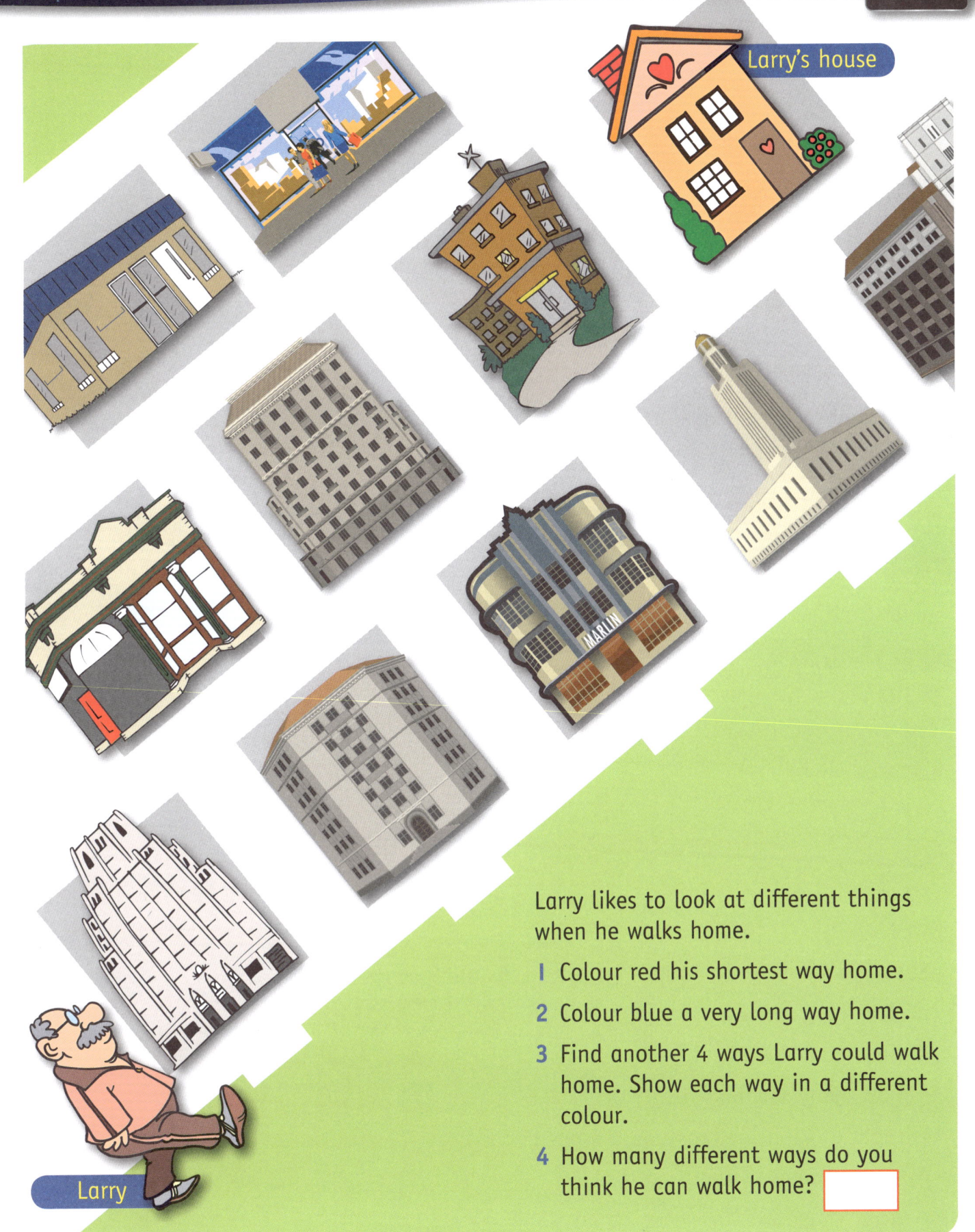

Larry's house

Larry likes to look at different things when he walks home.

1. Colour red his shortest way home.
2. Colour blue a very long way home.
3. Find another 4 ways Larry could walk home. Show each way in a different colour.
4. How many different ways do you think he can walk home?

Larry

ACMSP067 Chance • Conduct chance experiments, identify and describe possible outcomes and recognise variation in results.

179

Possible outcomes

Main Course
Spaghetti
Fish
Hamburger
Chicken

Dessert
Ice-cream
Cheesecake
Fruit salad
*

1 This is the menu for Claire's Cosy Cafe.

   a How many main courses are there? _____

   b How many desserts are there? _____

   c Hal ordered spaghetti. How many different desserts could he have with it? _____

   d Ivy ordered ice-cream. How many different main courses could she have with it?
   _____

   e List all possible combinations of meals.

Main Course	Dessert	Main Course	Dessert

2 Sam painted different shapes on some tiles and put them in a box.

   a How many circles? _____

   b How many triangles? _____

   c How many squares? _____

   Without looking, he took one tile out of the box.

   d What shape was the most likely? _____

   e What shape was the least likely? _____

Chance

1. a How many faces on a die? _____
   b Which three faces are showing on this die? _____ _____ _____
   c Which three faces are not seen? _____ _____ _____
   d If the die is tossed, what numbers could be on top?
   _____ _____ _____ _____ _____ _____
   e Is there any chance 7 dots could appear? _____
   Why? _____

2. Match one of the words in the list with each of these statements.
   a I will watch television tonight. _____
   b It will snow today. _____
   c The sun will rise in the morning. _____
   d I will grow taller than my mother. _____
   e I will see a horse on the road. _____

   impossible
   unlikely
   likely
   certain

3. a How many different outcomes are possible with this spinner? _____
   b Do all shapes on this spinner have the same chance of being selected? _____
   c Draw the shape that is most likely to be selected.
   d Draw the shape that is least likely to be selected.
   e True or false.
   ✚ is more likely to be selected than ★. _____
   ✦ has more chance of being selected than all the other shapes together. _____
   f What is the chance that the arrow will point to ◐ ? _____

Challenge!

Write down one event that will happen today.

Write down one event that won't happen today.

Write down one event that might happen today.

Revision Term 4

1 **4 7 1 8** p 142

Use the numbers to make:

a the largest number. _____

b the smallest number. _____

c an even number. _____

2 Round to the nearest hundred. p 143

a 468 _____   b 215 _____

3 Round to the nearest thousand. p 143

a 4695 _____   b 2398 _____

4 Use > or <. p 144

a 479 ___ 749   b 1280 ___ 1820

c 1005 ___ 1500   d 3600 ___ 3006

5 7426 is the same as: p 145

a ___ tens ___ ones

b ___ hundreds ___ tens ___ ones

c ___ thousands ___ ones

6 a 7 ×5   b 3 ×9   c 10 ×4   d 5 ×8   p 146

7 What is the product of: p 149

a 3 and 7? _____   b 5 and 10? _____

8 Colour the multiples of 4. p 150

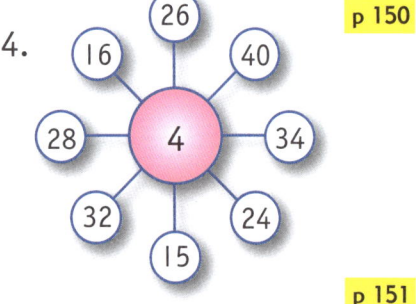

26, 16, 40, 28, 4, 34, 32, 24, 15

9 What do seven 5c stamps cost? _____ p 151

10 a 40 ÷ 10 = _____   b 18 ÷ 2 = _____   p 153

c 21 ÷ 3 = _____   d 55 ÷ 5 = _____

11 p 153

Divide the stars into:

a 2 groups. 1 group = _____

b 3 groups. 1 group = _____

c 9 groups. 1 group = _____

d 6 groups. 1 group = _____

12 Write these from largest to smallest. p 156

$\frac{1}{4}, \frac{1}{8}, \frac{1}{2}, 1, \frac{7}{8}$ _____

13 Colour the fraction. p 157

a $\frac{1}{5}$ b $\frac{1}{2}$

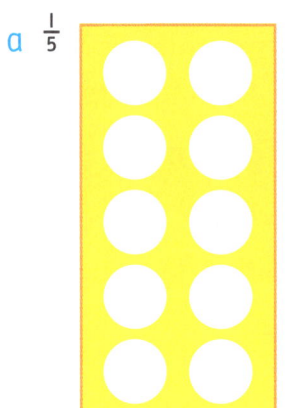

14 Circle the largest fraction in each pair. p 158

a $\frac{3}{5}$ $\frac{3}{10}$ b 1 $\frac{1}{10}$

c $\frac{1}{5}$ $\frac{1}{10}$ d $\frac{3}{5}$ $\frac{3}{10}$

Revision Term 4

15 How many centimetres in: `p 161`

    a 2 m? _____

    b $\frac{1}{2}$ m? _____

16 How many millimetres in: `p 161`

    a 5 cm? _____

    b 12 cm? _____

17 a Draw a line 38 mm long.   `p 161`

    b Measure this line in mm.

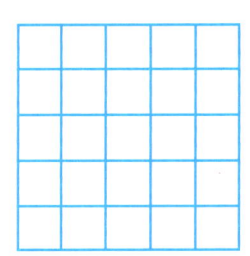

    _____

18 Draw a shape with an area of 20 squares.   `p 162`

19 True/false? If you measure the area of your desk with Base 10 flats (100s) and again with Base 10 longs (10s) there will be more Base 10 flats because they are larger.   `p 163`

_____

20 This magic machine changes numbers four times to make a sequence.   `p 168`

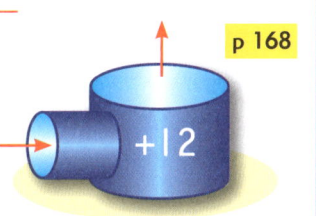

+12

What will these numbers become?

    a 7 ____, ____, ____, ____

    b 25 ____, ____, ____, ____

These number sequences came out. What number went in?

    c 28, 40, 52, 64 _____

    d 42, 54, 66, 78 _____

21 True or false?   `p 169`

    a 6 × 8 = 8 × 6 _____

    b 32 ÷ 8 = 8 ÷ 32 _____

22   `p 170`

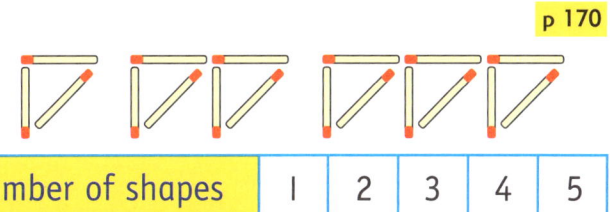

Number of shapes	1	2	3	4	5
Number of matches	3				

23 Draw: `p 171`

a a sharp angle.	b a blunt angle.

24 Write two places where you can see a right angle.   `p 172`

    a _____

    b _____

25   `p 173`

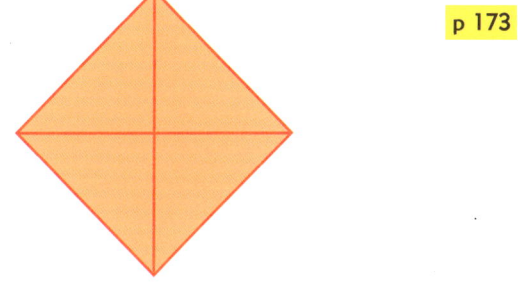

Which statement is true about this diagram? _____

    a There are 8 right angles.

    b There are 4 right angles and 8 sharp angles.

    c There are 8 right angles and 8 sharp angles.

183

Revision Term 4

26 p 174

3:30	Finish school
3:45	Afternoon tea
4:00	Play with Jan
5:10	Homework
5:30	Have bath
6:00	Watch TV
6:35	Eat dinner

This is part of Bill's timetable for Monday.

a Is it am or pm? _____
b What did he do at $\frac{1}{4}$ to 4? _____
c How long did he watch TV? _____
d What else did he do between 5:30 and 6:00? _____
e How long was it from finishing school to eating dinner? _____

27 p 175

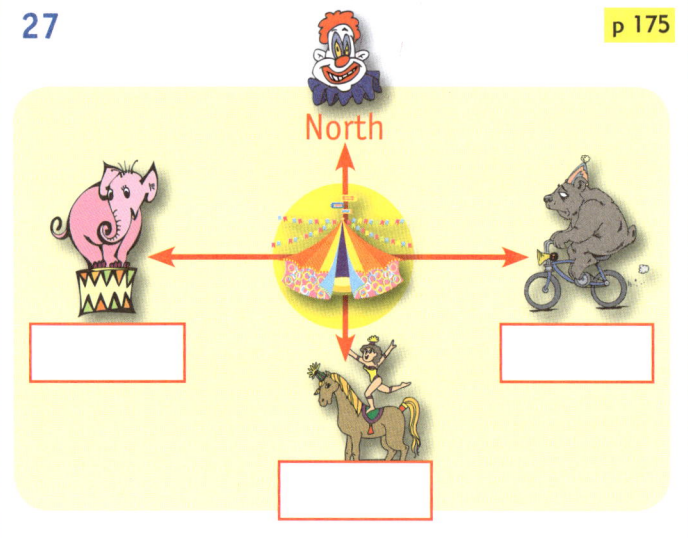

North

a Write in the other compass directions. From the circus tent in which direction is:
b the bear? _____
c the elephant? _____
d the horse? _____
e the clown? _____

28 Draw the path by following the directions. Start at ✱ and move: p 176

a 1 up   b 3 right
c 2 up   d 1 left
e 2 up   f 2 left
g 2 up   h 2 left
i 2 down

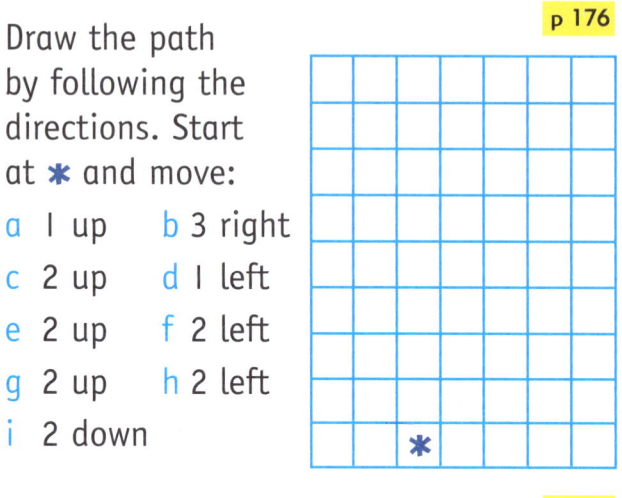

29 p 177

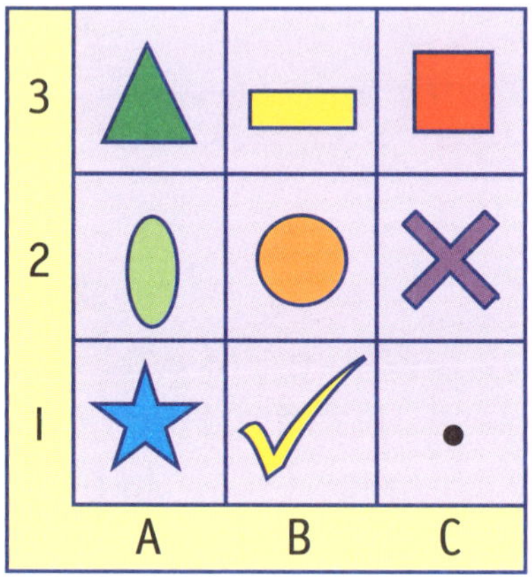

What is at:
a A3? _____
b B1? _____
c C2? _____
Where is:
d the star? _____
e the circle? _____

30 Helen has cheese, tomato, ham and lettuce for sandwich making. What are the different two-filling sandwiches she can make? p 180

_____   _____
_____   _____
_____   _____
_____   _____
_____   _____

31 Sam wanted ham with one other thing. How many different sandwiches could he have? p 180

184